Wringing Success from Failure in Late-Developing Countries

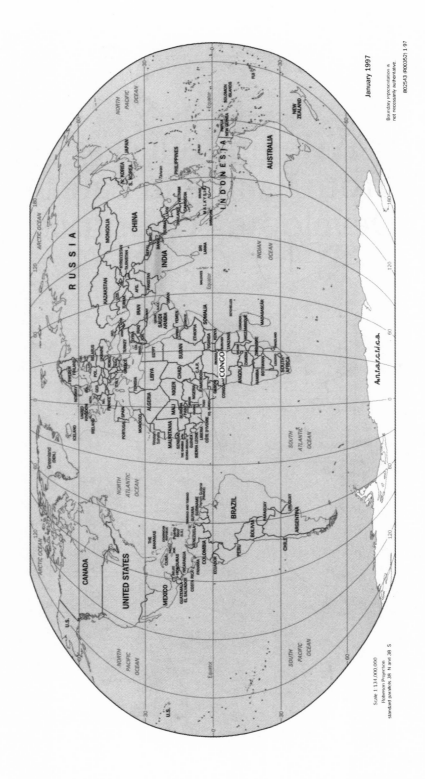

January 1997

Boundary representation is
not necessarily authoritative.

802543 (R00352) 1-97

Scale 1:134,000,000
Robinson Projection
standard parallels 38°N and 38°S

Wringing Success from Failure in Late-Developing Countries

Lessons from the Field

Joseph F. Stepanek

Westport, Connecticut
London

Library of Congress Cataloging-in-Publication Data

Stepanek, Joseph F., 1943–
    Wringing success from failure in late-developing countries :
lessons from the field / Joseph F. Stepanek.
        p.   cm.
    Includes bibliographical references and index.
    ISBN 0–275–96505–8 (alk. paper)
    1. Economic assistance—Developing countries.   2. Developing
countries—Economic conditions.   3. Developing countries—Economic
policy.   4. Poor—Developing countries.   5. Rural poor—Developing
countries.   I. Title.
HC59.7.S794   1999
338.9′009172′4—dc21   98–31075

British Library Cataloguing in Publication Data is available.

Library of Congress Catalog Card Number: 98–31075
ISBN: 0–275–96505–8

First published in 1999

Praeger Publishers, 88 Post Road West, Westport, CT 06881
An imprint of Greenwood Publishing Group, Inc.
www.praeger.com

Printed in the United States of America

The paper used in this book complies with the
Permanent Paper Standard issued by the National
Information Standards Organization (Z39.48–1984).

10 9 8 7 6 5 4 3 2 1

for Caroline

Contents

Tables

Preface

The Golden Gate bridge was high overhead, gleaming bright orange in the setting sun. World War II had been over for two years when my mother, my brother, and I sailed across the Pacific to China. It was 1947, and I was standing on the deck of a recently converted troop ship, the U.S.S. *General Gordon*. We met my father in war-torn Shanghai and from there flew in a tattered DC-4 to a bomb-cratered dirt strip in Hunan Province for his United Nations small industries assignment. My father's career carried us from Hunan, where we lived from 1947 to 1949; to Jakarta, from 1951 to 1953; to Rangoon in 1956 and 1957; and on to New Delhi, from 1959 to 1961.

A childhood spent in China and other distant places, sandwiched between seaboard passages and innumerable flights, led to a broad perspective and broader aspirations. I did not know then that I would become a willing captive of a government career in the United States Foreign Service, or that being a witness to global poverty would fire a heart-felt commitment to challenge it, which has not dissipated since youthful exposure. What might have been just another American childhood and just another government job became a passion and a continuing source of fascination, pride, and anger. Village China began a life-long love affair with development, and with foreign countries and cultures. I was captivated, even captured, by a chance encounter.

Asia's rice paddies turned from green to gold and to green again with each passing monsoon. Seasonal cycles became timeless. Life abroad in eleven poor countries, first in Asia and then in Africa, and as a visitor to dozens of others, stretched my horizons backward and forward, beyond normal time frames. My adult life as a professional aid practitioner (or aid *wallah*, a Hindi word for office functionary) exposed me to the immediacy of world poverty and world history. The broad events of a century were imprinted upon me—the colonial land grab of Africa, the Great War, the Great Depression, World War II, and the end of the cold war—all events that continue to shape the world today.

I write to share my story and my convictions with the American public, and with a younger generation, who may need to be convinced of the value of poor-world development, of foreign aid, and of their own personal commitment to noble goals. I am fortunate to have served development up close. It is my hope, therefore, to convey through this work the lessons I have learned from a career spent wringing success from poverty and failure in the poor world.

My story is drawn primarily from lessons learned during a twenty-five-year career with the United States Agency for International Development (AID). My family and I lived in Bangladesh from 1972 to 1977, in Indonesia from 1979 to 1983 (a second time for me), in Kenya from 1983 to 1987, in Tanzania from 1987 to 1991, and in Zambia from 1994 to 1996. By serving in distant countries that were not at the center of cold war pressures, my assignments enabled me to remain an optimist. I saw turmoil and failure of course, but I also saw first-hand what works when development and aid are effective.

In the relatively short time span of my travels, the population of some countries has nearly tripled. I grew up with indelible impressions created by the explosively growing populations in Asia and Africa. My professional life has been concerned with justice—with, to borrow a phrase from Abraham Lincoln, the sweat of other men's faces. Behind one sweaty face stood millions of others. I recall being bounced along by rickshaw through the crowded, broken streets of Hunan in the late 1940s. Twenty-five years later my family and I witnessed lifeless bodies from Bengal's latest famine being laid gently upon street meridians for carts to carry silently away. Why was there such poverty? We flew regularly from Dhaka to Calcutta in the early 1970s for breaks from oppressive poverty only to be met by an even more desolate reality—a skeletal frame dragging himself along a crowded Calcutta sidewalk to avoid his own excrement.

Constant travel can make a muddle of formal education. Kindergarten by correspondence in China ended with high school by correspondence in New Delhi. I attended an international school in Jakarta, founded by my mother, Antoinette. Her school, conducted first in a sweltering garage, is today the largest of its kind in the world. Ultimately, my travels caught up with me. A freshman year at Yale University suggested that I pursue a more productive course back home in Boulder, Colorado. It was at the University of Colorado that I earned a B.A. and a Ph.D. in economics in 1965 and 1971, respectively, with an M.A. in economics from the University of Minnesota in 1967 sandwiched in between.

The best teacher of all, however, has been the constant exposure to Asia and Africa through trips to the field. My first trip was through the rice paddies of Hunan on a tiger hunt. I carried the rope, my brother Jim, the sack. In Bangladesh years later, my AID colleague, the late Nizam Uddin Ahmed, and I visited farmers' fields across the same flooded plain every month for five years. With each trip impressions and thoughts accumulated and coalesced into lessons and prescriptions.

This book-length story treats development and foreign aid together because aid donors are contributing most of the development resources for poor, late-developing countries. In fact, donors may be funding as much as 100 percent of a poor country's development budget where private talent and private investment are constrained—even driven away. Economists tend to ignore discussions of mismanagement, corruption, poor world dependence on foreign aid, and even democracy. Too often village life has been dramatized in isolation from a national context. Too often multiple and conflicting motives have been ducked or hedged. I have been intimately involved in battles to shape AID's contributions, contradictions, and consequences. Serving AID required challenging the status quo; contributions had to be sorted from myths and mistakes.

Where do our foreign aid dollars go? Why should we be concerned about poor Africans when we have our own troubles at home? There are innumerable questions about development and foreign aid. My subject matter is not complicated but it is diverse; it is simple stuff but not easily simplified. It is best to tell a full story of development and foreign assistance than to cut corners; better to prepare the groundwork fully for understanding and reform than to overlook key actors and forces. This story builds toward a handful of principles that are needed for development and democracy, and for effective foreign aid. Justice demands a telling in full.

Acknowledgments

I bring you a story set on a stage peopled with the poor of this world. Yet for all the tales of woe and disappointment reported here, none of these weigh in the balance against AID's noble purpose and the opportunity it gave me for initiative and creativity. Townsend Swayze hired me at AID in 1971. What can I possibly say to him but, "Thank you." For my parents who took me to China, no words express gratitude for a chance encounter.

My AID career is now a memory. What irony to have been a member of a modest federal bureaucracy, to have worked on social struggles debated for centuries, by deadening bureaucratic rules described by Max Weber long ago, and yet to find a rewarding career in public service. As I said on my AID retirement as Caroline and I departed Lusaka in October 1996, "Imagine a government like mine hiring a person like me." I am, nonetheless, grateful. I will have been successful in these pages if I move a few hearts and minds, and if I attract a few young professionals to serve development overseas.

Throughout the entire enterprise I am grateful to my wife Caroline. Her commitment to our larger purpose enriched our work overseas and has kept me focused through dark mornings on cold Metro buses headed to downtown Washington, D.C.

For my schooling at odd times and places, there are too many to thank. For my final years of education I thank Ruben Zubrow and George Zinke at the University of Colorado, Vernon Ruttan at the University of Minnesota, and John Mellor, an early director of the International Food Policy Research Institute (IFPRI) who placed the institute on the map.

Per Pinstrup-Andersen, IFPRI's Director General, and Raisuddin Ahmed, director of the markets division, welcomed my book-writing enterprise by offering me the good offices of IFPRI in Washington, D.C. I am deeply grateful for their committed development purpose yet warm environment and for IFPRI's library and computer support. I thank you all, especially Elizabeth Daines, Chris Delgado, Lisa Grover, Mary Mastroianni, Carolyn Roper, and John Williams.

Chuck Mohan and I wrote *Crisis To Crisis* together in Lusaka, from which several ideas sprang. His initial and continuing support are appreciated. Chuck's friend Bob Myers became mine. I am grateful to Bob for forcing me to see what I had been looking at for years: "Joe," he said, "You are a credit to your race." Ben Hawley also contributed early and in earnest, with a scathing Jesuitical critique of a first draft.

In addition, many people commented along the way. More than their specific contributions, or whether we agreed, I thank them for their enthusiasm for my efforts.

For our Dhaka days, and for food and agricultural issues, I thank Joe Toner, Jim and Molly Gingerich, David and Dorothy Catling, David Atwood, Don McClelland, Fred King, A.S.M. Jahangir, Chuck Johnson, Ousmane Badiane, Nick Minot, Bruno Barbier, Nurul Islam, and our daughters Julie, Ahlia, and Vanessa.

For our days in Dar es Salaam, and for those good works, I thank Lucas and Flora Chogo, Kari Karanko, Terry Kramer, Liz Loughran, Fred Guymont, Zach Hahn, Mulugetta Yohannes, Hedwiga Mbuya, Daniel Ngowi, Wyn Owen, Joel Strauss, Arne and Gabi Strom, Peter and Stella Wood, and Abe Weisblat.

For days in a troubled Lusaka, I thank Theo Bull, M. K. and Hal Cope, Tom Carothers, Mary Kazunga, Freda Luhila, Jim Polhemus, Lise Rakner, and all the members of the Non-Group. I also thank the editors and staff of Lusaka's *The Post* for defending freedom of public expression and discussion. I thank Cynthia Bryant, Mambepa Kalwani, Pamo Kangwa, and Curt Wolters of the AID mission for assistance.

I thank Praeger Publishing for rescuing my draft from the oblivion of a desk drawer (where my critics believe it should have been left), Jim Sabin for deleting but one of my stories, and Bobbie Goettler for pressing the text into shape. Lastly, I thank my editor Terry Anderson for helping me do what I set my heart on doing and for converting drafts into a respected language. I alone am responsible for its content.

1

Poor People in a Poor World

MY PURPOSE IN TEN CHAPTERS

Since World War II mankind has been determined to alleviate poverty. Remarkable efforts to do so have been made in the fifty years since the end of the war, yet half of mankind remains poor; a fifth is very poor.

Poverty is not a state of nature, but it can be ascribed to man-made institutions that reflect self-serving and self-indulgent ideologies, poorly tested theories and policies, weak governments, and even poorly adminis- tered programs to alleviate poverty. Too often, institutions that were expressly established to aid the poor slip into policies and practices that are aimed at bureaucratic self-preservation.

My thesis has two parts: First, that well-designed development strategies and foreign assistance programs that draw thoughtfully on the lessons of the past can stimulate growth and reduce poverty in poor, late- developing countries; and second, that poverty in the late-developing world cannot be successfully alleviated without understanding and challenging all of its causes. Poverty has no one cause, no one solution. Furthermore, western governments, international development banks, and donor agencies must reexamine how they design and administer foreign aid, and they must realistically examine the problems that are endemic to late-developing countries that imperil poor people, including poor-world governments that squander talent, good will, and resources.

A quote from Abraham Lincoln's second inaugural address captures the essence of my overseas experience: "It may seem strange that any men should dare to ask a just God's assistance in wringing their bread from the sweat of other men's faces." I believe that poor men and women can profit from their own work, and that we can reverse the trend of the rich gaining at the expense of the poor, but only if we honestly address all the indigenous causes of poverty as well as the successes and failures of foreign aid programs. Foreign assistance has been so smothered in political interest, bureaucratic barnacles, and foreign policy controversy that its declared purpose and actual contributions can be hard to fathom. Multiple interests and motives must be untangled.

PRIMARY THEMES

I discuss development and foreign aid in general and specific terms, from their historic and theoretical roots to their present and practical application. Each chapter illustrates my development experience from a different perspective; each contributes to what I hope will be a compelling argument for development solutions and effective aid. Each chapter illustrates the vitality of ownership; many stress the importance of markets. One chapter is devoted to the challenge of democracy in Africa.

Because AID resources have been central to the implementation of U.S. foreign policy in the developing world, chapter 2 begins with a discussion and critique of AID in Washington. This much-berated institution, seen from within the famed Beltway of Washington, D.C., presents a study in good intentions gone awry. Because AID has been controlled by vested and divisive interests since its inception, poor countries have often ended up serving the Washington imperial imperative. I also examine the relationship between Congress and the Department of State—a necessary precursor to meaningful prescriptions for aid's reform.

Chapter 3 examines development theory and practice. In retrospect, many development theories have been shown to be more fad-like than usefully enduring; a few were based on neither evidence nor reason. Now that the cold war has receded in importance as a force that drives foreign policy, I identify post–cold war development principles that are best suited for guiding development in the next century. Africa's continuing plight and Asia's recent financial crisis underscore the imperative of adhering to economic and democratic principles.

Food production successes show up in unlikely places. Powerful people in powerful capitals labeled Bangladesh a "basket case," for example, and called for "triage" at its independence in 1971. Golden Bengal now grows its own food, as described in a heartening chapter 4. The cultivators of Bangladesh have taken the world by surprise, from which we can draw reinforcement for important growth enhancing and poverty alleviating principles.

In chapter 5, I direct the reader's attention fully to Africa. I review donor aid for its shortcomings and contributions from Dar es Salaam, the capital of Tanzania. I introduce the field perspective that is missing from most discussions of aid and I explore a variety of donor procedures that might contribute to Tanzania's ownership of its own development. Because aid in Africa will remain an important feature of its landscape, aid administration in Africa warrants close examination.

In chapter 6, I examine Africa's agricultural potential for initiating and sustaining its own green revolution. The heretofore untold story of American generosity to Bangladesh can, in turn, contribute to a success story for Africa; the lessons of the 1970s can yield important lessons for a new agricultural vision in drought-prone, bureaucratically controlled Africa. Market-led principles of openness and hard-won food aid lessons, combined and tested in Bangladesh, can guide African agriculture.

Macroeconomic reform in Africa is now in hand—or certainly at hand. Almost all of Africa is struggling to implement market reform, the principles of which are introduced in chapter 3 and are made relevant for Africa in chapter 7. Aid dependence, however, has engulfed African policy-makers. Few experts have examined World Bank and International Monetary Fund (IMF)–led causes of this dependency. Western bilateral donors and international investors appear to be turning their backs on this last, poor continent, just when Africa's policy-makers are recognizing the importance of trade and investment, of public debt forgiveness, and of controlling their own destinies.

Chapter 8 explores basic issues of democracy. Democracy is not easily imported and implanted, but it has arrived in Africa. Most African leaders are disturbed by the challenge of democracy; the appropriate role for outside assistance is daunting. But as Albert Camus said, the day of the "voiceless masses of people . . . going through their lives leaving barely a trace of their existence," is over.[1] Can democracy be transplanted to African cultures with few traditions supporting individual rights or institutional pluralism? I argue that development is neither owned nor sustainable without the participation and consent of the people involved.

Education and training can create African ownership, as we explore in a penultimate chapter 9. Americans can be justly proud of their educational and training contributions in many parts of Asia and Latin America; not so for Africa, however, where many of the same contributions have yielded costly failure. With failure as the result of great effort, it is difficult to imagine African educational institutions serving a population that is expected to double between 1990 and 2025. Donors must begin again; candid assessment is the first step.

My last chapter offers an opportunity to reflect. I have tried to be optimistic, yet candor dogs my heels. Helping a poor world overcome its continuing poverty as rapidly as have other, now rapidly developing countries, is a daunting task—daunting, but not impossible.

The world has changed dramatically since the 1950s, and is continuing to change, probably faster than our aid-giving institutions can learn and adjust. Aid mistakes are being repeated. Hundreds of millions—even billions of dollars, are being spent for poorly understood and misguided purposes. Aid continues to be wasted; sadly, as much in the form of good will as in the dollars themselves. AID's many motives and innumerable interests make murky that which is best in American generosity. Still, I believe the United States must continue to be a firm and creative voice for effective foreign aid.

DEFINING DEVELOPMENT AND AID

Development and *foreign aid* are often bandied about by aid recipients and donor institutions alike without a clear understanding of how the terms are used. Their use is confused further because established (if shop-worn) definitions give way to new ones faster than popular understandings become commonplace. Nor can we define these terms without defining foreign policy mandates and aid priorities. What is this development that is so commonly described and found wanting in so many countries? What is this foreign aid that is said to be useful, or useless, depending on one's orientation?

Development is defined as material benefit and progress for individual families and for nation states. I have seen that development means food security, clothing, housing, schooling, and new opportunities to make life better than it was. For young countries, the visual impression counts for a lot: luxuriant rice fields spread to the horizon; solid communities; well-maintained roads and bridges; new hospitals, shiny new airports; and especially healthy, smiling children.

The visual impression of material well-being has stood the test of time because it is basic and easily understood. It follows that economic growth results from the capacity to organize and use knowledge, resources, and institutions that promote material well-being. People are well-off because they work hard and work effectively, and because they enjoy the fruits of their labor. Growth, jobs, and higher incomes can lead to improvements in real wages; all of which can point to poverty's alleviation and improvements in the distribution of income. With development, countries and households are able to spend far less, proportionately, on food and other basic necessities than they do on things that make life more comfortable.

New concepts are frequently superimposed on the basic definition of development: Specific mandates for economic reform, for children and women, for environmental preservation, for sustainability, and for democracy and human rights. Newer still are aspirations for freedom of communication, intellectual property rights, preservation of the world's ethnic riches, conflict resolution, and responses to crises.

Because late-developing countries are so dependent on foreign aid, development is often defined by what aid donors seek to fund. Donor dollars and donor objectives often drive development in these countries. The matter of who owns development—donors or the countries themselves—therefore arises early in the analysis.

Each new development priority, added to earlier ones, can trip on prior aid aspirations. Earlier aid priorities are inevitably reduced in importance and may even be set aside. More and more material objectives are supposed to be met by overburdened poor governments and stretched aid budgets. The longer the list of priorities, the more complex the actions required and the more likely that unintended consequences arise.

Just as the basic definition of development can be reworked according to a particular donor's agenda, so can the term *foreign aid*. Aid, like development, can reflect aspirations of societal well-being generally, or it can focus on funding particular and special priorities without regard to ownership and sustainability by the recipient population as a whole.

I define foreign aid as the purposeful effort to change a disappointing status quo into family dreams for sustained betterment within the nation state through the transfer of materials, advice, and training. Aid can be given by one government to another, by one nonprofit or business organization to others, or by combinations of these. Given by generosity but owned by the recipient. Aid, when provided on less than commercial terms, represents experience and resources packaged in good will.

DEVELOPMENT PRINCIPLES—ESPECIALLY OWNERSHIP, A *SINE QUA NON* FOR SUCCESS

Development and aid are complicated subjects. There are no shorthand ways to describe poverty or ensure its alleviation across countries and continents. Diversity and complexity are the rule. Both the reader and the development practitioner may wish for simple categories and simple answers. In development, not only is everything related to everything else, but matters of causality, such as "aid finances development," are filled with qualifications and exceptions. Experience notwithstanding, I shall try to simplify and clarify.

This book is guided by a handful of development principles, with one—ownership—being the most important. I will show that each of the other principles described must be "owned" by the people in whose name development and aid are directed. Ownership, or responsibility, of national well-being by government, and of government by its people, is the proven route to sustained development and the alleviation of poverty. Foreign aid's effectiveness is tested by ownership.

I analyze the importance of ownership in these chapters as well as other conditions that are necessary for economic growth: principles of markets, market-determined prices, investment, and the environment that fosters investment. People must be enabled to invest in themselves. Closely related to market principles are democratic principles that are derived from western experience, such as pluralistic sources of power and decision-making, governmental checks and balances, and transparency of governmental processes. Equally important are the rights of individuals in markets to own property and secure contracts. These rights in turn can only be exercised freely provided they are founded in law and monitored by institutions that guarantee broad human rights, which encompass security of person, family, and community, and freedom of expression and religion.

The Rationale for Foreign Aid

Foreign assistance, like development itself, must be reassessed and rejustified to shape its relevance for the poor world. Much of aid's original justification remains valid. Traditional, that is, post–World War II purposes, retain their importance. The world remains a dangerous place. American security interests, despite multiple changes since the end of the cold war, remain paramount. International risks of terrorism, weapons proliferation, and drug cartels create great demands on America's domestic programs and law enforcement services, as well as on its traditional security and intelligence capabilities overseas.

American commercial interests follow in importance. Because foreign aid can and does contribute to the development of international markets, new markets for U.S. exports create U.S. jobs. Americans know this. In 1997 the U.S. economy was one-third trade related. In 1986, 74 percent of Americans agreed that economic growth in developing countries benefited the U.S. economy; in 1993, 83 percent agreed. A strong developing world greatly benefits the U.S. economy.[2] The downside risks of a modern Asia, such as the recent "Asian contagion" series of stock market crashes, should serve to broaden appreciation for market and democratic principles that underwrite enduring global ties.

American aid in the form of technical advice and training (as opposed to dollars) benefits the United States as well. American technical contributions to the developing world are often available, in turn, to the United States. New knowledge, for example, stimulates U.S. trade and investment. American training of foreign professionals leads to the demand for even more American training, and to joint ventures and exports to developing countries.[3]

Not only does food aid help create commercial export markets for American grain and other products, but technical assistance for the world's seed system rebounds to America's benefit as well. The $134 million the United States has invested in wheat and rice research centers, in Mexico and the Philippines respectively, has returned $14.7 billion from all public and private sources to the U.S. economy. One-fifth of our wheat acreage and more than 70 percent of our rice acreage are grown with seed varieties that were strengthened at these international research centers.[4]

Americans increasingly understand that the state of the world's health can affect their own personal health. Nowhere is the interrelationship more clear than with airborne diseases. A microbe that afflicts a community in the Congo, or chickens in Hong Kong, can reach Wyoming tomorrow and can lead to a global pandemic in a week. Even more frightening, we now know that viral strains can mutate and spread, faster, apparently, than they can be controlled.

America can protect its interests by supporting the growth of late-developing countries. It is better to help nations grow than to rebuild, whether from natural or man-made disasters. It is less costly to prevent, preserve, and create than to rebuild from ruin. As is particularly relevant in El Salvador and South Africa today, it is more permanently constructive to defuse tensions and deep-seated suspicion than to allow hatred to burst into bloody conflict again and again, as has occurred repeatedly in Burundi, Rwanda, Sudan, and Somalia.

No one claims that development forestalls all risks. As a simple matter of economics, it is far less expensive for the United States to strive to prevent crises than to share in the costs of military operations, peacekeeping, humanitarian relief, or even financial bailouts. When America is forced to contribute all these costs, the bills skyrocket. Rwanda is a case in point. Despite years of cold war aid, the present conflict and genocide have cost donors more than $2 billion.[5]

To the traditional arguments for foreign aid must be added new ones. America's borders once protected us; today, they are more open. The world of nearly 190 nation states is more integrated than anyone imagined in the 1940s and 1950s. Once foreign countries were dealt with distantly, formally, state to state. Today, individuals by the hundreds of millions travel the world and many risks follow them home. Disease, uncontrolled migration, global pollution, trade restrictions and trade wars, and urban and international terrorism fill the daily headlines. Even foreign stock market corrections follow us home. Each risk can reach into communities, factories, and individual lives across the United States.

Problems not addressed overseas are increasingly making their way across America's borders. According to one study, nearly 60 percent of countries considered to be late-developing were gripped by conflict during 1990–95, compared with the 14 percent that were considered to be developing well.[6] The Indonesian forest fires that brought a thick haze to much of Southeast Asia in 1997 and 1998 are a precursor of what the burning of China's soft coal reserves could do to the global atmosphere.

It is in America's interest to see that the world is at peace and that countries prosper and trade; a promise that is kept through development. Most important to my mind, are two additional reasons for strengthening America's foreign assistance: First, America must sustain its continuing ability to define the international agenda of global issues. Agenda setting requires an active foreign policy, one that is broadened to encompass complex developmental issues that face the poor world. Second, development itself makes it possible, even necessary, for late-developing countries to embrace global issues as their own. With development, America's global interests become shared interests.

As was often said of the Marshall Plan, so it is with America's interests today: An effective aid program is good for us, it is good for them, and it is true to our values. America must continue to share this promise with late-developing countries.

BILATERAL AND MULTILATERAL DONOR INSTITUTIONS

The immediate postwar world of the late 1940s was one of devastation, poverty, and poor, distant colonies. Though victorious as allies, war-torn Europe and Russia reflected little of their inherent institutional strength.

Victory gave new life to old ideals. The allied leaders seized upon a second opportunity to create a new world order, unified by like-minded commitments. Mindful of the failure of the League of Nations, and concerned with worldwide depression, rearmament, and debt, western leaders sought a framework for avoiding the errors of the past. From their vision, a United Nations was born. Its remarkable charter embraced universal values of worldwide development and human rights, and the role of government on a global scale.

What was then seen as a largely poor world—blank spaces on the map—became highly differentiated. The then red-colored portions of world maps, depicting England's colonial empire, gave way in the 1960s to dozens of independent countries in Asia and Africa. The Caribbean and South Pacific also broke into numerous independent states. New countries sprang up everywhere, at first a dozen, then 50, then 150. Most new states are tiny and are developing well; most late-developing countries are very poor and large. Aid-giving institutions were founded and multiplied as well; a few at first, and then one for almost every cause and crisis in the 1980s and 1990s.

The Beginnings of American Aid

Secretary of State General George C. Marshall, in a May 1947 speech, planted the idea for what became known as the Marshall Plan for the reconstruction of Western Europe and Japan. The Economic Cooperation Act (ECA) of 1948 established an Economic Cooperation Administration to implement the Marshall Plan; the Act was later expanded beyond Western Europe to include Turkey and Greece, which were threatened by Soviet expansion.

In his inaugural speech in 1948, President Harry S Truman announced what was soon known as his Point IV Program, which broadened U.S. material and technical assistance to the developing world at large. Point IV led to the Mutual Security Act of 1951, which was notable for combining U.S. technical assistance with U.S. military interests for the first time.

President John F. Kennedy, together with the founding of the Peace Corps, established the Agency for International Development, in 1961. AID subsumed the functions of previous aid administrations into one.[7]

The U.S. government was not the only source of American largesse. In Asia the Ford and Rockefeller Foundations played early and notable roles in agriculture and family planning. John D. Rockefeller III toured Asia in the early 1950s to determine the best use of the family's fortune; personal impressions gained during these travels led to the founding of the Population Council and the Agricultural Development Council.

The U.S. government matched its resolve and idealism with significant resource commitments immediately following World War II, and throughout the postwar era. Between 1946 and 1961 America distributed $85 billion overall in economic and military loans and grants: $13 billion for immediate postwar humanitarian relief (1946–48), $28.7 billion for the Marshall Plan itself (1949–52), and $43.4 billion for the successor Mutual Security Plan (1953–61).

Following AID's creation in 1961, $400 billion was authorized for economic and military assistance around the world for the thirty-five-year period up until 1997. Overall, between 1946 and 1996, U.S. assistance totaled $480 billion, of which $314 billion was for economic assistance, and $165 billion was for security and military-related priorities.[8]

Fear of war's resurgence, and then of communism, as well as European reconstruction and United Nations idealism, drove the popularity of the Marshall Plan and its successor programs. With a Democratic majority, Congress used fear as much as obligation and generosity to build domestic support for European reconstruction and what proved to be a protracted allied stand against communism. Increasingly, generosity and idealism were tempered by cold war hostilities.

Many countries rebounded economically after World War II sooner than they might have because of American aid, and many newly independent countries received an important and necessary boost. America can take pride in having contributed to the development and the graduation from aid of nearly fifty countries in the 1950s and 1960s, including those of Western Europe, Japan, South Korea, Taiwan, Turkey, Tunisia, and Venezuela. Experts recall criticisms of old that Portugal, Greece, Spain, Argentina, and Chile held little possibility for prosperity. Today Botswana, Costa Rica, India, Thailand, and Tunisia are considered successfully developing countries. Foreign aid is no longer a significant feature of their landscape.

Whatever pride the United States may have in its foreign aid accomplishments, however, must be tempered by subsequent developments. We now know that American aid may have contributed to development but it did not cause development. We now know that country reversals can occur and, indeed, are commonplace. Argentina probably heads the list as an example of a country once considered developed that then slipped backward. The failed-state list has mushroomed; in 1984 AID directors met to hear of a "successful" AID program in Rwanda. No one can speak unguardedly of Africa's prospects, given the uncertainty surrounding four of the continent's largest countries: Kenya, Nigeria, Sudan, and a new Congo. Nor can anyone speak unguardedly, as we did until recently, of Asia's prospects.

The steadfast feature of AID over many decades has been its reliance on overseas staff resident in the developing world to conduct most of its field work, from design to agreement to implementation to evaluation.

Today this tradition of resident, decentralized authority, rooted first in President Franklin D. Roosevelt's Lend-Lease support of a war-besieged Europe and later in the Marshall Plan's administration, continues to give AID an edge over other donors in the form of influence, creativity, and accountability. These attributes remain at the heart of an American partnership with the poor world and of their ownership of mutual aspirations.

America's Food For Peace Program

In 1954 Congress created "Food For Peace," or "P.L. 480," as the public law is commonly known, to supply American food for humanitarian and relief aid overseas, to reduce food stock surpluses, and to promote other U.S. foreign policy interests. Historically, Title I of P.L. 480 has been administered by the Department of Agriculture. American food is exported under this title on concessional terms; that is, on less than commercial terms, to recipient countries. Title I provides American corn, rice, wheat, and edible oils at a price discount, in exchange for modest "self-help" measures to ensure that recipient governments agree to strengthen their own agricultural systems. Like dollar aid, food shipments have been justified as much to promote U.S. security and commercial interests as to address hunger.

Title II of P.L. 480, which is administered by AID, provides humanitarian relief and food on grant terms for food crises worldwide, and to help alleviate chronic food deficits in poor countries. A Title III was added to P.L. 480 in the late 1970s, which offered recipient countries the opportunity to negotiate with AID for American food on grant terms, in exchange for more rigorous self-help measures. American food aid overall provided $57 billion in food, food shipping, and related handling costs between 1946 and 1996.[9] As with dollar assistance, food aid has its share of controversy.

Other Bilateral and Multilateral Donor Institutions

As European countries began to recover in the 1950s, they founded aid programs of their own. Many of these aid programs drew upon American aid practices and so appeared, at first, to have few distinguishing characteristics. Upon closer examination, however, Europe's aid programs evolved with distinguishing features that reflect their own unique economic and political philosophies.

Great Britain is the lead donor for its former colonies, expressing a certain degree of protective possessiveness toward them. France uses its aid almost exclusively to protect commercial, military, and cultural interests, particularly in West and central Africa. With fewer colonial interests as natural partners, Germany emphasizes technologies and exports worldwide. Denmark leads the European donors in aid as a percentage of gross national product (GNP) by achieving an aid level equal to 1 percent of its GNP.

The Scandinavian donors often act in concert and are usually led by the Swedish International Development Agency, SIDA. The Scandinavians tend to be strong proponents of governmental approaches to development; most target a limited list of countries and focus on poverty alleviation. The Netherlands and the Scandinavian countries are strong supporters of the U.N. family of specialized aid-giving agencies. Finland's aid program, FINNIDA, despite its small size, shows a new toughness in requiring effectiveness, not simply largesse. As with all donor programs, Scandinavian programs mirror the prevailing philosophies of the party in power. Canada's aid plays a unique role in fostering its disinterested support for universal human values. Canada was the first donor to stress partnerships with the poorest countries in the administration of its aid. The largest donor today is Japan. Despite the large scale of its aid, Japan still looks to other donors for guidance on development priorities and administrative methods.

The Europeans themselves established the Organization for Economic Cooperation and Development (OECD), in Paris in 1948, to administer its side of the Marshall Plan. In 1960, at the conclusion of the Plan, the OECD invited the United States and Canada to join it as it evolved to coordinate trade and development policy among the western industrialized nations. Within the OECD, a Development Assistance Committee (DAC), which is chaired by the United States, focuses attention on the latest development priorities, such as transparency and corruption, on keeping aid resource flows high, and on consistency of donor terms toward the poor world.

Where AID and its predecessor agencies once dominated the foreign assistance landscape, America now contributes less than 6 percent of the worldwide total of foreign aid spending. AID country programs today are usually ranked sixth or seventh in dollar size among the bilateral donors, using Kenya and Zambia as examples. All donor countries are gradually moving toward a focus on Africa; the need is great, as are the risks to the world of its continuing food crises and political instability. Donor countries often voice a moral obligation toward Africa; several see a developing Africa as a promising market.

United Nations Agencies

The United Nations system of cooperating member nations and specialized development agencies was founded immediately after World War II, as were the International Bank for Reconstruction and Development (IBRD, or more simply, the World Bank) and the International Monetary Fund. Each of these three global institutions, the U.N., the World Bank, and the IMF, plays an important role in fostering stability and development in developing countries.

The United Nations development agencies were founded to assist war-ravaged countries in the mid-1940s, beginning with the United Nations Relief and Rehabilitation Administration (UNRRA), which drew my father to China in 1946. Today, a panoply of specialized agencies, headquartered around the world, is coordinated by the New York-based United Nations Development Programme (UNDP) and its representative UNDP offices in poor-country capitals. The major United Nations agencies include the Food and Agricultural Organization (FAO), based in Rome; the United Nations Fund for Population Activities (UNFPA), in New York; the United Nations Children's Fund (UNICEF), in New York; the United Nations Educational, Scientific and Cultural Organization (UNESCO), in Paris; the International Labor Organization (ILO) and the World Health Organization (WHO), in Geneva; the United Nations Environmental Programme (UNEP), in Nairobi; and the United Nations Industrial Development Organization (UNIDO), in Vienna. Coordinated by the resident UNDP representative, each agency provides advisory services to developing countries on grant terms (that is, as gifts).

The World Bank consists of three institutions that span the needs of the developing world for concessional (soft loan) and commercial (market rate) investments. The IBRD provides loans on slightly less than commercial terms, the International Development Association (IDA) provides highly concessional loans, and the International Finance Corporation (IFC) finances commercial investments through nonconcessional lending or equity financing (that is, the IFC may take a percentage of stock in a poor country investment).

The World Bank is governed by its 180 member nations and is housed in seventeen polished block buildings clustered around Pennsylvania Avenue, immediately West of the White House. The IMF is located next door.

The World Bank has forty-four resident missions based primarily in the poorest countries; authority for approving loan agreements, however, resides in Washington. Almost all of the World Bank's lending operations are as loans, and all loans must be repaid.

The IBRD lends roughly $15 billion annually to nearly 140 countries, and borrows from the world's capital markets to finance its lending. IDA lends $6 billion a year to fifty of the world's poorest countries. Its lending ability depends upon capital grants of roughly $3 billion a year from thirty-two wealthy nation donors. Between 1946 and 1996 the IBRD lent a total of $280 billion, IDA lent $97 billion, and the IFC financed $42 billion of private capital.[10]

The World Bank's original purpose, as its full name implies, centered on reconstruction and development following World War II. Its loans for European recovery complemented and enhanced resources that were available under the Marshall Plan. Since the 1960s, and primarily through IDA, the World Bank has greatly expanded its soft loans to the developing world for dams, roads, schools, and more recently, for broader (and more costly) programs for economic stability and reform. As the World Bank has moved away from investment-grade projects, its portfolio has been subject to greater and greater criticism.

Like other donors, the World Bank has become enculturated by the need to spend money. "Money spent" has become a proxy for development success, thereby fostering bureaucratic pressures to keep financial flows moving. Robert McNamara, one-time World Bank president, initiated this unintended culture. Like AID, the World Bank is subject to many of the same congressional and parliamentary pressures that shape all donor priorities.

The IMF has a different purpose. It was established to advise and prescribe good financial management guidelines for all countries, as well as to facilitate financial stability, which is a precondition for development. Hence the IMF's short-term, commercial-rate loans are conditioned upon agreement to balance budgets, expand revenue, control expenditures, liberalize foreign exchange controls, and management debt prudently. Like those of the World Bank, IMF loans must be repaid on schedule. Although the IMF is not, strictly speaking, a donor or aid-giving institution, its operations are integral to any comprehensive analysis of development and foreign aid.

Big governmental and government-like institutions have been joined in the development business by hundreds of foundations, private voluntary organizations (PVOs), and other nongovernmental organizations (NGOs) with broad and narrow mandates. Mostly government-funded, NGOs often play significant roles in supporting social sectoral priorities.[11]

POOR COUNTRIES ARE MOSTLY IN AFRICA

The poor world today is not the poor world of the 1950s. After World War II the world's population was less than half of what it is today, and there were fewer than fifty independent countries. In the 1950s many of the world's poor people lived in colonized and poverty stricken countries. With the subsequent independence of dozens of former European colonies, and with their development beginning in the 1960s and 1970s, a smaller proportion of the world's population today is poor, as compared with the 1950s. Today there are nearly 190 independent nation states, but fewer than a third of them are ranked by the World Bank as being poor or low-income (see Tables 1.1 and 1.2). These states are home for nearly 1.3 billion poor people.

The poorest countries today are defined by the World Bank as those with $730 or less in annual per capita income (that is, countries where people live on roughly $2 per day). Many people in these countries are very poor; they live on half this poor-world income standard, of only a dollar a day. The world's low-income countries are concentrated primarily in Africa—some thirty-four of an estimated forty-eight. There are ten low-income countries in Asia, five in Central Asia and the Middle East, and only four in Latin America and the Caribbean.

Today we see developed and developing countries almost everywhere. Postwar Europe surpasses the United States in many social indices, such as literacy and longevity; the newly rich countries of East Asia have become heated trade competitors. Each year another country that used to be poor adds its name to the list of those that are developing rapidly.

Classifying developing countries into two groups, those that are developing rapidly and those that are developing late or low-income, is not easy. There are no standards or even firm definitions. Each country and its problems are special.

Some countries' successes were hard to imagine only a few years ago. South Korea, for example, in the 1960s ranked as very poor, along with Bangladesh. Bangladesh today is faring better than most experts had predicted in the 1970s. If the development history of the 1960s and 1970s is a guide, we will witness significant improvements in coming decades among the low-income countries listed in Tables 1.1 and 1.2.

It is striking that so much has been accomplished; the then-poor world of the immediate postwar era is, in short, history. The hundreds of millions of poor people today—1.3 billion out of 6 billion people as estimated by the World Bank—serve to dramatize the reality of successful development

Table 1.1
Africa's Poor Countries

Country	Population, mid-1996 in millions	GNP per capita 1996 dollars
Mozambique	18.0	80
Ethiopia	58.2	100
Congo, Dem. Rep.	45.2	130
Chad	6.6	160
Tanzania	30.5	170
Burundi	6.4	170
Malawi	9.8	180
Rwanda	6.7	190
Sierra Leone	4.6	200
Niger	9.3	200
Burkina Faso	10.7	230
Nigeria	114.6	240
Mali	10.0	240
Madagascar	13.7	250
Guinea-Bissau	1.1	250
Angola	11.1	270
Uganda	19.7	300
Togo	4.1	310
Central African Republic	3.3	310
Kenya	27.3	320
São Tomé and Principe	0.1	330
Benin	5.6	350
Zambia	9.2	360
Ghana	17.5	360
Comoros	0.5	450
Mauritania	2.3	470
Equatorial Guinea	0.4	530
Guinea	6.8	560
Senegal	8.5	570
Zimbabwe	11.2	610
Cameroon	13.7	610
Lesotho	2.0	660
Côte d'Ivoire	14.3	660
Congo, Rep.	2.7	670

Source: World Bank, *1998 World Bank Atlas*, pp. 16–17, 24–25.

for many countries and development's continuing importance for late-developing countries. Poor countries and poor people are just as poor as they were in the 1950s, if not more so, but there are fewer of them and their poverty is differently understood.

One reason there are fewer low-income countries is that the world's population is not growing as rapidly as was once projected. "Standing room only" is no longer the inevitable grim prospect that it was thought to be in the 1950s. Population projections into the next century now indicate that with shared development and family planning, the world's population will stabilize at around eight billion people, two billion more than today's six billion.[12] Fertility rates continue to decline worldwide, from an average of 6.0 children per woman in 1970 to 3.6 in 1993.[13]

This earlier-than-expected population stability dramatizes the glaring nature of poverty in the remaining poor world. Partly because of declining population growth rates, social well-being is improving. Infant mortality has declined from 180 per thousand births in 1950–55 to 69 per thousand in 1990–95, or illustrated more dramatically, infant deaths have fallen from nearly one out of every five babies to fewer than one in fourteen. Average life expectancy in developing countries has increased by half, from 40.7 years in 1950–55 to 62.4 years in 1990–95.[14]

We are becoming an educated globe.[15] Schooling has become nearly universal at the primary level in developing countries. Ninety-seven percent of all children attend primary school, and half of all children are in secondary school. Schooling for girls has also expanded dramatically; primary school enrollment has nearly doubled in South Asia, from 50 percent in 1970 to 93 percent in 1992.

The good news from developing countries must not distract from our ability to face the challenges and risks that remain for poor, late-developing countries. These macrodata disguise serious, even explosive problems—the gross mal-distribution of income, food insecurity, widespread squalor, and massive underemployment in most of the world's cities.

According to the United Nations, the poorest 20 percent of the world's people saw their share of global income decline from 2.3 percent to 1.4 percent in the past thirty years. The proportion of poor people experiencing negative growth more than tripled, from 5 percent to 18 percent of the world's population. Incomes in sub-Saharan Africa began to decline in the late 1970s; twenty of these countries are still below their per capita incomes of twenty years ago.[16] Literacy is declining; nearly 60 million children in Africa leave primary school early.[17]

Table 1.2
Poor Countries in Other Regions

Country	Population, mid-1996 in millions	GNP per capita 1996 dollars
Asia		
Nepal	22.0	210
Bangladesh	121.7	260
Vietnam	75.4	290
Cambodia	10.2	300
Mongolia	2.5	360
India	945.1	380
Lao, DPR	4.7	400
Pakistan	133.5	480
Sri Lanka	18.3	740
China	1215.4	750
Central Asia and Middle East		
Tajikistan	5.9	340
Yemen Republic	15.8	380
Azerbaijan	7.6	480
Kyrgyz Republic	4.6	550
Armenia	3.8	630
Latin America and Caribbean		
Haiti	7.3	310
Nicaragua	4.5	380
Honduras	6.1	660
Guyana	0.8	690

Source: World Bank, *1998 World Bank Atlas*, pp. 16–17, 24–25.

Furthermore, countries can prosper temporarily, then collapse. The term *failed state* is now common. Successful development entails robust governments and markets that are capable of weathering economic and political setbacks. Development comes with no lifetime guarantee. The failed states of Somalia and Sudan are joined by those of the new Congo (formerly Zaire) and Liberia. Several of Asia's successes have faltered.

We should also look to our own backyard; slippage has occurred with alarming regularity among our southern neighbors. The relatively high income levels in Latin America have declined over the past decade. Eleven countries out of the twenty-six experienced declines in per capita incomes over the twenty years between 1975 and 1995.[18]

Finally, the difference between recognized developing countries and still-poor ones offers confirmation that development is now the norm and not the exception. That is good news. But it is also true that the scale and complexion of poverty remain serious. Eighty million people are added to the world's population each year, primarily in Africa, South Asia, and China. It is Africa, however, that is least able to handle these burgeoning numbers. Unlike the rest of the world, which is approaching population stability, Africa's population will double in the next two generations.[19] The development record, taken as a whole, is a good one. Now, can Africa come to embrace every expectation for its own prosperity?

NOTES

1. Albert Camus, quoted in Robert Royal, "The Other Camus," *The Wilson Quarterly*, Autumn 1995, p. 52.

2. The Council on Foreign Relations, *Financing American Leadership: Protecting American Interests and Promoting American Values*, January 1997; and USAID, *Polls and Public Opinion: The Myth of Opposition to Foreign Assistance*, January 23, 1995.

3. USAID, Office of Reimbursable Development Programs, *Benefits to the United States from American Technical Assistance Activities Abroad, Some Case Studies*, 1972.

4. Philip G. Pardey et al., *Hidden Harvest: U.S. Benefits From International Research Aid*, International Food Policy Research Institute (IFPRI), Food Policy Statements, September 1996, preface and p. 11.

5. John Eriksson, principal author, *The International Response to Conflict and Genocide: Lessons from the Rwanda Experience, Synthesis Report*, The Danish Government and the Organization for Economic Co-operation and Development, Development Assistance Committee (OECD, DAC) Joint Evaluation of Emergency Assistance to Rwanda, 1996, pp. 25 and 34.

6. D. Smith, *The State of War and Peace Atlas*, Third Edition, London: The Penguin Group, 1997. Quoted in IFPRI, *The World Food Situation: Recent Developments, Emerging Issues, and Long-Term Prospects*, October 27, 1997, p. 25.

7. Throughout the book I use *AID* to refer to the United States Agency for International Development—often referred to officially as "USAID." I prefer the term AID, spoken as "A–I–D." I use *aid* to refer to donor assistance generally, including bilateral donor governments, multilateral development banks, the World Bank, the IMF, and the specialized United Nations agencies.

8. USAID, *U.S. Overseas Loans and Grants and Assistance from International Organizations*, July 1, 1945–September 30, 1996, p. 4.

9. Ibid, p. 4.

10.   Ibid, p. 225.

11.   For reviews of multilateral and bilateral donors see the annual OECD, DAC reports (for the DAC's aid database, see www.oecd.org/dac); John W. Koehring, *AID's In-Country Presence—An Assessment*, USAID, Center for Development Information and Evaluation (CDIE), October 1992; and Peter J. Schraeder, Steven W. Hook, and Bruce Taylor, "Clarifying The Foreign Aid Puzzle—A Comparison of American, Japanese, French, and Swedish Aid Flows," *World Politics*, 50:2, January 1998.

12.   David Seckler and Michael Rock, *World Population Growth and Food Demand to 2035*, Washington, D.C.: Winrock International, September 1996, p. 1. See also David Seckler, *Trends in World Food Needs: Toward Zero Growth In The 21st Century*, Winrock International, 1994; and David Seckler and Gerald Cox, *Fertility Rates and Population Projections: Why The United Nations Low Population Project Is Best*, Winrock International, 1994.

13.   World Bank, *1996 World Bank Atlas*, pp. 18–19.

14.   World Bank *Atlas*, for 1996 and 1997; and James W. Fox, *What Do We Know About World Poverty?* USAID, CDIE, Evaluation Special Study Report No. 74, May 1995, p. 2.

15.   Fox, 1995, pp. 9–10.

16.   United Nations Development Programme, *Human Development Report 1996*, New York: Oxford University Press, 1996, p. 2.

17.   Kevin Watkins, "Life and Debt Situation," *The Financial Times*, January 23, 1998.

18.   Inter-American Development Bank, *IDB 1996 Pocket Profiles*, pp. 6–27.

19.   Seckler and Rock, 1996, Table 1 and p.10, and Per Pinstrup-Andersen, Rajul Pandya-Lorch, and Mark W. Rosegrant, *The World Food Situation: Recent Developments, Emerging Issues, and Long-Term Prospects*, Washington, D.C.: IFPRI, October 27, 1997, pp. 5, 15, 49, 50.

2

Washington's AID Program

EVOLUTION OF AID PROGRAM PRIORITIES

America was once the lone donor providing foreign assistance. Today, dozens of bilateral, multilateral, and NGO aid donors fill the poor world. This chapter examines America's aid priorities as they are defined and directed by Washington pressures. AID, like all donors, is fundamentally a creation of domestic political interests.

The Marshall Plan's focus on rebuilding European cities and heavy infrastructure such as factories, ports, highways, and railways led to similar programs in Asia and Latin America. While much of this infrastructure still functions today, it gradually became clear that the economic "trickle down" of predominantly urban and industrial growth—from large factories and heavy infrastructure—did not benefit or trickle down to poor populations in poor countries.

As development theorists and aid planners began to realize the shortcomings of trickle down theory in the 1970s, legislated assistance priorities began to shift. Hard infrastructural programs gave way to soft, people-oriented programs. Since 1973 AID has been mandated by Congress to emphasize poverty reduction directly by focusing assistance on small farm households; on the poor majority (mostly rural); on the informal sector of small businesses (mostly urban); and on education, health, and family planning.

In recognition that dollars alone and even specialized programs do not necessarily equate with development for people, AID began to broaden its focus to encompass the enabling environment; that is, the economic environment in which public policy and administrative practices in poor countries encourage private investment and individual well-being. The concern for an enabling environment was motivated in part by oil price shocks in the late 1970s and the subsequent declines in economic growth and corresponding increases in debt burdens. Attacking poverty at its roots, we realized, required an enabling environment to promote businesses of all shapes and sizes. In the 1990s AID priorities expanded further to emphasize education for girls and women, the environment, and democracy.

Inevitably, the number of AID priorities has grown over the years, from building bridges and ports to planting trees, rural health, and prosthetics for the war-torn. New priorities are added annually; none are removed. In total today, AID's congressional authorization stipulates thirty-three separate goals and seventy-five priority areas.

Misleading lessons had been drawn by experts from the success of the Marshall Plan. For AID in Washington, the resource-centered lessons explain many of Congress' frustrations with the aid business: All this money spent and yet so many people remain poor! The Marshall Plan led to unintended difficulties in later years because the plan's success for Europe fostered the idea that development was primarily a matter of financial and material largesse. The institutional and educational preconditions existing in Europe that made dollar and material transfers so effective simply do not exist to the same degree, nor can they be easily created in or transferred to, the poor world. Late-developing countries do not have the deeply rooted traditions of open markets and democracy that made possible Marshall Plan contributions to European recovery. Africa, for example, does not have Europe's trained manpower or vast educational system.

Today, despite all the congressional pressures and aid lessons learned, the idea that material largesse is necessary and even sufficient for development remains fixed in the popular and policy mind alike. The story of development and aid, my story in these chapters, is one that addresses squarely this complex and vexing issue.

From the beginning, America's aid programs have served multiple foreign policy objectives, not just developmental and humanitarian mandates. Foreign assistance has always served the objectives and interests of other federal government departments besides AID. The Departments of State, Defense, Agriculture, Commerce, and the Environmental Protection Agency have learned that economic assistance legislation offers a useful way to obtain complementary resources. Because of their own related but independent agendas, several departments and agencies take a keen interest in the budgetary outcome of each foreign assistance bill.

America's domestic support for foreign aid translates into food grain export opportunities; college and consulting firm contracts; and air, shipping, and other transportation services. To these broad commercial and academic interests must be added the interests of social, ethnic, and religious organizations pursuing specific agendas involving poverty alleviation, health, human rights, and conflict resolution. AID-funded exports and AID-funded university and business contracts are shared with nearly every one of our fifty states; three or four receive more than $100 million a year in AID-funded contracts and grants.

AID's priorities are therefore inevitably and ultimately shaped by the participation of diverse interest groups. Each has its say, and generally its budgetary reward, in the form of contracts and grants that implement AID's program priorities.

Domestic and foreign policy interests often become blurred as they become entangled with and written into foreign aid legislation. The cold war served to dilute and divert America's generous development resolve during the decades following the Marshall Plan. Increasingly, the foreign affairs budget has been used to support our worldwide security interests. Consequently, congressional consensus building often has a stiff price. Each department involved with foreign affairs and each interest group command a share of the aid budget with the consequence that aid flows as much to our many foreign policy interests and to its supporters as it does to poor people overseas. AID's development objectives can be diminished in the finely negotiated compromise.

THE FOREIGN AID BUDGET

AID has more than one master within the Washington Beltway. Like other democratically derived programs built on leadership and consensus, the mission, programs, and budgets of this agency are complex. A full understanding of AID requires knowledge not just of its history but of its annual congressional authorization and budget process.

Although the U.S. Constitution gives authority for the conduct of foreign affairs to the president, the president in turn has delegated daily responsibility in this area to the Department of State, where AID is, by statute, located. However, given AID's status as a subcabinet level, even temporary agency, its authorization to exist must be voted anew every year, as must its annual budget. Congress, therefore, exercises considerable authority in both foreign policy and foreign assistance.

In practice, Congress and the president hold the Department of State and AID primarily responsible for carrying out America's foreign assistance policies. However, the total foreign assistance budget is administered by several other federal departments, not just by State and AID, which often leads to fierce budget battles on Capitol Hill. The foreign assistance budget, the "150 Account," is where the real battles take place. It is sharply scrutinized throughout the year by both the executive branch and Congress. Table 2.1 illustrates the principal budget elements in the fiscal year (FY) 1998 foreign affairs account. The 150 Account, totaling $19 billion, makes up slightly more than 1 percent of the overall federal budget of $1,672 billion for FY 1998. The shape of the budget reflects both the shape of our foreign policy priorities and of power in Washington.

Table 2.1

The Foreign Affairs "150 Account" Budget for Fiscal Year 1998,
in billions of dollars

World Bank, MDBs, United Nations agencies and programs, IO&P	1.723
AID, including portions of other programs	3.687
P.L. 480 Titles II and III	.867
Economic Support Fund	2.420
Foreign Military Financing	3.363
Migration and Refugee Assistance	.650
Peace Corps	.226
Export-Import Bank	.696
U.S. Information Agency, other media	1.133
State Department, conduct of foreign affairs, and other programs	4.267
Total	19.032

Source: FY 1998 estimates contained in the USAID, *FY 1999 Congressional Presentation.*
Note: MDBs—multilateral developments banks; IO&P— international organizations and programs.

The annual 150 Account contains the funding for the Treasury and State Departments, AID, the United States Information Agency (USIA), the Peace Corps, and several other departments involved in foreign affairs. In addition to departmental allocations, the 150 Account is loaded with dozens of special programs and interests, enough to do a Christmas tree proud.

Budget battles are compounded by the multiple departmental responsibilities, assigned by Congress, which are expressed within this one budget, as the principal line items in Table 2.1 indicate. In addition to AID's budget and administrative responsibilities, the U.S. Treasury is responsible for U.S. policy guidance for and budget contributions to the World Bank, the

IMF, and other multilateral development banks. The Treasury Department, not State, was deemed responsible for serious money—namely loans. Grants, which did not have to be repaid, and which could therefore be treated less seriously, were handed to the State Department and AID—with telling consequences for aid creativity and debt, as detailed in later chapters.

The State Department is responsible for crafting policy and for making grants to the United Nations specialized agencies and other international organizations and programs. AID's bilateral budget of $2.4 billion in FY 1998 contains programs defined by Congress as *development assistance.* Within this category, major subcategories include child survival, family planning, funds for micro and small enterprises, urban and environmental credits, and disaster relief. In addition, AID administers other budget elements of the 150 Account, country by country, with varying degrees of State Department involvement and approval. These include the Economic Support Fund (ESF) ($2.4 billion), development assistance for Eastern Europe and the independent states of the former Soviet Union ($1.3 billion), and Titles II and III of P.L. 480 ($867 million). In sum, AID administers $6.9 billion, or a third of the 150 Account.

Security assistance, in the forms of ESF and foreign military financing (FMF), are packaged with foreign assistance where their security and military nature are less easily perceived. ESF may be used for bona fide development programs in some countries, but this account primarily serves long-standing security agreements for the Camp David Peace Accords and for access to military bases (in Turkey, for example). The United States, the world's military power and watchdog, is often criticized by domestic interests and other donors for using its aid budget in this manner.

The Camp David Peace Accords consume the lion's share of the 150 Account. The Accords, funded through ESF and FMF, provided Israel and Egypt with $5.1 billion in FY 1998, the largest share of the combined annual budget of $19 billion. This level of funding, stable over many years, remains an open-ended commitment. These resources are transferred to Israel as cash, and to Egypt for policy and project-based development programs administered by AID in Cairo.

Of the $3.7 billion allocated expressly to AID within the 150 Account, only $2.4 billion, or 70 percent, is directly allocated for development assistance across the developing world. Viewing the 150 Account as a whole, only 13 percent of the $19 billion total is directed as America's support for poor countries. Overall, $1 billion is for Africa.

Contrary to the impression given by a first reading of the 150 Account, portions of security assistance are programmed by AID to ensure development impact. Dollar and food programs in fact serve multiple purposes. It is in this complex resource environment that AID strives to achieve aid impact in late-developing countries.

Funding for the 150 Account fell by half in real terms between 1985 and 1996. Broad budget cuts to balance the domestic budget have hit foreign policy especially hard. Several regional and country programs have been cut prematurely because of resource constraints in Washington. Consequently, AID has been forced at times to "graduate" countries, that is, terminate aid assistance early, often placing promising development programs in these countries at risk, as in the cases of Venezuela and Costa Rica.

AID has had as many as 110 offices overseas at any one time; some have been staffed with a handful of American Foreign Service career officers; a few with hundreds of career staff, contractors, and national support staff. AID staff levels peaked at 17,600 American career officers in the late 1960s during the Vietnam era. Staff levels have declined to around 4,000 today (with 2,500 overseas), partly because of U.S. budget pressures and partly because of the perception in some quarters that aid does not work.

The total number of overseas AID missions has also declined since the 1970s, from a high of 110 missions and offices in 1992 to fewer than 80 today. This tends to have a negative effect on other donors, who often follow the lead of the United States. Reflecting our own budget cutbacks, worldwide aid levels fell by 40 percent between 1991 and 1996.[1]

Each year two or three AID missions close as countries graduate. They may then turn to commercial loans and investments to fund development, or they fail, in our eyes, to deserve continuing assistance and therefore may be graduated for this reason. At the same time, one or two missions open each year, following resolution of political, humanitarian, or ethnic crises, when requested assistance can be effectively used for economic recovery.

Programs and dollar levels, divided up for individual AID country recipients, are fought over in often heated meetings between AID and State Department officials in Washington throughout the fiscal year. At the same time, embassies and AID missions are frequently kept off balance, defending programs and dollar levels that were promised to host countries, striving to work with congressional program directives, and hoping that promised monies will be allocated and formally signed with country recipients before the fiscal year runs out on September 30th at midnight.

Much tension is created because there is little to go around after special mandates and interests are satisfied. Ceaseless budget tensions help to explain the "we-they" syndrome that has long characterized the differences in perspective between Washington and its far-flung embassies and AID missions.

HAMSTRUNG AT THE START: CONGRESSIONAL MICROMANAGEMENT

The executive branch is being increasingly hamstrung by congressional directives to spend foreign affairs money in specific ways. In the 1960s and 1970s, Congress allocated money for general categories of development, such as agriculture and education. In more recent years, however, congressional micromanagement has led to earmarks . . . to legislated requirements to spend for specific activities, even by country and type of contractor, such as American voluntary agencies, and American colleges and universities.

Consensus-building on Capitol Hill can and does define foreign policy to a degree that reduces the ability of the executive branch to represent America's interests overseas. Congress often tells AID to go forth and do good, and by the way, spend x dollars for priority y with contractor z. The intent of earmarking may be idealistic (such as promoting better child health in Africa), but it can also be less than transparent, such as assigning contracts and grants for special interests and specific constituents. Consequently, field experience and bilateral agreements are often jeopardized.

Similar to earmarking, "holds" are frequently used by Congress to delay executive branch spending for issues of congressional concern. Under this common practice, AID and the State Department must testify to the Hill's satisfaction on all manner of issues, large and small, or else a particular project's funding will remain blocked. Holds are often used as proxies for larger foreign policy issues, for example, for a democracy project in a country that violates human rights. Like earmarks, holds can lead to incoherent planning and haphazard implementation of executive, even congressional intent.

Earmarking and holds have grown in importance, step by step, year by year. Because AID must win support on the Hill every year simply to sustain its operations, its administrators are naturally anxious to please. Because the State Department is responsible for foreign policy, it sees AID dollars as its own and therefore supports approval of AID's budget. State Department and AID management often plot with congressional and outside interests to reach consensus. Accommodations have to be made.

In order to secure funding and special priorities of their own, and to compete against other foreign assistance supplicants, AID staff may be found on the Hill dealing directly with congressional staff outside of authorized agency channels. Conversely, if an AID manager threatens to cut a poorly performing but special interest project, the phones at AID will ring within the hour.[2]

What has long been a major problem for AID has become a major problem for foreign policy in general as Congress increasingly ties the aid budget to its priorities. Earmarking and holds have grown into an industry, and in some cases so completely define aid dollar use that an executive branch objective for a policy, program, region, or country must be abandoned. On this problem, the White House, the State Department, and AID agree.

Congressional earmarks and holds also tend to kill professionalism and render project evaluation futile. Professionals in the field and at AID headquarters are frustrated by mandates based on scattered congressional priorities rather than on analysis, field experience, and recipient needs and requests. In the words of former Deputy Secretary of State Larry Eagleburger, "earmarks are killing us."[3]

Examples of special interests and earmarks illustrate the kinds of distortions criticized by Deputy Secretary Eagleburger:

First is the earmarked funding for the Israel-Egypt Peace Accords, which were reached at Camp David in 1976, more than twenty years ago. Economic and military grants of $5.1 billion a year represent more than a quarter of the overall foreign affairs budget, and have escaped budget cutbacks despite domestic pressures for a balanced budget. All other items in the 150 Account have been cut to protect these open-ended peace accords, with both immediate and potentially far-reaching consequences. The American people have been told for years that we are very close to a comprehensive peace (in the Middle East)—now is not the time to cut these levels. Yet a majority of Americans, 56 percent, would curtail aid for Israel and Egypt (and 52 percent would curtail military aid in general, world-wide).[4]

As a direct consequence of the Camp David Accords, AID has trimmed numerous programs in other regions, especially in the former Soviet Union, Asia, and in Central and Latin America, and has tended to graduate some countries prematurely. The sanctity of the accords means that AID's overall food and agriculture budget is effectively "scraped to the bone" to protect commitments to security interests.[5]

A second, smaller yet common, example is provided by the AID program in Zambia. In fiscal year 1996, AID in Zambia received twice the funding for health that it could usefully spend because of special interest influences. Three other AID priorities—on agriculture, democracy, and privatization—were cut in half with deleterious consequences for Zambian development.

A third example is found in Latin America, where eleven countries are experiencing per capita income declines while the war on drugs continues unabated and unsuccessful. U.S. assistance was cut by two-thirds during the early 1990s. For more than forty years the United States contributed $30 billion in development assistance to Latin America. The cut in U.S. aid to the region from roughly a billion dollars down to 300 million per year is jeopardizing trade's growth, not to mention the drug war. Similarly, in the former Soviet Union, AID budget cuts have seriously compromised democracy promotion, economic stability, and the control of nuclear and chemical weapons. Many experts believe that such risks are unacceptable.

A final example illustrates how American food aid created opportunities for our commercial food exports. In FY 1996 the U.S. agricultural trade surplus reached $35 billion, the bulk of which was exported to Asian countries. Of the fifty largest buyers of U.S. farm goods over the years, thirty-four have received P.L. 480 food in the past. South Korea now buys as much from American farmers *in one year* as it received in twenty-five years as a P.L. 480 recipient. While the Agriculture and Commerce Departments have active U.S. export enhancement programs, AID is the only federal agency that works directly to promote economic viability in developing countries, which enlarges their trade. Earmarks have served to cut funds for AID's growth priority programs, which has resulted in deleterious consequences both for recipient countries and for U.S. trade. The same kind of growth-oriented development efforts, with dollars and food aid, are still required in Africa.

Earmarking and holds are symptomatic of the continuing tensions between the legislative and executive branches. These tensions have their genesis in the Vietnam War and more recently in various Central American and Middle Eastern adventures. Congress has good reasons to exercise control over foreign policy, above and beyond oversight. When there are policy differences between a president and Congress, foreign assistance earmarks and holds serve as one way to question and even redirect presidential priorities. However, the question for development theorists and aid administrators is whether the ultimate effect of checks and balances is a dilution of America's commitment to the alleviation of poverty.

Examining AID from inside Washington helps to explain its relations with Congress as well as problems that are of AID's own creation. Over the years AID has been vigorously criticized for waste, mismanagement, and sometimes criminal conduct. We may now understand that some waste reflects congressional or cold war security priorities, as illustrated in earlier examples, or even a vested interest. By law and executive branch decision, AID has disbursed large amounts of public monies down foreign rat holes. Congressional interests written into law force AID to bend to political pressures, rather than to serve the interests of the people AID is authorized to serve.

Many AID staff spend their careers in Washington defining and defending AID programs. Even overseas staff spend an inordinate amount of time meeting congressional requirements. Few critics of AID differentiate between AID's real internal problems, its palpable external pressures, and the consequences of both for foreign policy. In short, AID has remained an easy target. Hardly a study is written prescribing its reform without the same simplistic mistake being made: If only AID would serve the national interest and poor people in poor countries. But AID cannot serve multiple and often conflicting goals.

AID AND THE STATE DEPARTMENT—TROUBLE IN FOGGY BOTTOM

AID's difficulties stem not only from its relations with Congress but also from its subservient role to the Department of State. State Department priorities are expressed in major speeches and on a daily basis through diplomatic channels. Its career officers serve national objectives of promoting alliances, fostering markets and trade, promoting peace, strengthening democratic values, and protecting the world community against transnational dangers. These objectives are primarily served through diplomacy. Most Department objectives are dealt with over the short-term; some of them entail funding. Many of these objectives have implications for longer-term development and staff.

But in facing multiple foreign policy goals and pressures, the State Department has remained static in the postwar storm of change. Like AID, the State Department is subject to a number of internal and external forces, but more are inbred and are of longer standing.

The Department's authority within the U.S. government has been severely eroded since the end of World War II. Many of its responsibilities have been siphoned off to other departments and agencies. Examples include delegating the responsibility for directing the World Bank, the IMF, and the other development banks to the U.S. Treasury; delegating commercial matters to the Department of Commerce and the Foreign Commercial Service; assigning trade to a newly created Office of the Trade Representative, which now manages U.S. relations with the even-newer World Trade Organization; and the Department of Agriculture's management of P.L. 480 Title I concessional agricultural sales. All of these delegations have implications for our foreign policy interests and for those of the developing world. The Defense Department has development strategies to guide its worldwide preparedness priorities, knowing well that many kinds of conflict are rooted in poverty. The Defense Department understands the dilemmas of its new peacemaking and peacekeeping functions in a development context, in marked contrast to the State Department's failure to conduct diplomacy on the basis of medium- to longer-term analyses of the world, developmental or otherwise.[6]

The State Department's embassies offer overt and covert platforms for other federal interests be they AID, the Library of Congress, the FBI, the IRS, the Drug Enforcement Agency, or the intelligence services. As many as forty federal agencies can be represented in an embassy and need to be coordinated by an ambassador and functional and administrative staff. Not all agencies pay attention to an ambassador's coordinating responsibilities.

Competition in the formulation of foreign policy increasingly comes from vested domestic and foreign interests, which further restricts the State Department's authority and flexibility to define agenda priorities and to implement policy. Examples are found in Israel and other Middle East countries; and China, Mexico, and Cuba; not to mention new forces, such as transnational corporations and international capital markets.

Because of the complexity of international relations, dozens of federal agencies, state governments, and global corporations deal directly with foreign governments and multilateral institutions with hardly a nod to the Department of State. In short, competition to control foreign policy remains the State Department's constant preoccupation.

MERGING AID FURTHER INTO THE STATE DEPARTMENT?

There has been considerable debate inside the Washington Beltway over the merging of AID and other international agencies, such as USIA, with the State Department to better coordinate foreign policy and foreign assistance. But as the previous discussion makes clear, AID is already merged with State. The Department and its ambassadors approve AID budgets, country programs, and overseas staff.

Few critics acknowledge that the basis for tensions between AID and the State Department rest with Congress, for it is Congress—not State or AID—that authorizes AID's long-term commitment to development, in part to curb the Department's historic tradition to deal in short-term goals, for which flexible policies and spending authority ("walking around money") are said to be needed. In this sense, the State Department's issues are more with Congress than with AID.

Deputy Secretary of State Larry Eagleburger understood the value of the present AID-State status quo when he said, "we don't want you!" The State Department already has sufficient control of key AID policy decisions. Why should it take on special congressional interests by the hour, be responsible for AID project design and implementation and, in particular, be accountable for AID's budget? Partial mergers of the State Department and AID geographical functions have occurred in the past, such as for Latin America, but they did not work and were dissolved.

A few development experts and AID proponents have recommended an independent agency free from extraneous influences. Only once did Congress pass legislation separating AID from the State Department. President Jimmy Carter and Congress, in part to honor Senator Hubert Humphrey, agreed to the International Development Cooperation Act (IDCA) of 1979, which established AID directly under the president. International and domestic crises at the time prevented the Act from becoming operational; IDCA remains a shell—an entry in the AID telephone book.

To be even-handed, the picture is not as bleak as I paint it. There has been merger progress of the kind that counts. The State Department established a bureau for global issues that gives selected worldwide problems an organizational focus that, in turn, strengthens ties with AID because these issues may be addressed through development. The Department's Bureau for Human Rights makes the same organizational contribution to the Department's broadened vision, and to AID's work in promoting democracy. AID and State now have more reason to coordinate and to cooperate.

As if to guarantee that no one gets carried away with the possibility of a more effective relationship, AID has moved out of the State Department building, its home for nearly fifty years, to new quarters on Pennsylvania Avenue, closer to Capitol Hill.

AMERICAN FOREIGN AID—MYTHS AND REALITIES

A Washington view of AID provides a vital but incomplete picture of how AID serves and is shaped by America's foreign assistance interests. Myths abound in the aid business.

The first myth has to do with AID's dollar claims on the federal budget. Roughly $18 billion to $20 billion a year during the 1980s and the early 1990s, AID cost less than 1 percent of the federal budget; yet one aspiring

Congressman campaigned on a claim that the first thing he would do when he got to Washington would be to cut $300 billion from the aid budget.

The second myth is that Americans are against foreign aid and that they believe far too large a share of their taxes are wasted on give-away programs. A University of Maryland opinion poll found the opposite. Most Americans believe that aid should account for 5 percent of the federal budget and that there is a strong commitment to humanitarian and development aid and a willingness to question the use of aid for strategic, military, and other foreign policy interests. Furthermore, most Americans support government aid as a moral obligation and not simply for use as commercial or economic interests. An overwhelming majority reject the idea that the United States should give aid only when it serves national interests. A strong majority see recipient development as a way to avoid the necessity of American relief, and that poor countries need to be helped to address their own disasters. Americans state, according to the Maryland poll, that if they could be assured that their money was being spent well, and not to prop up corrupt regimes, they would be willing to pay more; a few respondents said considerably more.

One has to conclude that Washington myth-making has been success-ful. The negative images of American aid have been created by AID's supposed supporters—Congress, the media, and even private voluntary agencies and contractors. The American people pay the price for the lack of comprehensive representation. One poll makes it clear that Americans see an America more actively engaged in the world today than it was during the cold war.

No case is made in these pages for more foreign aid dollars, but it should be gratifying for an agency under siege to know that the American people support what it does, even though Congress belies that manifest commitment. A government accused of watching public opinion polls and shaping its policies accordingly appears to have overlooked a source of support for foreign assistance.

REFLECTIONS ON A WASHINGTON PERSPECTIVE

Even with the best of Washington intentions, and the best is usually voiced by the U.S. government, foreign assistance raises tough questions. America's national interests depend upon worldwide defense, commercial development, and, as I argue in these pages, development policy. These must be backed by resolve, professionalism, and resources.

How do we justify and implement these interests today? Few would claim that development is such a sure thing for guaranteeing universal stability and well-being that it obviates the need for a strong defense, or that defense obviates the need for development. Few would argue that global commerce is the complete answer.

America has yet, as a matter of strategic interest and guiding policy, stated that development can and does reduce the manifold risks of divisiveness and instability, or that development enhances commerce worldwide, or, even more importantly, that development helps a country address global issues. And within these interests and issues, that late-developing countries require special attention.

There is plenty of skepticism around. What about a still-poor world in which, having already contributed a great deal, the United States has little to show for it? Some critics point out that we have already spent billions for development over several decades, yet crises have been the reward. If aid contributed to the heading off of trouble between 1971 and 1994, then what of Haiti (which received $3.1 billion in U.S. aid during this period), or Burundi with $4.1 billion, Rwanda with $4.5 billion, Zaire with $7.8 billion, Somalia with $8 billion, and Sudan with $13.4 billion?[7]

Did American aid compound their present predicament? Probably. It was aid of the cold war variety. Using American aid largely to serve nondevelopmental interests is a lesson we cannot afford to repeat. And yet we are. Forty-three government agencies have already spent $290 billion to control and interdict the international drug trade.[8]

A foreign policy not founded on a longer-term, developmental understanding of global change is one that risks being caught in daily crises. The United States is not going to withdraw from the world (but we are sending troops in harm's way less frequently). To cut foreign affairs funding further, which is our diplomatic, nonmilitary foreign policy instrument, provides the president and Congress with fewer options than they have at present. The lack of a strong developmentally oriented strategic vision by the executive branch leaves policy vulnerable to the vagaries of politics, to ad hoc policy implementation, and to the open-ended use of the United States military. Doing little for development in the fractious, still-poor world guarantees the further need and immense cost for military, for humanitarian aid, and, ultimately, for development itself. Deterrence must be based on development.

Broad development issues have a personal immediacy. What kind of AID can attempt to carry these burdens? I joined AID in 1971 and was told by my new colleagues that morale had never been lower. I soon learned that development, life even, was in the field—overseas. And as much as Washington determines AID's budget, its very existence even, the field has always been where the action is. With each return to Washington the realities of morale, budgets, and agency survival were driven home. From 1971 to 1972 I worked on the Pakistan and Bangladesh desks in Washington; from 1977 to 1979, after I returned from Bangladesh, I worked on rural development and food aid issues; and from 1991 to 1994, after living in Indonesia, Kenya, and Tanzania, I worked on Latin America. With each return my colleagues voiced the same refrain, that morale had declined further. Upon retiring from AID in 1996, following two years in Zambia, morale was said to be still lower.

The erosion of American presence overseas has its parallel in Washington. Downsizing AID and the State Department sounds like a good idea (who can be in favor of bloated bureaucracies?), but downsizing during the 1990s has also served to disguise a serious erosion of AID's field experience and authority. Why is morale down? Economic growth and employment have not been the politically correct flavor during the 1990s. AID budgets have been redirected to serve congressional interests and not hard-won development lessons from the field. Senior-level signaling within AID makes it clear that experience, staff discussion, and individual courage are not welcome. New computerization, with old technology, has cost $100 million already and has yielded little. Congress and the State Department continue to increase their involvement in AID's daily project activities. AID staff training has been discontinued. Field analyses and authority appear to get in the way of special interests; AID staff appear to get in the way of World Bank and IMF macroeconomic prerogatives. In short, AID is witnessing an erosion of its own strategic vision and capability.[9]

These reversals in hard-won AID capacities are not the stuff of leadership and innovation for new international challenges or for America's global interests. Best development and aid practices must be institutionalized and sustained. The spark of American experience and presence overseas must be respected and strengthened.

NOTES

Material has been drawn from publications of USAID's Office of Legislative and Public Affairs; from *State 2000—A New Model for Managing Foreign Affairs*, by the U.S. Department of State Management Task Force, December 1992; from USAID's FY 1997 *Congressional Presentation*; and from Vernon Ruttan's study, *United States Development Assistance Policy—The Domestic Politics of Foreign Economic Aid*, Johns Hopkins University Press, 1996. See also United States Foreign Assistance Oral History Program, *An Interview with Joseph F. Stepanek*, 1997, Association for Diplomatic Studies and Training, Arlington, Virginia.

1.   Per Pinstrup-Andersen, Rajul Pandya-Lorch, and Mark W. Rosegrant, *The World Food Situation: Recent Developments, Emerging Issues, and Long-Term Prospects*, Washington, D.C.: International Food Policy Research Institute (IFPRI), October 27, 1997, p. 21.

2.   AID, senior officer, personal communication, July 6, 1994.

3.   Address to State Department and AID staff, January 15, 1993.

4.   Steven Kull, principal investigator, *Americans and Foreign Aid—A Study of American Public Attitudes—Summary of Findings*, Program on International Policy Attitudes, a joint program conducted by the Center for the Study of Policy Attitudes and the Center for International and Security Studies at the Maryland School of Public Affairs, The University of Maryland, January 23, 1995; and Steven Kull and I. M. Destler, principal investigators, *An Emerging Consensus—A Study of American Public Attitudes on America's Role in the World— Summary of Findings*, with the two centers cited above, University of Maryland, July 10, 1996.

5.   Ruttan, 1996, p. 469.

6.   Author's notes from the State Department's Senior Seminar, 1991–92.

7.   "Opposing View," *USA Today*, November 12, 1996.

8.   *The Washington Post*, June 8, 1997.

9.   Sharon Epstein, E-mail on AID reforms, July 25, 1996; U.S. General Accounting Office, *Foreign Assistance—USAID's Reengineering at Overseas Missions*, September 1997, p. 4; Frank Miller, *New Management System a Financial Black Hole*, USAID American Foreign Service Association (AFSA), E-mail, February 23, 1998; and AID's "New Management System," AFSA E-mail, March 18, 1998.

3

Why Asia Is Developing and Africa Is Not

DO DEVELOPMENT THEORIES MATTER?

Asia floods the world with its outpouring of modern products. Africa exports raw materials and traditional handicrafts, when it can. East Asia and, increasingly, the newly industrializing countries of Southeast Asia, have heated up the international corporate world of high-tech competition. The United States and Western Europe buy from these one-time poor world countries and witness the restructuring of their own industries as global competition grows. Meanwhile, African handicrafts are shown at Saturday neighborhood markets, interest a few buyers, and bother no one.

How has this happened? A recent Harvard University study of the East and Southeast Asian economic "miracle" noted that it was Africa, not Asia, where "national independence brought a wave of optimism that anything could be done."[1] It was Africa that was noted for its resource riches after World War II, not Asia. Today, Africa is naturally rich—but remains poor.

What growth model is East and Southeast Asia using? Notwithstanding the economic crises of 1997 and 1998, why have their levels of poverty fallen so dramatically? What are Asia's lessons for growth and poverty reduction? Can late-developing countries, in Africa particularly, learn from these successes? What does the Asian miracle—even accounting for "Asian contagion"—teach the world?

Fifty years is a long time to debate the theoretical and to assess the practical. A great deal has been learned about development, yet it appears that we may have misunderstood, or possibly ignored, lessons we might have learned. Africa continues to fall behind.

Does western development theory guide development, or even explain very much? Does foreign aid matter? If foreign assistance is to be justified in a new century, we must move beyond the present degree of uncertainty between theory and practice, between aid and impact. Many accidental relationships dreamed up by western theorists—by accidental tourists—do not stand scrutiny. Development and aid must be guided by the evidence of what works.

We find in this chapter that theoretical forces have influence on development thinking and aid priorities just as political forces have influences in our capital cities. The best of each theoretical contribution needs to be assessed to sort practical successes from shortcomings. I venture a preliminary conclusion in this chapter that field-tested market principles are of considerably more value than the advice of public planning theorists or priorities that are set in donor capitals. Riches gained from this practical experience—blending market principles with a few public sector lessons—lead to conclusions that have special importance for Africa's development, for the effective use of foreign aid, and for Africa's ownership of both development and aid.

OPEN MARKETS OR PUBLIC PLANNING

Two schools of western theory have guided development in the poor world. One school relies on private markets to guide development priorities, and the other relies on public planning. One trusts the market; the other does not.

Adam Smith eloquently spelled out the principles of laissez-faire, market-based development in his 1776 treatise, *Wealth of Nations*. Others would expound his principles and extrapolate from them during the two centuries that followed. "An invisible hand," and not government planning, motivates and directs production, commerce, and the creation and sharing of wealth. Many theoretical contributors since, drawing from Smith's work, focused on development as a growth process, which was guided by this invisible hand. Smith's economic model drew from European history. Market-determined specialization and growth made nations develop from pastoral to settled agriculture, which set the stage for higher levels of commerce, and then industry.

If achievement of successive stages is the right strategy for getting ahead, how does a poor country quickly move from one stage to the next? Models of these stages influenced development thinking and policy direction in the newly independent countries during the 1950s and 1960s. It is obvious that a poor country needs resources to move to higher growth stages. Many development proponents saw growth theory as a fundamental challenge to mobilize and direct resources. In the early 1950s the development debate focused on government planning to initiate this mobilization. Market-based approaches were ignored.

In the 1960s Walter Rostow, one of stage theory's famed advocates, postulated a view of market stages that could, if they were followed, lead to the final take-off to development. The traditional pastoral setting would lead to the preconditions for take-off, to the take-off itself, then to the drive for maturity and to the age of mass consumption. Rostow and other market theorists identified the complicated economic and political elements—the preconditions—of market society and market forces that would guarantee development. Most theorists acknowledged that more was required for development than just resources. Social and political preconditions had to be in place and choices had to be made.

Whether stage thinking was fundamentally sound or not, it laid the foundation for other theorists and policy-makers in rich countries to argue for a resources approach to finance development and therefore, to foreign aid. Stage models, whether plan-based or market-based, either explicitly or inadvertently played into the hands of larger political forces that controlled post–World War II, cold war resources. The economists' qualifications and assumptions that underpinned theoretical, market-based reasoning—the preconditions for development, or the fine print, if you will—were swept aside by broader forces.

Countervailing Forces at Work

Smith's exposition of the market's invisible hand might have played a more influential role in postwar development thinking and practice if it had not been for several concurrent and countervailing influences.

First, the depression of the 1930s altered for decades the perceptions of laissez-faire capitalism, and hence the role of government. Because domestic and international market forces had failed to ensure growth and employment—as was so obviously the case for both rich and poor economies at the bottom of the depression—the public looked then to government for answers. Public expectations in many countries led to large public programs and many five-year plans.

Second, World War II and the subsequent founding of the United Nations promoted the idea, first espoused by the League of Nations, that governments had major international responsibilities. Equally important was the Marshall Plan, which demonstrated—even proved—that government and public resources ensured development.

Third, related to these forces, concerns for social well-being from across the political, ideological, and academic spectra held capitalism and free markets in suspicion and viewed government as the protector of the poor.

As we can now see, these developments led to the institutionalization of public responsibility on behalf of the general welfare. Institutions such as the World Bank, the IMF, and the United Nations, reflecting American liberalism, have today become sufficiently robust that they have taken on lives of their own. Public bureaucracies and their public plans, as found in India, China, Africa, and the former Soviet Union, remain deeply entrenched despite the changing shape of the world economy.

Cold war policy-makers certainly welcomed theoretical ammunition that justified the use of rich-country resources to buy poor-world allegiances. More money, more development, and, as a result, higher stages of development would soon be achieved for the good guys in a cold war. The prime role for aid—to finance successive growth stages—became fixed in the minds of policy-makers and the public alike for decades. Postwar forces cemented a public-planning-with-public-resources approach to the conduct of government responsibility. Most, but not all, western donors and recipient governments saw the problem and its solution the same way: public planning with public resources. The resources problem could have meant wide acceptance of private investment as the key to development, à la Adam Smith and his growth-oriented successors, but a cold war was on.

The five-year plans in India, China, and the Soviet Union directed the construction of almost all of their heavy infrastructure and industry. Their plans mobilized hundreds of millions of workers in the postwar period as the central effort that promised the long denied prosperity. Much was accomplished in these countries and dozens of new countries followed suit, especially in Africa. Even new economies that remained largely private in their orientation, as in East Asia and Latin America, established plans to achieve better health and education and more physical infrastructure. Many fledgling economies took planning to great lengths. The nationalization of "the commanding heights" of poor economies became the vogue in South Asian countries and for most of Africa. Governments controlled, or took command, of all major industry and the strategic "heights," such as mining, steel, power, even commerce and trade. International capitalism and trade were not to be trusted to serve the poor.

To serve their own ends, Africa's colonial powers built public institutions to control trade, domestic commerce, and agricultural marketing. A newly independent Africa, inheriting administrative models and motives from a colonial age, embraced and reinforced these approaches to public responsibility. Further, it was widely believed that the international economic order was designed primarily to extract wealth from the poor world. Africa, finally independent, sought to protect itself.

Resource Gaps—Real and Imagined

If poverty was the problem, and it could be overcome by rapid advances through the stages of development, then money for public planning was the solution. Development experts hypothesized that two resource gaps had to be met—domestic and foreign. First, domestic savings in poor countries had to be mobilized to meet the domestic investment requirements that were envisioned in planning targets. But these countries were poor and had no domestic savings. Second, if domestic efforts to save were insufficient, as was thought to be true in most poor countries, foreign funding, that is, aid, would bridge the savings and investment gap—the dollar gap between generally modest export earnings and the imports needed to meet the plan. Many development experts argued for large investments to fund what was then known as the "big push" to move developing countries rapidly through development stages.

To mobilize capital, poor governments introduced plans and budgets to direct productive investment and to attract and channel donor assistance. A one-percent-of-GNP rule for rich countries was popularized by the Netherlands and the Scandinavian countries to quantify moral suasion behind aid giving. Aid, like private flows, would contribute directly (and only) to plan targets.

Prices were set to ensure the "right" distribution of income for people and the "right" planned-for investment decisions. For many new countries, prices for basic goods and strong currencies, such as the dollar, became set by bureaucratic procedure. Price controls to protect people from the vagaries of domestic and international markets became the rule. Planning energies focused primarily on one factor: financing. Other factors necessary for development, such as food and trained people, didn't matter because government ministries would take care of agriculture, employment, education, and health. It was financing that turned plans into reality.

Markets and market prices, therefore, were turned on their heads. Because governments could supply all plan and consumer needs (assuming the ready availability of financing), the prices of principal commodities and wages could be fixed. Attractive prices and salaries were not needed to motivate teachers, farmers, bakers and bankers, domestic savers, or even foreign investors. Market prices were not allowed to equate the supply of bread with its demand, or the supply of financial funds with opportunity.

Plans, rather than interest rates and foreign currency rates, as examples, would mobilize and ration development financing. The demand for financing would be met by governments (and donors), not by market-motivated savers, producers, and traders. Governments would supply bread at low, fixed prices that people could afford. Supplies of financing and goods mattered; prices did not. Governments would act in lieu of markets.

Many policy-makers and development experts believed that poor people were too poor to save and that rich countries would choose not to help. This resource pessimism reinforced a protectionist orientation in public development philosophy. The resource pessimism was reflected in concerns by planning ministries for low international prices of commodities and restrictive trade practices by rich countries toward poor ones. It also served to reinforce the prevalent view that growth came from heavy industry directed and owned by the public sector. Only later would poor people benefit from the trickle-down of jobs and income that would be created by planned industrialization and urbanization.

The consequences of overcontrol are now well known. Governments and donors approved of price controls and subsidies because, they claimed, poor people could not pay for market-priced necessities and private investments would not be forthcoming. Experience finally taught us a different lesson. Poor people *will* pay for food, water, energy, and even health care and education if given a chance, and private investments will be made if markets are allowed to function by government. Controlled prices, as experts eventually learned, cost governments and donors, and benefit, generally, the urban elite and middle class.

Planned economies became closed economies, protected from the outside world. Little thought was given to domestic incentives and motivation, to international comparative advantage, to specialization, or to global dynamism. Poor countries cut themselves off from new technologies and ideas, and gradually went broke with the help of their donors.

AFRICAN PUBLIC PLANNING HITS THE ROCKS

After World War II rich nations committed themselves to a 5 percent growth target for the developing world in a First Development Decade of the 1960s. This one United Nations target was supposed to fit all newly independent states. UNESCO and WHO called for universal education and health care by the end of the 1960s. Poor countries achieved the growth target (largely because of high, not low, prices for exported commodities), but saw little positive improvement for their people. Unemployment increased and inequality rose.

A second development decade could not be like the first. Sobriety had started to set in. The poor world was complicated and diverse; no one target or planning model would fit all countries. Still, international leaders and theorists remained determined to find public solutions to "the obscene inequalities that disfigure the world."[2]

During the 1960s and 1970s, developed countries, whether eastern or western, were more alike in promoting and funding statist development models than anyone today would care to admit. The cold war served to unify resource intensive, public sector support for African development (and to curry allegiances). Donors funded ministries, institutes, and parastatals by the hundreds across Africa. Few outside voices were raised against public control of the commanding heights in poor countries.

African government officials, trained in the West as well as in then eastern-bloc countries, staffed their newly established planning commissions. Armies of public servants made five-year plans the vehicle for development, medium-range planning, and state intervention. Plans became a nation's symbol of modernity and independence. They were sovereignty itself.

Stark stories reveal stark realities. One expert learned that Zambia spent more to educate its embassies' children overseas than for all of its primary school children. Zambia's governmental elite flew free to South Africa for free health care. Mike Wallace's interview of me for a *60 Minutes* segment set me back: He could not grasp that Tanzania would buy a fleet of sixty new cars for a conference, and then hand them over to the party faithful.[3]

There is wide agreement today that public plans in most poor-world economies accomplished far less than had been hoped, especially in Eastern Europe, the Soviet Union, and in Africa. Ideals exceeded capacity; commitments led to excesses as well as to lethargy. Plan targets not met were revised downward again and again. Command of the commanding heights had extended to the slopes and valleys of several already poor economies. Governments had nationalized far too many businesses, including, in a few African countries, dry cleaning stores and restaurants. Farm cooperative crops rotted as cooperative managers drove new cars. Billions of dollars and an immense amount of goodwill were lost. There has now been a downsizing of public expectation of untold cost and disappointment.

African public planning yielded neither the rate of growth nor the equity promised in the laboriously designed plans. Instead, poor economies experienced little growth, public payrolls burgeoned, debt mounted, and corruption set in. Public investment became public consumption for the relative few who were employed in government. Public plans led to governments that were larger than their tax bases could support; to public employment greater than revenue could sustain. Social programs served populations poorly. Donor dependence grew in scope; it is common still to see a headline such as "75 Percent of Zambia's 1995 Budget is Donor Funded." Plans, price controls, and an all-controlling public apparatus drove away private investment and talent. Even the United Nations has estimated that billions of dollars have been moved from sub-Saharan Africa to foreign banks.[4]

Little thought was given to effective responsibility and management in Africa; governments and donors alike assumed that public dedication, innumerable staff, and public training courses would be an adequate substitute for private ownership and private management. Experts gradually learned that public decisions were made as much on the basis of client favors and rent-seeking opportunities (for personal profit) as they were for the national good. Price controls, the tip of the bureaucratic iceberg, opened the door wide to rent-seeking and other forms of corruption.

Starting in the 1970s little moved in governmental Africa without a hidden (donor) hand. Ministry officials were driven in donor-financed vehicles, to donor-sponsored seminars, and to attend donor-initiated training (on good governmental management). Donor per diems of $100 for these officials swamped public salaries that averaged $50 per month. Public control, in extreme form, proved to be a bad idea. Planning in Africa had been given a chance to work because of donor faith and largesse. The planned-for development yielded stagnation and isolation. Reform followed collapse—often after many years of development delay and financial crisis.

Upon arriving in Dar es Salaam in 1987, I sought to understand African planning. I met Joan Wicken, a socialist and personal secretary to Julius Nyerere, founder and first president of Tanzania. I grew discouraged by the minute as we covered more and more ground. At last I hit on a subject I thought we might agree on—computers. Tanzania could modernize with computers, I said enthusiastically. Ms. Wicken, as lovely to meet as a favorite aunt, glared at me. "Computers," she said, "put people out of work, and besides, Tanzania is about to become self-sufficient in typewriters." I had hit the hard rocks of African reality.

Africa Is Forced to Reconsider

All of these forces influenced, ultimately, the course of donor thinking and the level of western generosity. More and more public loans were negotiated with donors, nominally for new investments but, in reality, just to keep African governments afloat. Some governments borrowed heavily to stay the public planning course, often with the concurrence of western advice. Other countries ground to a halt, realizing that they could not repay debts nor, for political reasons, could they curtail public expenditures. These factors conspired to lay bare the reality of public mismanagement, corruption, and the scale of donor aid dependency.

The oil crisis hit Africa hard in the late 1970s. African governments borrowed to sustain themselves. The World Bank and the IMF, at least at first, agreed to continue lending to sustain old habits. African countries could not pay off new loans let alone the mounting debt service charges for old ones.

If donor support for African plans did not help people, then direct programs would. Robert McNamara, president of the World Bank in the 1970s, redirected Bank lending for poverty reduction and for the macroeconomic and macromanagement policy reforms that enable employment enhancing growth and poverty alleviation. To accomplish these new goals following the oil crisis, the World Bank initiated global and country lending targets, and therein abandoned its bank-like investment discipline and its cost-benefit analyses. Defined project loans became loosely defined program loans. New loan approvals—to alleviate poverty—became the priority. Loan targets had to be met. But Africa needed new loans simply to pay old debts. Pressures mounted on all donors, including the World Bank and the IMF, to keep aid flows positive. Pressures to reform and to pay debt gave birth to ever more public program loans for Africa.

Policy reform in support of open markets and away from state control was the right strategy. But lending for reform became lending to serve other, less visible objectives. The World Bank and bilateral donors developed what became a deep-seated need to lend, driven in part by the magnitude of Africa's official debt and the consequent need for fresh loans to pay it off.

Aid dependency led gradually to the realization that donor practices had become unsustainable and that African ownership of development policies, processes, and even projects rested in the wrong hands. Donor assistance in effect allowed, drove a wedge even, between the development process and its intended beneficiaries—a theme of later chapters. African dependence on aid led in some countries to an unseemly and mutually self-serving culture. It reached beyond just loans and debt service to enculturate policy-makers and aid practitioners. Locally "owned" institutions grew poorly, if at all, in this development environment. Donors as a group became caught in a self-serving trap of keeping resources flowing to ensure the stability of frail African governments, to ensure the repayment of earlier loans, and to sustain the myth with their congresses and parliaments that more money was needed to help poor Africa.

The crisis in public planning played out during the 1970s and 1980s forced an historic reconsideration of the private sector's role in development. Dependence on government and outside resources was shown not to be the answer. The 1980s and 1990s saw the beginnings of reluctant change, of public decontrol of prices and markets, and of governmental downsizing, which preceded the collapse of the Soviet Union and the end of the cold war. The fall of Soviet communism deflated, even collapsed, Africa's hope for ideological and financial support from any quarter. The oil and debt crises also diminished the influence of African vested interests that were resistant to change. Africa had nowhere to turn but to the World Bank and the IMF.

First one theory of development was popularly acclaimed, then another. I will not forget the question of an exasperated Tanzanian during a seminar in Dar es Salaam: "Why don't you guys make up your minds?" His sincere outburst spoke for a generation of Africans who had grown too dependent on foreign donors for cash and for ideas.

Some countries saw the warnings early and moved quickly to reduce governmental controls and foster openness and trade. Most countries, having only accepted portions of the planning philosophy, did not have to do much to open their economies. Others, mostly in Africa and South Asia, and to a lesser extent in Latin America, had to change their deeply held convictions that government would create development for their people, to placing their faith in markets. Many African leaders still have not reversed their thinking. A few African countries have moved not at all.

At least in Africa, donors may be faulted for being too slow to criticize, possibly because most of the advice Africa took had been from western-trained experts. The warning signs had been growing within the donor community since the 1970s. Most donors eventually found that they could not work with weak African governments that had overcontrolled economies. A few donor programs were reduced; a few AID missions were closed. The World Bank and the IMF, at first sympathetic to the financial crises facing planned economies, were gradually forced to stiffen their determination that market-oriented reforms be reintroduced.

On leaving Tanzania in 1991, I spoke with the Minister of Finance, the late Stephen Kibona, who had by then become a friend. The stress of reversal and reform showed on his handsome face. He asked forlornly: "Do you think we can win?" I assured him that reforms would work.

Table 3.1 compares Asia with Africa. The table illustrates percentages of external debt to gross national product, per capita aid, and aid as a percent of gross domestic investment. Debt is relatively low in Asia, whereas aid dependency per capita and aid as a percentage of investment are high in Africa.

Practical Good Works from the Public Sector

Not all planning led to isolation and failure. Although it may not be popular in some circles to speak of the public sector's contributions to development in Asia or Africa, some of these are of considerable, even historic, importance. Across most of Asia, and much of Africa and Latin America, practical good works have been completed by governments in enormous numbers over the past fifty years: Cities and towns were built; harbors and airports expanded; roads, railways, and urban power supplies became commonplace; public buildings sprang up; and hundreds of thousands of civil servants were trained and assigned to prescribed governmental positions. Practical benefit was shared with hundreds of millions of people. I offer three examples to highlight their material contributions over many decades.

First is the famed green revolution. Genetically improved seed varieties have been developed and promoted to almost every crop and crop zone in the world over the past fifty years through public centers of agricultural research, seed distribution, and farm-level advice. One criticism of planning models, predicated primarily on industry, was that the models overlooked agriculture. "Food first" proponents challenged the prevailing wisdom that food for cities could be bought on the cheap from poor farms. Food crises in the 1960s, seen in retrospect, gave the green revolution a kickstart and reinforced public research and later public price and expenditure policies for small-farm-based food production. Millions of Asian farmers produced far more food than had been projected at the time. Despite early skepticism in Asia, the new seed revolution brought benefit to the landed and landless alike and promises to serve Africa as well.

A second example is family planning, which continues to make an equally historic impact worldwide, again, largely through public channels. As with agriculture, practical experience has surprised and gratified development experts and practitioners. Again, successes far exceeded those of the dreamers of earlier decades. Women worldwide want family planning services; when offered a choice, they welcome it.

The third example is health and education. Public health was combined early with family planning activities in most developing countries. Public health education attained acceptance and its impact was felt almost as widely as that of the green revolution. Primary education, as noted in

Table 3.1

Comparing Debt, Aid, and Investment in Asia and Africa, 1996

	External Debt as a Percent of GNP	Aid Per Capita in Dollars Per Year	Aid as a Percent of Gross Domestic Investment
South Asia			
Bangladesh	30	10	23
India	22	2	2
Nepal	26	18	39
Sri Lanka	41	27	14
Southeast Asia			
Indonesia	64	6	2
Malaysia	5	−22	−1
Vietnam	123	12	14
Africa			
Cameroon	106	30	28
Côte d'Ivoire	171	67	66
Ethiopia	149	15	68
Niger	45	28	135
Senegal	53	68	68
Tanzania	114	29	85
Zambia	161	67	120

Source: World Bank, *1998 World Development Indicators*, pp. 242–44 and 342–44.

chapter 1, is becoming universal. The U.S. government, other western donors, WHO, and UNICEF provided the world a great service by translating medical knowledge into practical services and technologies; populations in many regions of the world are healthier today as a result.

It is public planning behind these sciences and services that is ensuring a stable world population of 8 billion people. The green revolution and a host of social services were at the time, lest we forget, high-risk public experiments. Today they feed success upon success. All of these public contributions have delivered far-reaching benefits for the world, particularly for Asia. Africa alone faces burgeoning demands for food and public services as its population continues to double.

I emphasize these public contributions to force the point that governments have a continuing responsibility to serve development well-being.

Current calls for less planning and less government, in Africa especially, do not in themselves serve this purpose. We must pick our way carefully through this debate.

CRITICISMS OF PLANNING AND THE MARKET ENRICH THE DEBATE

Disappointment that poverty was still manifest around the world after two decades of development was palpable. Pessimism spread in the 1970s and fueled frustrations with orthodoxy of whatever stripe. Some critics gave up on both the market and central government. A chorus of voices remained suspicious of the efficacy of economic philosophy. Planning may not work, but markets do not work for poor people either! For many experts in the NGO community, a return to market principles was a betrayal of egalitarianism. Shrill criticisms were a measure of the failure of public responsibility. Many of these voices were heard in Congress and European parliaments; donor programs were redirected toward "people first."

Neither plans nor markets had benefited the poor in Africa. Large investments for large plans did not seem to benefit many people; benefits from employment, schooling, and health programs did not trickle down to the millions of very poor people. Poor people could see the bright lights, new cars, and modern buildings in major cities, but little benefit came their way. In the 1970s and 1980s a rethinking about what works for development began taking place, away from public dominance toward a renewed appreciation for less governmental responsibility, communities, and, particularly, nongovernmental institutions.

A few development advocates and leading NGOs were determined to direct development attention to basic human needs, and looked to the decentralization of responsibility, to voluntary associations, to church groups, to rural and suburban communities, and to appropriate technologies to accomplish these needs. NGOs added immeasurably to the range of the debate and permanently to development's inclusive nature. Innumerable governmental and nongovernmental pilot projects began to have an effect on mainstream development thinking. People, not "things," mattered in development. Not just central government, but all levels of government mattered. Not simply markets, but people with purchasing power and adequate diets mattered.[5]

It is noteworthy that the International Labor Organization stressed the importance of income and people as long ago as 1923 when it emphasized that people should have the income to purchase their basic human needs. In the 1980s and 1990s two NGOs, CARE and Bread For The World, stressed the same important duality: growth that creates jobs and income, and investment in human beings.

The value of education began to be seen more broadly. Education for women and girls was seen as valuable in its own right, and as a synergetic way to enhance household income, nutritional well-being, and child care. A new household-level theory of economics called for integrated goals and methods where other social sciences had gone their separate ways, and so had overlooked powerful conceptual contributions.

Many critics started looking beyond economic issues to politics and democracy. Some western critics demanded that all donors focus aid according to an index of economic freedom and noted the positive relationship between freedom and prosperity.

The many criticisms of public and market-oriented, trickle-down theories did serve to open doors to further thinking and reform. Multiple criticisms voiced during this era opened doors to people, to environmentalism, to decentralization and democracy, and to the nongovernmental world—all have become permanent contributions to development practice.

Criticisms of mainstream thinking led to improvement in the quality of the overall debate and, ultimately, of development and aid. The aid that had funded closed economies, and even corruption and elitism, began to fund inclusiveness. An era of centralized public planning—what once appeared to be mainstream thinking—proved to be but an interlude in the 1950s and 1960s. For Africa, however, great damage has been done, and its countries have far to go.

People First in Agriculture

Despite all the criticisms of mainstream development thinking, some of which continue to this day, one stream of thought placed people and agriculture first, and married the best of public responsibility with market incentives. Rooted in the green revolution experiment, long before its success was proven worldwide, Bruce Johnston and John Mellor postulated that agricultural productivity was the key to widely shared development. "Food First" and "People First" proponents had their theoretical underpinnings in the new seed technology and in growth linkages that create further rounds of growth. New seed varieties yielded greatly increased harvests per unit of land with irrigation and fertilizer.

New incomes created second and third rounds of investments in rural towns and ultimately for industry, urban centers, and international trade. More food grain yielded more household income, and more income was spent on nonfood consumer goods. This new income created demand for more fertilizer, new clothes, better housing, and household goods. Farm production and income, generated by the use of new seed varieties, help to create more off-farm jobs, through production and consumption spending.[6]

A household that spent 70 percent of its meager income on food was a poor household and had little left over to buy other necessities. A household that grew new crops found that, in time, it spent a declining share of its income on food, as little as 25 percent, and the rest on necessities and even luxuries, which were produced elsewhere. A once-poor household not only became well-off, but it became one that contributed to development in a country that spent less and less, proportionately, on food grains and other food staples. Sustained agricultural growth contributes to growth for the economy as a whole.

Seed-based growth linkages documented for the first time that growth and poverty alleviation go together—as a unified, win-win strategy. For an Asia of low incomes and large rural populations, agriculture was the only initial avenue open to growth and poverty alleviation. Small-farm holders are also winners in export-oriented strategies. In Africa lose-lose was coming to an end; Africa had lost both growth and poverty alleviation, while Asia's green revolution was a harbinger of market-oriented policies that had proven to work for all.

AN ASIAN DRAMA UNFOLDS

As public planning began to fail in Africa, and lost its luster across Latin America, market-oriented theorists and proponents started to note the bustling experience of several newly industrializing countries in East Asia.

Following Japan's lead, South Korea, Taiwan, and the city-states of Hong Kong and Singapore, the "Four Tigers," burst on the popular scene in the early 1980s, followed soon thereafter by equally aggressive countries in Southeast Asia. These countries became known collectively as the Asian Miracle; they have become models of market-oriented regimes that turned simple economies producing simple, often low-quality products like shirts, watches, and toys into a technological, communications, and financial services revolution.

Their increased trade and related competitive tensions caught everyone's attention and the world of development thinking was caught by surprise. Dynamism in East Asia and then Southeast Asia had gone unnoticed. Perhaps westerners were too focused on Africa, on public planning, and on aid. How did these countries explain their sustained growth rates in per capita incomes that averaged 5.5 percent annually during the twenty-five years between 1965 and 1990—considerably higher than for other developing regions? The Asian tigers used no model as such, at least not one from the hand of a famed theorist; and aid, which had never been significant, had long since departed.[7]

The proponents of aggressive free markets and free trade in these countries had carried the day. They had deliberately opened their doors to global market opportunities, which resulted in the successive adoption of progressively sophisticated industries—first textiles, then household electronics, then computers and financial services. Their economies had evolved from simple, labor-intensive manufacturing, to ones of capital-intensive exports, then to manufacturing of skill-intensive and technologically intensive global products and services. As older technologies gave way to newer ones, semi-skilled laborers became skilled professionals.

Explanations for Rapid Growth

Perhaps because of their own innate cultural orientations, and western training beginning in the 1950s, many Asian countries maintained strong markets and trade regimes throughout the era of public planning. Perhaps choice of growth model explains the difference. The once-poor world of East and Southeast Asia changed rapidly.

East Asia's success was at first assumed to be explained by aggressive industries operating in unfettered economies. Public planning, even in Southeast Asia, had been deemphasized early. As the successes of these Asian countries were examined more closely, however, different conclusions were drawn from the laissez-faire prescriptions that had at first been assumed. The lessons proved to be multiple. Outside experts found, for example, that there was close cooperation between government and industry (too close as we now know). Not just government and industry cooperated closely, but the major actors within society worked toward commonly held perceptions of the national interest. Public policy and economic interests across sectors supported aggressive export strategies.

Governments had been coordinating and biasing incentives in several forms toward consensus building, human resources, efficient production, and exports. Leaders in government, industry, banking, unions, the civil service, and politics met regularly. Economists were used to inform and direct policy but were otherwise insulated from political and self-serving behavior. Large firms and selected industries did not act alone but were part of a purposeful and less-than-transparent public structure. Underlying this early economic effort in the 1960s and 1970s was a common regional concern for national security. China and wars in Korea and Vietnam were constant reminders of risks to the region. Competitive firms and industries, therefore, served a coordinated national purpose. A very different picture started to emerge from that of a laissez-faire philosophy, which had been initially understood by the West.

For these Asian countries, positive government intervention, as a partner in development, had to be taken seriously. These governments had created a new type of development support, while at the same time keeping their hands off (it was claimed at the time) banking and industry decisions.

Asian governments had, first, kept their macroeconomic houses in order by controlling government deficits and inflation, and by keeping domestic prices and foreign exchange closely aligned with market conditions. Strategic industries and exports were targeted to receive subsidies. Credit, taxes, regulations, and moral suasion at cabinet levels were keyed by government to industry performance and the achievement of social objectives.

Upon further inquiry, economists drew additional conclusions. Primary education had been a priority as long ago as the 1950s. General education created a skilled labor force. The pattern of income and asset distribution was more egalitarian than in other countries at a similar level of development, which probably contributed to greater domestic savings and investment.

With the advantage of hindsight, it becomes apparent that the central concern for financial savings had, in these countries, taken the form of investment in people more so than in grappling with financial gaps (filled with other people's money). Fertility and mortality rates were almost uniformly lower than in other countries with similar levels of income, which also reflected an early commitment to social well-being. These initial conditions, primarily education and equality, more than simple economic openness, explain most of the growth in these countries. Why is this so? The British economist, Dani Rodrik, states that "Human capital makes investment more productive, facilitates the transfer and adoption of advanced technology from abroad, and enables the establishment of meritocractic, efficient, and capable public administration." American training, vastly more than is at first recognized, helped several Asian countries build robust institutions.[8]

Table 3.2 illustrates the gulf that exists between the two prevailing economic philosophies in Asia and Africa. Public planning in Africa has yielded low growth; markets in Asia have yielded high growth. The table reveals the declining share of agriculture in gross domestic product, and higher public investment in educating girls in a few African countries.

Stability, education, and rule of law were found to be fundamental preconditions for development—the preconditions that underlaid the

Marshall Plan's success. Indonesia, Malaysia, and Thailand had been growing quickly (up until Asian contagion), with Vietnam not far behind. India and Bangladesh are gradually liberalizing state controls on investment and trade. Unlike the original four tigers, the late-comers are resource rich.

Table 3.2
Comparing Economic and Social Indicators in Asia and Africa

	GNP Per Capita Growth 1995	Agriculture as a Percent of GDP 1985–95	Female Primary School Enrollment 1993
South Asia			
Bangladesh	2.1	31	105
India	3.2	29	91
Nepal	2.4	42	87
Sri Lanka	2.6	23	105
East and Southeast Asia			
Malaysia	5.7	13	93
Indonesia	6.0	17	112
Vietnam	—	28	106
Africa			
Cameroon	–6.6	39	89
Côte d'Ivoire	—	31	58
Ethiopia	–0.3	57	19
Niger	—	39	21
Senegal	—	20	50
Tanzania	1.0	58	69
Zambia	–0.8	22	99

Source: World Bank, *1997 World Development Report*, pp. 214–15, 226–27, and 236–37.
Notes: For Vietnam and Cameroon, primary enrollment data are 1980 figure; female school enrollment is percentage of age group.

ONE STRATEGY ENSURES GROWTH AND POVERTY ALLEVIATION

Beyond the Asian tigers, evidence began to accumulate that almost all countries that reduce and reform government controls are rewarded with growth, and that growth, in turn, alleviates poverty. Growth reduces poverty? Finally we have a clear answer: a resounding Yes, according to a Harvard University study of sixty developing countries.

National growth translates into income increases for the poorest 40 percent of a population. An annual growth rate of 10 percent overall benefits the poorest 40 percent of the population by increasing their incomes by 10 percent as well. Growth reaches widely. For the poorest 20 percent of a population, growth benefits them almost as impressively, with a 9 percent increase, on average, for almost all of the countries studied. Growth, according to the Harvard study by Michael Roemer and Mary Kay Gugerty, "is a powerful mechanism for reducing poverty."[9]

The same study states that direct efforts to alleviate poverty, such as public education and health projects, rather than the promotion of growth across the board, may result in less growth and more poverty. This striking conclusion contradicts another one of those stylized facts about the best of public planning intensions: "Forgoing growth is not the answer to the problem of poverty."

As we saw in chapter 2, development priorities that focus on health and education, and not on growth, have become the donor vogue in western capitals. The Harvard study supports the thesis that market growth, openness to the world economy, and sound macroeconomic policies alleviate poverty. Sectoral priorities alone do not contribute to either growth or poverty alleviation. This decades-old controversy between growth and equity may have arisen because growth in the 1960s meant steel plants and national airlines; whereas today, growth is more likely to be market-based, labor-intensive, and skill-using production and export—with a significantly different effect for poor people.

Open markets break open domestic economies and shift opportunity from the powerful to the powerless and the poor. Or, if not a shift, then at least a sharing. With an eye to the closed economies of the world, the Harvard study notes that open economies have, on average, annual growth rates as much as 2.8 percentage points higher than closed economies.

Country cases drawn from this study reveal a compelling trend. Incomes in Indonesia grew by 4 percent a year between 1970 and 1993; those in poverty fell from 60 percent of the population to less than 15 percent. It is this astonishing success that makes the present Asian contagion crisis all the more tragic. For Malaysia a more modest growth rate of 3 percent caused poverty to fall from 18 percent of the population to only 2 percent over the same twenty-three-year period.

For the first time evidence strongly supports the thesis that national growth and people are the twin beneficiaries of a unified development strategy. One strategy for growth and another for poverty alleviation conspire in practice to create no growth and no poverty alleviation.

Qualifications abound for an emphasis on growth but they do not detract from this central lesson.

What role has aid played? According to World Bank economists, aid can be used effectively to support both growth and poverty alleviation, provided a country is committed to open markets. In countries without open markets, however, aid has had no measurable effect. The evidence strongly supports this conclusion: Countries with open markets grew at 3.5 percent a year; countries without open markets grew at 2.0 percent only.[10] Markets can deliver the promised responsibility for reducing poverty.

DEVELOPMENT LESSONS FOR A FAST-PACED WORLD

Despite the good news that growth works to alleviate poverty, we live in a fast-paced world. Conclusions drawn today are qualified tomorrow. Asian successes, as well as Asian economic crashes of 1997 and 1998, demand reconsideration. Markets are not perfect nor can poverty's alleviation be assumed by growth alone. But it is better to be on the right track than on none at all. Asian contagion underscores the point that all development is work in progress; no conclusions are immutable or irreversible. What else must be learned?

Asian Lessons Reassessed and Reaffirmed

The economic collapse in some Asian countries will be detrimental to their growth and therefore to gains made to reduce poverty. Hundreds of thousands, possibly millions of Asian workers face certain unemployment for an unknown period. In Indonesia alone, the managing director of the IMF estimates that 20 million people have fallen below the official poverty line. Dozens of banks will close, so will hundreds of companies. Regrettably, all the good performance indicators cited earlier will now show declines and reversals.[11] How can Asian countries recover? Which policies should they keep? Which should they reform?

First, Asia has to stay the course. Open markets created growth for millions of Asians once; it will do so again. Asia's market-led principles are reinforced by the recent crisis. Macroeconomic stability has to be maintained. The importance of education remains the key to open market exploitation, employment recovery, and continued poverty alleviation.

Second, bad and inappropriate loans created the bad debt in the first place, so some reforms clearly are required. Openness of investment decision-making processes must be strengthened. Public partnerships with business must be transparent in all transactions. Government and corporate investments must meet market tests and further privatization of public companies is needed. Governmental as well as private trade and manufacturing monopolies must be reduced in number and they must be regulated. Government contracting must be open to competition.

It is now clear that a few Asian governments and major businesses have operated together too snugly, and some very large and very poor investment decisions have been a consequence. For too long, western development institutions and experts have known of these too-cozy, public-private ties, but have not questioned their costs or consequences. Sumitro Djojohadikusumo, Indonesia's senior macroeconomic advisor, sums up the situation for Asia: "There has long been a dichotomy between macroeconomic policies, which are by and large adequate and appropriate; and microeconomic policies, which are full of distortions and inconsistencies and marred by corruption and excessive protectionism."[12]

Adherence to these twin conclusions will restart economic growth on a firmer path among Asia's maturing tigers. Whether the path will be firm enough remains to be seen.

Third, Asian contagion raises troubling issues about international donor institutions; about their possible roles in contributing to a compounding of these crises; and about their ability to sustain corrective, credible policies, and new investment-quality loans. Critics argue that the IMF and World Bank invite private and government investment recklessness by rushing in too early with new loans. International investors and speculators know these institutions to be lenient; the lenders of first resort. If poor performers—be they investors or governments—are confident that the IMF and the World Bank will partially finance their debts and losses, then they will be inclined to persist with poor policies and investments.

A moral hazard is created when borrowers come to believe that central banks and the IMF accept excess lending risks. Borrowers know from experience at home and elsewhere that they will be partially bailed out if their ventures fail. They know that sufficient quid pro quo is seldom demanded by the IMF, the World Bank, or central banks. Corporate board members and political elites alike know they are likely to be spared great losses under the guise of sustaining domestic stability and international market confidence. They know this because their economic advisors know the loan-driven, debt-driven motives of the IMF and the World Bank. As one consequence, investors, speculators, and governments may spend more time watching IMF and World Bank policy practices than in pursuing credible government actions and wiser investment decisions.

The problems of recent Asian debt relief and corrective operations have been compounded by moral hazard. To avoid further compounding of the

African crisis, the IMF and the World Bank must shift their lending back toward investment performance and more stringent bail-out requirements. Donors must make reform conditions tougher so that investors and governments alike more fully accept market and transparency discipline, and carry their share of bad investments and closures.

Additional Lessons for Africa

More than forty African countries have started economic reforms. What is their story? David Sahn of Cornell University asks whether economic reform has hurt the poor in Africa. His six-country study concludes that reform generally has improved income distribution and has raised the incomes of the poor. His conclusion is similar to that of the tigers' experience. The losers in the African reform process have been civil servants and traders who have had access to rationed foreign exchange.

Sahn cautions, however, that while the general conclusion is that the macroeconomic and social reforms have little to do with causing poverty in Africa, they should not be expected to be the whole solution. Eliminating predatory and otherwise corrupt practices of the state and restoring good macroeconomic management practices are just initial steps in what is needed for Africa's development.[13] African countries—with their overcontrolled economies and closed borders—tend to drag each other down; with sustained reforms, they will help each other up.

For the broad development agenda, Africa should look to Asia. Africa, like Asia, must sustain open markets. Market openness, market prices, and private investment are keys to growth. But policy reform has to mean policy persistence, not hesitation. Policies cannot be on one day, off the next. Borders cannot be open one day and closed the next. Open-market persistence will lead to policy credibility by investors, which in turn will ensure, for the first time, that millions of people start to experience economic opportunity. Those countries that only discuss reform, or that take only a few hesitant steps toward reform, are finding that markets do not work well. Reforms have to be put in place wholeheartedly. Governmental seriousness is one key to reform. A personal commitment to national well-being by African leaders and policy-makers is the key to sustaining reform. The late Mancur Olson said it succinctly: "The best thing a society can do to increase its prosperity is to wise up."[14] No growth occurs when labor, financial capital, and natural resources are wasted.

We must ask ourselves whether aid for poor countries contributes to or delays reform. Countries that want aid generally misuse it. Those that pursue investment policies do not need aid and seldom depend on it.

Development is an issue of management and organization. Africa already knows the aid game and, therefore, knows well the issue of moral hazard. Africa's economies have stagnated for a generation as partial consequences of central control and donor aid.

Those who claim on Africa's behalf that market-based reforms do not work are probably seeing a world of half-hearted implementation and continuing aid dependency. Some experts claim that African markets will not work, while others say that Asia is special. African farmers are presumed to be unresponsive to markets and are unable to obtain credit. There is only one set of development principles for both Asia and Africa. Embracing open markets and transparency are fundamental to Africa's growth. There is no room for hesitation, qualification, or delay. According to Harvard's Jeffrey Sachs:

It might be argued that these [reform] changes are mis-directed; that Africa's problems are more fundamental than development specialists understand. This theme, that African countries are "special" and "highly complex" in ways that do not permit rapid growth have been common themes among African policy-makers who have been reluctant to undertake economic reforms. It is worth recalling (and emphasizing) that the same arguments were once used in the context of Asian countries in the 1950s and 1960s, before they adopted broad-based, market-oriented policies. Whether by design, institutional incapacity to change, or intellectual laziness, the donor community did not effectively challenge these views, especially during the 1980s. Instead, the donors continued to provide large amounts of balance of payments assistance to governments which were, at best, unconvinced of the need for, and value of, adjustment. Many [African] countries have lived on the dole literally for decades.[15]

Further lessons for Africa can be drawn from the Asian experience beyond the macroeconomic ones. Vernon Ruttan emphasizes that open markets open old avenues to growth as well as ones we can only dream about. Openness will tease open still-newer avenues that we cannot begin to see today but that will be major sources of growth, even for Africa, in a generation.[16] There is no "silver bullet" as the one solution to development, but innumerable opportunities and requirements that have been dramatized by Asia's high rates of growth—and its recent setbacks.

Unskilled African workers can one day become skilled professionals if governments are committed to education and openness. Financial savings and resource gaps must be replaced by an emphasis on enabling people, and on market-based uses of financing. Growth is based as much on human and managerial resources as it is on markets, financing, and technology.

The recent Asian experience demands that donors reassess their objectives and motives. There was a donor role of a particular kind in two of these tigers in the 1950s and 1960s. Experts now note a necessary development boost or kickstart offered by the United States, in the form of technical assistance and training, to South Korean and Taiwanese government policy-makers and technicians. There were no policy conditions nor budget support then—no dozens of donors tripping over each other. South Korea and Taiwan knew what their goals were. According to one evaluation of U.S. assistance to Taiwan, aid probably doubled the growth rate of GNP. The United States offered significant aid flows coupled with the salutary announcement that economic assistance would cease. In addition, food aid was seen early by Japan, South Korea, and Taiwan as potentially creating a risk of dependency. For them, foreign aid was useful but temporary.

Development thought and theory have been radically reformed; donor aid has not. Many African governments are struggling with reform while their donors are not. Donors know how to sustain weak governments but they know less about opening markets and sustaining transparency, and even less about ending dependency. Economic theory is ultimately and belatedly subject to field tests, but donor aid is subject to political truths at home.

The Asian gift to Africa, reaffirmed by recent crises, is that open market and education lessons are reinforced by hard-won experience.

NOTES

1.   David L. Lindauer, Michael Roemer, editors, *Asia and Africa: Legacies and Opportunities in Development*, Harvard Institute for International Development (HIID), January 1994, p. 1.

2.   Dudley Seers, "The Meaning of Development," *International Development Review*, 11:4, December 1969.

3.   Interview with Mike Wallace in Dar es Salaam, May 30, 1989; referenced in the author's *Monograph on Tanzania's Development—Discussion of Issues*, July 24, 1991.

4.   A United Nations study estimated that $200 billion fled Africa in 1991, quoted in *The New York Times*, February 4, 1996. Also note comment by Paul Collier of the Centre for the Study of African Economies, Oxford University, that 70 percent of Africa's private wealth is held offshore. IFPRI seminar, December 12, 1997.

5.   Several short studies had a considerable impact on development thinking in the early 1970s: James P. Grant, "Development: The End of Trickle Down?" *Foreign Policy*, No. 12, Fall 1973; Robert d'A. Shaw, *Rethinking Economic*

Development, Overseas Development Council (ODC), Washington, D.C., March 1972; Robert E. Hunter, James P. Grant, and William Rich, *A New Development Strategy? Greater Equity, Faster Growth, and Smaller Families*, ODC, October 1972; and William Rich, *Smaller Families Through Social and Economic Progress*, ODC, January 1973.

6.   Early agricultural growth studies include Bruce F. Johnston, "Agricultural Productivity and Economic Development in Japan," *Journal of Political Economy*, 59:6, 1951, pp. 498–513; John W. Mellor and Uma J. Lele, *Growth Linkages of the New Foodgrain Technologies*, Occasional Paper No. 50, Department of Agricultural Economics, Cornell University, May 1972; and John W. Mellor, *The New Economics of Growth: A Strategy for India and the Developing World*, Ithaca, NY: Cornell University Press, 1976. For an agricultural stages analysis, see Gustav Ranis and John C. H. Fei, "A Theory of Economic Development," *American Economic Review*, 51:4, September 1961, pp. 533–65. For an assessment comparing Asian and African agricultural policies, see C. Peter Timmer, *The Macro Dimensions of Food Security: Economic Growth, Equitable Distribution, and Food Price Stability*, Cambridge, MA: Harvard University, draft, June 1998.

7.   For discussions of the Asian miracle, see Dani Rodrik, *King Kong Meets Godzilla: The World Bank and The East Asian Miracle*, April 1994; Joseph E. Stiglitz, *The Role of Government in Economic Development*, Annual World Bank Conference on Development Economics, 1996; "Some Lessons from the East Asian Miracle," *The World Bank Research Observer*, 11:2, August 1996; Lindauer and Roemer; and Colin I. Bradford Jr., *From Trade-Driven Growth to Growth-Driven Trade: Reappraising The East Asian Development Experience*, OECD, 1994.

8.   Rodrik, p. 9.

9.   Michael Roemer and Mary Kay Gugerty, *Does Economic Growth Reduce Poverty?* HIID, Consulting Assistance on Economic Reform (CAER) II Discussion Paper No. 5, April 1997.

10.   Craig Burnside and David Dollar, "Aid Spurs Growth—in a Sound Policy Environment," *Finance and Development*, World Bank, December 1997, pp. 4–7.

11.   John Evans, *The Social Impact of the Asian Crisis*, Trade Union Advisory Committee to the OECD, 1998; IMF Managing Director Michel Camdessus, interview, *Agence France-Presse*, May 25, 1998.

12.   "Indonesia: Sukarno Seems Set To Accept 'Concrete' Economic Steps, IMF Aide Says," *The Washington Post*, January 13, 1998.

13.   David E. Sahn, *Economic Reform and the Poor In Africa*, Oxford, U.K.: Clarendon Press, 1996, pp. 21–22.

14.   Mancur Olson, Jr., "Big Bills Left on the Sidewalk—Why Some Nations Are Rich, and Others Poor," *Journal of Economic Perspective*, 10:2, Spring 1996, p. 21.

15.   Jeffrey Sachs, *A New Partnership For Growth In Africa*, HIID, Cambridge, MA: February 28, 1997, pp. 1, 8, 11.

16.   Ruttan, 1996, p. 481.

4

Bangladesh Grows Its Own Food

SKEPTICISM AT INDEPENDENCE

> "Hopeless, hopeless, hopeless"
> "An international basket case"
> "A clear choice for triage"[1]

Outsiders voiced little hope for an independent Bangladesh in 1971. There were simply too many people on too little land. Seventy million people lived in an area the size of Wisconsin. Famine-prone Bengal could not feed itself. Bangladeshis themselves sensed the mounting pressures on their *Sonar Bangla* (Golden Bengal). My associate, Nizam Uddin Ahmed, and I asked a farmer about the size of his family. Sensing our tone he replied bluntly, "Soon we will not even have land enough to bury our children."

Despite pervasive pessimism about Bangladesh in its first years, agriculture did begin to grow in the late 1970s. As the new country began to feed itself, the proportion of people in poverty declined, family planning began to be accepted, and there was even talk of ultimate food self-sufficiency. The agricultural economy grew at an overall rate of 4 percent during the 1980s, up from 2.3 percent in the 1970s. These achievements defied the expectations of even the few optimistic observers in the early 1970s. What happened during those twenty-five years to explain Sonar Bangla's agricultural success? How was Bangladesh able to address growth and poverty alleviation? How were massive food shipments translated into equally impressive harvests by her own farmers? What lessons can we learn to sustain Bangladesh's agriculture into the next century?

Perhaps the government recognized that dependence on outside food denied its own farmers a chance to succeed. How was it that food grown by American and other rich world farmers was gradually but surely displaced by Bangladeshi farmers producing for their own country? In retrospect it appears that the market-oriented principles that guided development in East and Southeast Asia also guided Bangladesh. The answers to these questions explain a developmental and foreign aid success story.

The Fields of Golden Bengal

Each year Golden Bengal turns green with rice, nurtured by the monsoon rains and flooding rivers. Silt-laden floodwaters rejuvenate the world's largest, most densely settled delta. Each annual cycle bears three rice crops drawn from rich soils. Mother Nature could not have more carefully designed a stage for the green revolution, and for a first, a second, then a third high-yielding crop a year. Some rice varieties have evolved to stay ahead of deeply flooded fields; these deepwater plants can grow by as much as fifteen feet. Farmers have also learned to irrigate their fields during the dry winter months. Bangladesh agriculture, one of the world's most ancient and complex, is also becoming one of the most modern.

I saw Bangladesh's agricultural potential for myself on a flight from Dhaka to Paris for a donors meeting in late 1974—Golden Bengal is golden green from above, but on the ground, looking westward across India and on for thousands of miles across Asia, the wintery land mass appears dead to the eye. It is no wonder that European explorers knew Golden Bengal's delta for its white muslin cloth, blue indigo dye, and golden jute as long ago as Marco Polo's twelfth century.

Competition for land is intense. Nearly all of the delta's roughly 22 million acres of cultivated land are planted with rice. Jute fiber for sacks and carpets has, historically, been the region's key money earner, but it is grown on only 7 percent of the land. The more jute that is planted means that less rice can be planted, harvested, and consumed.

Bangladesh had 12 million farms in 1990, averaging 1.8 acres in size; farms that were already down a third in size since independence, twenty years earlier. Malthusian theory was going to be tested in Bangladesh during its first decades because population appeared to be growing faster than food.

Bangladesh faced a calamitous cyclone that swept up the Bay of Bengal in November 1970, a year before independence. A major humanitarian tragedy led to international food aid on a massive scale. The twin challenges of a cyclone and an independence struggle focused the new government's attention on the vulnerability of its public food system, which was reinforced by still another food crisis in 1974. These tragedies together define to this day the government's food priorities.

Private traders have been blamed for Bengal's frequent famines as much as war, political and religious turmoil, and the monsoons. First the British, then Pakistani, and then the Bangladeshi governments have faced innumerable food crises. Long before independence, the famine of 1943 across greater Bengal prompted the establishment of a public food system and focused public planning priorities thereafter. Even before the famine of 1943, earlier famines had led the British to draft a Bengal Famine Code of 1865, which contains many of the remedial lessons used to this day to address food shortages and village suffering.

As each crop is harvested and consumed across this densely populated delta, rice prices can spike upward, grain can disappear from markets as people hoard, and poor villagers can starve. Balanced between golden harvests and starvation, Bangladesh was born on the edge. In 1971 the population of Bangladesh was 70 million people; in 1998 it is nearly 130 million.

The government of Bangladesh began anew to strengthen its publicly controlled economy and its public food and agricultural systems, which were funded and supplied by a generous international donor community. The government's policies in the first few years were, therefore, similar to those of other countries, at least as far as public planning was concerned. As occurred elsewhere in the developing world, the demands on public systems burgeoned in the late 1970s and through the 1980s, and began to bankrupt the government's budget.

As early as 1973 the government set rice self-sufficiency as a goal. Public planning, it was assumed, would win this achievement. In practice, the new government looked to food aid first to keep its towns and cities fed. Free food aid, sold in Bangladesh, also generated revenue for the budget. However, a combination of pushes and pulls on public policy started an economic reform process in the late 1970s, well before market-based principles became commonplace around the world. These reforms helped rationalize general economic policy and agriculture policy specifically, and, as a result, brought the beginnings of prosperity to the Bangladeshi people.

AID'S FIRST YEARS IN BANGLADESH

Because the United States had been involved in the development of both East and West Pakistan, it was in a position to work with the new Bangladesh to support relief efforts following the 1970 cyclone and the 1971 independence struggle. America supported the country generously as did other food donors, such as Australia, Canada, the European Union, and the United Nations.

We in the AID mission in Dhaka saw an irony in the country's agricultural potential juxtaposed with the massive tonnage of P.L. 480 food arriving monthly. Rice was being imported into a rice-producing country. In those early years between 1975 and 1980, 1.5 million tons of grain were imported each year, of which 80 percent was as aid, and half of that as P.L. 480 food. Donors and the government gradually began to see the importance of getting on with development in an obviously rich deltaic setting.

The AID mission used the expectation of P.L. 480 food aid and AID dollar projects to begin multiyear discussions with the Bangladesh government about tapping the country's agricultural potential. We designed and negotiated a food and agricultural policy strategy and food aid and dollar programs to implement it. The AID mission's contributions to agricultural reform became known as "food for development," by which we meant placing Bangladeshi farmers first in the government's food and agricultural priorities.[2]

High Risks of a Heady Vision

The AID mission pushed a Bangladesh agricultural self-help vision into action, sensing the risks, and hoping for the best. We recognized then that only with hindsight would we know whether the country could grow its own food and wind down its dependence on food aid. As we said to ourselves in the early 1970s, we "looked forward to looking back."

A small AID mission staff was in the hot seat during most of the 1970s. First Tony Schwarzwalder and then Joe Toner, the first two AID directors, guided what became a major, innovative, and risky effort. Marrying large food aid imports, infamous for their price-depressing effect on local production, with an equally large agricultural potential was the challenge. Passively importing American food surpluses might have led to further food aid dependency and possibly to disaster if Bangladeshi food production declined as an inadvertent consequence of the dumping of imported food. Food aid could also run out because of poor harvests in rich-world countries, or could be diverted to other claimants just when another humanitarian crisis befell the country.

In the 1970s we had not yet learned reliable development lessons to guide food aid's best use or to give confidence to a successful outcome. America dumped its food surpluses, often with few self-help conditions attached. Everyone knew it. But we were not going to just deliver food dockside and not follow through on its distribution or market effect. We knew we had few good choices; issues and risks faced us at every turn.

Our best intentions, large amounts of food aid, and a proclivity to get involved brought the U.S. government nose to nose with Bangladesh on a central issue; namely, donor support for its political and economic survival. We believed that Bangladesh could survive and grow by feeding itself. Our food-for-development vision was predicated on an agricultural growth process wherein government would gradually reduce its reliance on food aid and look first to its own farmers to grow enough food for self-sufficiency. Bangladeshi and international seed scientists were already at work tailoring new rice and wheat seed to deltaic conditions.

We also knew informally that senior Bangladeshi officials actively resisted food self-reliance, preferring instead to rely on free food and the cash that its sale generated for the government's budget. Senior officials saw food aid rather than domestic production as the way to fill a growing food gap created by modest prospects for domestic production and an ever-growing level of food consumption. Donor budget support helped, as did American rice for a volatile middle class. The new government did not trust its farmers, traders, or nature—nor did it pass up the advantages of American generosity.

Joe Toner led the early design effort and called the first meetings to coordinate the policy-linked uses of food aid. America's food aid tonnage was used early in the 1970s as leverage to encourage discussions of an active, pro-growth, domestic food and agricultural policy with the government of Bangladesh, World Bank and IMF representatives, and other food donors—an unheard-of step at the time.

AID used each P.L. 480 Title I agreement to advance its food-for-development vision by stressing specific self-help steps, which were discussed with planning, agriculture, and food ministry officials starting in 1973. The AID mission believed that government should reduce its budgeted subsidies for food rations to the public and for fertilizers, pesticides, and agricultural equipment. Such a step-by-step plan would lessen the burden on the budget and expand market opportunities for farmers and traders. Some key ministers agreed with our vision; most resisted. A few officers sensed that the green revolution was indeed about to revolutionize agriculture. Reluctantly at first, the new government gained confidence in this vision.

Other elements of our strategy included experimenting with ways to stabilize grain prices in order to reduce the government's fear of sky-high prices, low stock levels, and famine. The government had to gain confidence in the market if it was to redirect its control of rice purchases and sales. To modernize agriculture we envisioned a more effective use of the public grain stock, an expansion of agricultural credit, and the decontrol and privatization of fertilizer distribution.

My field trips across Bangladesh with Nizam Uddin Ahmed served to bolster my early optimism for the green revolution's potential. Our field work across innumerable fields, villages, and towns taught us first-hand about the new seed, and multiple crop and marketing systems. These trips fed the food-for-development vision.

Conflicts over Policy Priorities

Our early discussions with the Bangladesh government were often tense. They found talk of food self-sufficiency as being, primarily, not a source of growth, but a source of instability. While we talked of growth, they kept asking if the United States would meet its food aid pledge and when the next food shipment would arrive. It took years to reduce these fears, and even today, they often resurface. The Bangladesh government's ability to foster domestic growth and alleviate poverty was, and remains, tied to the fundamental perception that food security comes first.

America's food aid, mostly rice in the first years, fed urban people, the government, and the military. This use of America's food aid became a source of tension. When I first learned that our food was being allocated almost entirely for the urban middle class I recall being upset. Only 7 percent of all food aid was for hungry people who were too poor to buy their own grain. The rest was sold at low prices in urban centers, to the civil service, and to the military.[3] What about the rural poor, I wondered? What about those who were starving?

As the food donors began to appreciate how their food aid was being allocated, Bangladesh was hit by famine in late 1974. Domestic and international market forces more so than natural conditions caused the famine, when 20,000 people died.[4] Deaths were not caused solely by crop and marketing failures but by governmental manipulation to protect cities and towns. Bangladesh had appealed to donors and sought commercial food imports, but international prices were sky-high.

Famine was not what I thought it was. I was learning. Food aid served the relatively well-off first. I had failed to read the Famine Code of 1865; poor people are routinely priced out of the market because they have no cash. The stock of grain was available in 1974 to feed the poor, but traders and rich households hoarded; and the government, low on its own stock levels, did not release sufficient quantities to the poor until it was too late.

Donors were blamed for not keeping the public grain stock level high enough. A year and a half later some government officials still claimed that three-quarters of the public stock was being released to poor people in rural areas; a few officials feigned ignorance of their own system.

Tensions between food donors and the government grew during the late 1970s. Why did so much food aid need to be imported when good harvests occurred regularly in Bangladesh? Why import food and sell it at low prices to those who can afford it? It was easy to understand that a stable government would need stable supplies of rice and wheat—but it came at a high and an open-ended cost to the Bangladeshi poor, and to food donors. It was equally obvious that donor aid was financing the entire development budget and much of the operating budget as well. Only gradually and with continuing AID insistence was the proportion of public grain shifted to poorer people.[5]

Food issues were connected early with population growth. Were massive food aid shipments for Bangladesh just helping to, as we said at the time, "grow more people"? The dual development challenge facing Bangladesh had to be faced squarely; we questioned the government's commitment to family planning. AID staff in Dhaka began stressing family planning as early and as earnestly as it did food policy. Joe Toner made family planning a priority with senior officials in the Bangladesh government and, on a personal mission, took the issue to donor capitals in 1975—a second, unheard-of step.

While seemingly unsuccessful at the time, Toner's personal mission helped plant an idea that has paid historic dividends. By 1976 family planning had become a governmental priority. Donors helped the government establish a major program that introduced women as family planning counselors. The new country's fertility rate fell from 7 children per woman in the 1960s, to an average of 3.4 in 1994. In 1996, 45 percent of married couples used contraceptives. Mike Jordan, the AID family planning officer, helped the government to lay the groundwork for this achievement.

Food crises forced the donors to act in an increasingly coordinated manner. Placing conditions on aid to support public-sector-directed policies and programs increased. With each round of discussions, coordination between the government and donors improved, and food and family planning issues gained further acceptance and urgency. Aid conditioning grew more exact and useful as donors learned to associate themselves with like-minded Bangladeshi officials. The IMF was with the AID mission in spirit. The AID mission came to rely heavily on the strategic and macroeconomic work of Fred King, Basil Kavalsky, and the late Carl Jayarajah of the World Bank.

Using Wheat for Price Stability?

The matter of who ate American food in Bangladesh was a symptom, not a cause, of Bangladesh's broader food dilemma. Government confidence in Bangladesh's own farmers was the broad challenge; gaining this confidence was possible and could be achieved a step at a time. But how?

The government's priority was to ensure adequate food stock levels to secure stable prices. Senior officials went to great lengths to manipulate the stock level so that the food gap was always as large as possible. The United States did not always have a rice surplus, nor the budget to send unlimited supplies. We asked about using wheat. Wheat in rice-eating Bangladesh? An unlikely combination; but, that is what AID proposed.

The 1974 famine provided an opportunity for a food pilot. The AID mission deputy director, David Wilson, suggested that planting wheat in the upcoming dry season would create badly needed rural employment and would expand a new dry-season harvest for destitute people. Wheat is also cheaper and more plentiful than rice on the international market. Bags of wheat seed came by air freight from Egypt in early 1975. The Ford Foundation in Dhaka helped to fund this pilot.

We were not sure that wheat would be accepted in the cities. East Pakistan's urban consumers had long since accepted wheat products because wheat had been introduced by the Pakistan government and was grown in drier West Pakistan. The risk of introducing wheat was twofold: First, would new, high-yielding wheat seed be accepted by Bangladeshi farmers? And second, would wheat sold in urban markets, mostly in Dhaka, effectively dampen a sharp rise in the urban price of rice, where it mattered most?

Lots to worry about and worry we did! Charles Johnson, the AID program officer, wrestled with this idea and embarked on analyses and negotiations with Bangladeshi officials. In practice, a simple idea proved to be complex in its implementation. In concept, the introduction of wheat was fundamental to the food-for-development vision: A green revolution for Bangladeshis, protect poor cultivators and poor people with farming incentives and direct food assistance as needed, and reduce the risks of market price extremes. We were not confident that poor farmers would accept wheat as a crop, or whether wheat supplies in the major markets would dampen peaks in rice prices. The food donors did not have unlimited supplies of wheat or rice, nor did the government have an unlimited capacity to administer a wheat-based sales operation. But the government was starting to see that it could not rely endlessly on donor largesse.

The shadow of past famines hung over these discussions; but, with a nudge from Charles Johnson, the government agreed to try it. A wheat sales pilot program started in May 1976 was expanded into a retail sales operation in 1978.[6] The finance and food ministries were obviously taking a risk. AID was on the point. We had the support of the World Bank, the IMF, and our food aid colleagues, and we also had our fingers crossed for good measure.

The U.S. Congress passed new P.L. 480 legislation in 1977, which tied food aid to stronger self-help measures. The first Title III agreement in the world was signed with Bangladesh in mid-1978; it traded U.S. wheat for Bangladesh's conduct of this wheat sales pilot program. Congress also passed the Bellmon Amendment, named for Congressman Henry Bellmon, which stipulated that AID had to certify that American food aid would not spoil upon arrival nor cause a substantial disincentive effect on local production. The wheat sales idea found strong congressional support. We were now officially armed to trade food aid for policy reform.

The Bangladesh government had been relying on price controls rather than the market to stabilize food prices. The public system was costly to administer and theft was rampant. Grain was stolen from public warehouses and retail shops.[7] A price-based, wheat sales operation could give the government greater efficiency in stabilizing grain prices and could lay the basis for encouraging Bangladeshi cultivators. Wheat sales, at higher than traditional ration-system prices, would feed the cities. Wheat sales in the cities, we believed, combined with less reliance on subsidized rice sales by government, would ultimately lessen the need for publicly supplied rice.

Several factors combined, even conspired, to force this wheat sales experiment and to make it a success. All these factors convinced the Bangladesh government and the food donors alike that they were on the right track.

First, Bangladesh is blessed with able civil servants who have been willing to try development experiments of all kinds. Innovation was not new to government.

Second, the 1974 flood and famine and skyrocketing international grain prices in the mid-1970s left few food experts in doubt about the unsustainability of the donor-dependent food system.

Third, and as if to underscore that Bangladesh could not rely on American food aid indefinitely, the U.S. government objected strongly when Bangladesh sold jute bags to Cuba during 1974 and 1975 by suspending food shipments for a short period.

Fourth, and on a more positive note, the sweet smell of a green revolution was in the air in the mid-1970s.

Less than a year after wheat sales started in January 1979, AID and the Bangladesh government conducted a joint evaluation of this first trial of wheat sales. The results were in. Government officials were pleased; wheat production grew and the rice price had been kept below a predetermined maximum by the sale of wheat. Wheat sales did, indeed, work to stabilize rice prices. We had opened the door to reducing the ration system's cost and scope, and for relying on Bangladeshi farmers.[8]

Beginning in the late 1970s, donors grew increasingly concerned that they, and not the Bangladesh government, were doing far too much of the analytical and prescriptive work. Despite asking the government to make its own choices for Title I self-help steps in 1973, the collegial process did not work well. AID suggested that Bangladeshi staff be charged with these analytical responsibilities in early 1976. Ultimately, a ministry of food monitoring office was accepted and funded by the World Bank so that government, and not the food aid donors, would conduct the analyses and evaluations, and create the policy options. Later, IFPRI and the World Bank contributed analytical staff and financial support to the office. An AID report from the early 1980s noted that the government accepted the principle that public food stock levels could be halved. This is another payoff of analysis, policy dialogue, and risk-taking. Making food aid work for development under difficult conditions required donor presence and, according to Vernon Ruttan, "determination, experience, and negotiation."[9]

OPEN THE DOOR AND GET OUT OF THE WAY
—THE GREEN REVOLUTION

The new Bangladesh government had inherited and embraced public planning as its principal approach to development, a carry-over from the Pakistan government. The government took first a few steps, then many to decontrol and devolve its responsibilities, which were straining the budget. In retrospect, Bangladesh began redirecting its economy toward market-based growth on the heels of the Asian tigers, and well ahead of Africa, which was still committed to public planning.

The country's budget was an even more serious matter than food. The World Bank was obliged to help Bangladesh secure promises of financial support. Food, fertilizer, and pharmaceuticals, for example, which were sold at reduced prices, supported almost the entire budget. But because these donated commodities were being sold well below their true value, and because of pilferage, the actual revenue from them was meager.

Soon after independence the government and the IMF were at loggerheads over an unsustainable budget deficit and price controls. The new government, feeling nationalistic, had taken over several privately held jute companies and agricultural estates. Nor was the government about to liberalize, that is, float, the value of the new national currency, the *taka*, downward to a realistic international value. A financial crisis in 1974 occurred because the government did not have enough dollar reserves to hold the taka's price steady. Donor assurances to support the budget and the taka were forthcoming but Bangladesh had to agree to the further decontrol of prices and parastatals. By March 1975 the taka had been devalued by nearly 60 percent, which made Bangladeshi exports, namely jute, more competitive on international markets.[10]

In August 1975 the country was wracked by a bloody coup and then two counter-coups. Tanks rolled in the streets of Dhaka. The coups were not only political and bloody, but came to represent a gradual change in economic direction. What had been nationalized was now denationalized, or at least the process of decontrol was started. A market-oriented military was back in power. Most of the Bangladesh government's reforms, like its food and agricultural reforms, took place between 1976 and 1991, when the military was in power.

Throughout the late 1970s and early 1980s, the government remained under severe budget constraints and was forced constantly to negotiate financial relief and economic reform packages with the World Bank, the IMF, and the major donors. The government, gradually and begrudgingly, removed restrictions on private imports and reduced tariffs on exports. A more flexible exchange rate policy was initiated in 1979 following the 1975 devaluation, which slowly reduced the exchange rate and therefore the price bias against agriculture, and began opening Bangladesh to the global economy.

Just as Bangladesh had inherited a public food ration system, so too did it inherit parastatal trading companies that had been set up by the Pakistan government in the 1950s and 1960s. These companies ensured that farmers had adequate supplies of fertilizers, pesticides, and irrigation pumps. Fertilizer remained in short supply and was inevitably sold to those who could pay a premium to obtain it. Publicly supplied agricultural inputs, particularly credit, were similarly controlled, priced, and scarce.

The government's monopoly on agricultural inputs, primarily irrigation pumps, tubewells, and fertilizers, was relaxed and eventually eliminated. An AID-funded experiment proved to the Bangladesh government's satisfaction, like the wheat pilot before it, that private traders could deliver fertilizer to farmers. A parastatal that had controlled fertilizer for a generation was reduced in scale and cost.

Many of these national-level economic reforms had a direct and positive effect on agriculture and private business opportunities in towns and villages. By 1995 only a third of the public grain sales was sold through the old ration system, and two-thirds were sold through the new market operation. The gradual reduction of costly subsidies for food and agricultural inputs favored farmers on balance because the reforms created opportunities for retail suppliers of food grain, inputs, and services at lower cost and better reliability.[11]

Private trade could now legally serve agriculture. There was an explosion of food and agricultural retailers in the early 1980s, employing well over 100,000 businesspeople. The private importation of wheat and irrigation equipment was allowed for the first time. Irrigation pumps and tubewells in all shapes and sizes sprang up, displacing traditional, hand-powered techniques. Irrigated cropland doubled from 17.1 percent in 1980 to 33.9 percent in 1994. Fertilizer use more than doubled as well in the same period. Input prices fell dramatically as the reforms took effect and private businesses competed to serve rural Bangladesh.

The Bangladeshi people and their government began to see the fruits of reform. The evidence of impact was clear as can be seen in Table 4.1. By 1985 one-third of the rice crop and all of the wheat crop were planted with new, high-yielding seed varieties. The dryland rice crop was 80 percent planted with new varieties and was nearly 100 percent irrigated. The government did "open the door and did get out of the way."[12]

The green revolution, finally free to operate in practice as in theory, caused food production to nearly double since independence. Food harvests grew by 2.7 percent a year, exceeding population growth for more than two decades—a remarkable accomplishment.[13] By 1992 Bangladesh was nearly food self-sufficient. In fact, it was widely said that Bangladesh cultivators could produce 1.5 million more tons of rice if there was a market for the harvest (or if the government would buy it).

The production gains were shared across Bangladesh. The cost of rice fell nearly by half between 1974 and 1995, with most of this benefit accruing to poor consumers who, at independence, spent as much as 70 percent of their income on rice.[14]

In addition to macroeconomic and agricultural policy reforms, Bangladesh, like the Pakistan government before it, invested heavily in rural infrastructure such as roads, irrigation ditches, and earthen embankments to create off-season employment and to complement the introduction of the new seed into this flood-prone world. The phrase *flood prone* does not quite convey this reality. Every year 60 percent of Bangladesh normally floods. These public investments in rural water control are entitled to some of the credit for the country's agricultural growth. Several NGOs, led by CARE, were instrumental in administering food-for-work projects and in designing and evaluating new pilot projects and social safety nets to alleviate poverty. Rural electrification for villages and irrigation pumps also contributed to rural productivity.

Bangladesh made food self-sufficiency its first goal and has sustained good harvests, but this could not have happened without the reforms of the 1980s. Although Bangladesh is not yet self-sufficient, its agricultural growth has been impressive, and a sense of confidence has grown with this achievement.

With the relaxation of trade and investment controls, Bangladesh discovered a new source of growth. Investors, with sewing machines in hand, began arriving by the dozens from East Asia. The production and export of shirts and jeans became a new growth industry, which was fueled by secure food supplies and an economy that encouraged private investment. Textile exports by the mid-1980s were generating more foreign exchange than were jute fiber exports.

Table 4.1
Broad Changes in the Bangladesh Rice Market

	1960s	1970s	1980s	1990s
Total rice crop in millions of metric tons	10	12	15	18
Winter crop as a percent of total	7	18	26	37
New seed use as a percent of total	1	23	36	58
Grain marketing as a percent of production	12	27	34	49
Grain distribution as a percent of public share	30	15	11	7
Number of marketing agents	6,155	11,592	43,691	50,868

Source: Adapted from Nuimuddin Chowdhury and Steven Haggblade, "Evolving Rice and Wheat Markets," in Raisuddin Ahmed, Steven Haggblade, and Tawfiq-e-Elahi Chowdhury, *Out of the Shadow of Famine: Evolving Food Markets and Food Policy in Bangladesh*, IFPRI, September 30, 1997, p. 160.

ORIGINS OF THE GREEN REVOLUTION SEED

The introduction of new rice seed took on personal meaning for Bangladeshi officials and donor staffs alike. It is a delight to recall the excitement during the 1960s and 1970s when researchers were developing new varieties. Donors in Dhaka followed the testing and release of each new rice or wheat seed as closely as if it were the development of their own children. We asked where it was being planted, if it would stand up under its larger load of kernels, and if villagers would like its taste.

Today there are nearly twenty international research institutions that add immeasurably to world food growth, analysis, advice, and security. The centers include, first and foremost, the Centro Internacional de Mejoramiento de Maiz y Trigo (CIMMYT), in Mexico, which conducts research on corn and wheat. CIMMYT began in the 1940s with funding from the Rockefeller Foundation. Then came Asia's equally famous International Rice Research Institute (IRRI), in Los Baños, the Philippines, starting in the 1960s with funding from the Rockefeller and Ford Foundations and AID. The American seed scientist, Hank Beachell, among a handful of other scientists, founded this rice revolution. Since then nearly twenty other specialized agronomic, animal, fisheries, irrigation, and genetic research centers have rounded out the public agricultural research system.

Today most developing countries have their own seed research centers. Bangladesh has been a direct beneficiary as well as a contributor. The Bangladesh Rice Research Institute (BRRI), for example, adapts outside varieties with local trials. Tied to IRRI, BRRI in turn has adapted thirteen rice varieties for use in Bangladesh and twelve other countries.

Starting in 1975 these various scientific research centers have been coordinated by the Consultative Group on International Agricultural Research (CGIAR). IFPRI, also based in Washington, acts as an analytical arm of CGIAR to promote global and country-specific analyses of food security, consumption, and nutritional well-being.

My first walk through a rice field took place in China's Hunan Province in 1947—long before I knew any of this. Without appreciating what I was looking at then, traditional rice varieties yielded two to three tons per hectare at the most. During my professional years in Asia, in the 1970s and early 1980s, green revolution rice varieties yielded an exciting five to six tons per hectare, with an amazing nine to ten tons just around the corner. Today, scientists are developing varieties of rice that yield ten to twelve tons per hectare.

WHAT OF THE BANGLADESH POOR? WHO BENEFITS?

It is one thing to describe the origins of Bangladesh's agricultural success, it is quite another to document who is benefiting. Bangladesh is farmed by absentee land owners, by farm owners-as-operators, by tenants, and by millions of landless laborers. The poorest are believed to have no access to land at all, even as laborers.

During the 1960s and 1970s the available evidence revealed a grim picture. Poverty was widespread between 1963 and 1974, and was increasing. Those people who consumed fewer than 1,935 calories per day increased from 42 percent to 56 percent of the rural population as a whole, and from 25 percent to 48 percent in cities. Twenty-seven percent of the population was very poor, consuming fewer than 1,805 calories per day.[15]

A different picture emerged in the 1980s as surveys began to capture the positive effects of the green revolution. An early study illustrated a broad, positive picture. Rural poverty is reported to have actually declined by 51 percent between 1982 and 1986; the absolute size of the

poverty group, despite population growth, decreased by about 15 percent, from 53 million people in 1982 to 45 million in 1986.

While the numbers of poor people remained large, the incidence of
poverty declined from 92 percent to 48 percent of the population between 1974 and 1992.[16] Wage surveys, albeit incomplete, also show a
positive picture. Real wages were reported to have increased between
1982 and 1986; another wage report stated that rural wages had tripled in
some areas. These surveys appeared to capture the sharp and beneficial
declines in the price of grains. The real price of rice fell by half over the
last twenty years, benefiting most of the population who were net buyers
of food grain, including marginal farmers, the rural landless, and the
urban poor.

This productivity-induced price decline can also be illustrated by
examining farm size. Twenty years ago it required 1.2 acres to feed a
family of six; in 1994 enough food grain could be grown for that family
on 0.4 acre of land. The green revolution was clearly paying off for poor
laborers and owners of small farms.

Rural works also helped the rural poor. Workers were paid both cash
and food for construction of earthen works such as minor roads, river
embankments, village ponds, and irrigation ditches. A sample of villages
showed that household income had grown by a third, that rural wages
almost doubled, and that landless laborers and small-farm owners gained
the most from increased crops, higher wages, and more livestock and
fish, while large landowners gained the most from their rural businesses
and industries.[17]

By the 1990s there was agreement from researchers from across the
political spectrum that the poor people in Bangladesh did, indeed,
benefit from the green revolution. It is striking, perhaps deceptively so,
that the ready availability of grain would have such a major, positive
impact on the alleviation of poverty. The good news, however, is tempered because 40 million people still live in poverty. Further, studies
have concluded that the investment in rural works has provided neither
the income nor the consumption impact that is required to eliminate
poverty. The consumption benefit of food as wages, which provided only
a 10 percent increase in annual income, is said to be negligible. Nor has
food aid overall, a portion of which is used as payment for rural works,
reported to have had a significant nutritional impact.

There is a risk that recent surveys have captured only the best news
from the field, that of productivity gains from the new seed and an
associated decline in the cost of food. Because rural poverty in Bangla-

desh is so intimately tied to land tenure, land use patterns must be examined before a summary can be made on the plight of the poor.

Farm Tenancy and the Green Revolution

Fundamental to agriculture development theory is the western belief that farms have to be large to be successful, and that farmers who own their land will increase their production when they can make money because they have an incentive to use modern seeds and fertilizers. Western experts widely assumed that Asian tenants and laborers, who worked small plots, would not benefit as directly from the green revolution and hence would not invest as heavily in modern inputs.

I too drew the conclusion that there was little hope for the green revolution benefiting most of the actual Bangladeshi cultivators because its incentives and profits would be enjoyed by the landowners and not by tenants and laborers. Owners not only owned the land and had cash but had easier access to all the new inputs. They would be the first, and possibly the only ones, to enjoy the new harvests.

In retrospect, I was wrong. A few western experts had spent their careers arguing the farm size issue, and the owner-as-cultivator case for the green revolution's adoption in Asia; they too were proven wrong. Stylized facts were shelved.[18]

First, the historic evidence from several Asian countries shows that new seed and modern inputs are neutral to farm size. Neutral means that a farm does not need to be a certain minimum size to use a new seed, as would be necessary for the efficient use of a tractor, for example. (On Java I often saw terraced, irrigated plots no larger than a square meter.) This first issue was laid to rest early.

Second was the issue of ownership. One reason the green revolution was thought to be such a boon to Bangladesh was that the country was farmed almost entirely by owners of small farms, or so it was thought at the time. Furthermore, Bangladesh, it was officially reported, had no large farms and nor were there many tenant farmers. With new seed, the right inputs, and favorable prices, harvests and profits would multiply. Fine in theory, and in practice it did work.

During my five years in Bangladesh, Nizam Uddin Ahmed and I talked to villagers about tenancy and landlessness. In time we learned the vernacular and asked the right questions. By 1975 we came to realize that 80 percent of the country was not actually farmed by landowners but by tenants and laborers. The reality was the reverse of the official land tenure picture. Tom Jannuzi and Jim Peach of the University of Texas at

Austin and A. K. M. Ghulam Rabbani of the Bangladesh Central Bureau of Statistics documented this unpopular reality.[19]

Nonetheless, field evidence showed that poorer Bangladeshi farmers, tenants, and laborers *did* share in the overall revolution. Rich farmers were the first to adopt the use of new seed, but poorer farmers and tenants also used new seed and eventually caught up. They paid higher prices for inputs and obtained lower market prices at harvest than did wealthier farmers, but they were part of the revolution. Land use surveys from 1979 report that nearly two-thirds of tenants interviewed used fertilizers and many used irrigation equipment. In short, another western assumption (and official government statistic) had to be set aside.

So how do we assess this land tenure situation? All farmers accept the green revolution—this is a fact. New rice and wheat varieties are being widely accepted, as has the market and all of its associated reforms. Most Bangladeshis share in the revolution's benefits: landowners, tenants, laborers, and consumers. A new rural middle class is benefiting as well, but it remains true that tens of millions of people are still very poor.

Several hypotheses might explain the present situation. First, perhaps landowners direct their tenants to use new seed effectively. Perhaps competition for land is so intense that no one can afford to cut corners by not using the right seed and the right amount of fertilizer. Use of new seed is labor intensive. Perhaps underemployment has been so severe that laborers are working twice the hours they used to on the new crops, and so their annual wage income is increasing.

Second, perhaps traditional village work, tenant, and food sharing mechanisms still operate despite the introduction of labor and tenant contracts. Perhaps higher wages reflect sharing as well. Taking these two hypotheses together, we might surmise that the very poor are simply being carried along by traditional work-sharing arrangements that are still functioning during the green revolution's early years.

Third, perhaps rural poverty surveys simply have missed the plight of the poorest people. Surveys might be measuring the favorable impact of agricultural production and price changes rather than the actual income status of the very poor. Data analyses do not always capture answers to the subjective question, "How are you doing?"

Raisuddin Ahmed and his colleagues at IFPRI are not at all sanguine about the plight of the poor in their 1997 study. The rural poor's lack of access to land creates an "increasingly tenuous claim on a key productive asset [that] reduces not only earnings power but also the ability of the poor to weather setbacks emanating from ill health, disease, or natural calamity." They conclude that "the green revolution food grain technology has not been able to solve Bangladesh's deep-seated poverty singlehandedly."[20]

In summary then, if agricultural growth is sustained, and if real rural wages continue to increase and this index is broad-based across Bangladesh, then experts should be reassured. These are big ifs. For my part, I left Bangladesh in 1977 discouraged, primarily because I thought tenancy practices were so pervasive that they would slow and even prevent acceptance of the green revolution by the very groups of poor people for whom the green revolution showed the most promise. No one should wait for another humanitarian crisis to learn more about the plight of the poor. Surveys will always be needed to guide still-newer growth enhancing and poverty alleviating policies and programs. No one should assume that sharing mechanisms of old and new agricultural practices, whatever they are, will benefit all of Bangladesh.

LOOKING BACK ON A HIGH RISK AID PROGRAM

Through AID the U.S. government stayed the course with Bangladesh over several decades; it pressed for and financed wide-ranging economic reforms while simultaneously providing humanitarian relief and political stability of sorts in the face of continual food and political crises. The AID mission worried about the risks of policy creativity and resource commitments. These were primarily risks for the Bangladesh government, and secondarily for donors. We did not see the total donor cost in eventual food tonnage and project dollars. But then, we did not appreciate the government's eventual willingness to experiment and succeed, even if budgetary and donor pressures played a role. The American taxpayer might argue that the costs of helping Bangladesh were too high and our aid lasted too long. However, Bangladesh was born in an era of public-directed development and large food surpluses.

AID could not have run a better program in the face of the political risks, the monsoons, the floods, and the vagaries of our own commitments and those of other donors. The AID mission benefited greatly when Title III of P.L. 480 and the Bellmon Amendment were passed. We could not have delivered food and then ignored what happened to it, as much as some Bangladeshi officials would have liked, because food spoilage would have caught up with us quickly.

Up until the mid-1990s the United States gave Bangladesh $2 billion in food aid, or 41 percent of all the country's food aid, during the preceding twenty years. The absolute amount appears huge, but not when it is viewed in per capita terms of $12—and declining—or when it is compared with the amount of aid that goes to other, equally poor countries. American food aid leverage occurred in Bangladesh by supplying only 4 percent of its total, domestic and imported, cereal supply.[21]

The AID mission had the benefit of the world's best development thinkers. Visitors included John Mellor, René Dumont, Gus Papanek, Chester Bowles, John Thomas, Akter Ahmed Khan, John Lewis, and Gus Ranis. Herbert Rees, the AID Regional Director for South Asia in Washington, had the good sense to route all development thinkers who were interested in Bangladesh through the AID mission in Dhaka. While on a visit to Dhaka in 1973, Herb told the mission that we were to draft a comprehensive development strategy and that it was going to be the best one in the world, and he slammed his hand on the table for emphasis.

The AID directors at the time, Tony Schwarzwalder and then Joe Toner, and the many that followed, might have been disinterested in innovation and risk; they might have designed standard programs by the rule book. Or, as is common, each director could have changed course simply to imprint his or her name on the program. All have resisted this temptation. For twenty-five years the AID mission has wisely focused on structural adjustment, privatization, and broad-based growth long before their efficacy was proven.

We had important allies at the time. The World Bank and the IMF were not thinking about agricultural reforms at first, yet they and the United Nations and the major donors made AID's initial work their own. I recall that a few expatriate advisors, including Trevor Page of the World Food Program and Hugh Brammer of FAO, had ties with the Bangladesh government and were fully supportive of AID's food policy proposals. Even an American ambassador or two helped out. There were also allies in Congress. P.L. 480 legislation was under review in the late 1970s, key congressional staff came to Dhaka to listen, and Title III, Food For Development, was born.

At the time, those of us at AID believed, despite all the risks, that we had little choice but to innovate. We went to the flooded fields and to markets to learn, we helped the government try pilot projects of various kinds, and we helped implement development policy by virtue of being resident in Dhaka. Our presence added principles and value to more than $1 billion in food and project aid, with definable, propitious consequences. Perhaps AID's good work was more serendipitous than planned. Who is to say? A retrospective story such as this one can provide only a few of the answers for a country where tens of millions of people remain very poor.

Carrying Field Lessons Home to Washington

Following five years in Dhaka, I returned to Washington in 1977 to work on food aid policy worldwide. There I worked for Alex Shakow, head of AID's policy and planning office. We acted to implement the new Title III legislation and I traveled to Jakarta, Kabul, Khartoum, and Mogadishu to help design country programs; I completed a draft food aid policy paper; and served on the staff of the White House World Hunger Working Group.

I had an opportunity to apply lessons from Bangladesh. Shakow strived to depoliticize P.L. 480 by judging food aid proposals by their intended purpose as being either political, developmental, or humanitarian. By doing this he nudged the State Department into revealing that its interest in food aid was primarily as a gap-filling dollar reward rather than humanitarian or developmental.

I helped AID design and negotiate several Title III programs and cut a few ill-conceived proposals off at the design stage. Again, small steps in the right direction. My food aid policy draft sat on a superior's desk for two years, possibly because it had the word "policy" in its title.

Working in a White House atmosphere, fresh from flooded fields, was both fun and shocking. What were then battles over the conflicting uses of P.L. 480 are standard development positions taken for granted today. We had built a Washington consensus required for the developmental uses of P.L. 480.[22]

FACING THE TURN OF THE CENTURY

Crises will continue to befall Bangladesh, but the country has built a basis for confidence, recovery, and sustained growth. Perhaps food aid has not just "grown more people." Perhaps families have grown more confident that their children will be fed and will find work, and that government is confident that it too will survive. As David Atwood, an AID agricultural economist, has said, the country is at a crossroads that government sees as its own.

Bangladesh government officials have taken large risks in promoting market-based agricultural growth. They have undertaken structural adjustment in the middle of humanitarian, economic, and political crises; and have implemented radical reforms despite floods and droughts, coups, and counter coups; and despite food, budget, and foreign exchange crises. Bangladeshi officials would not have embraced reform without sharing in the ultimate vision.

However motivated and tumultuous, the manifest national bounty stemming from the reforms are being shared: The real price of rice has fallen by half over twenty-five years, family planning acceptance has grown dramatically, real wages may be increasing, and new industries have come to life. Although tens of millions of Bangladeshis remain poor, the beginnings of sustainable growth and further poverty allevia-tion are in place.

This story does not stand in isolation from its present context, however. These pages are a retrospective on food and agricultural policies that were formulated during the 1970s and 1980s. During the mid- to late 1990s, Bangladesh has cause for worry. The government continues to face political fractiousness, which has allowed dilution in its commitment to reform. One consequence has been a sharp decline in the rate of agricultural growth, from 2.7 percent per year during the 1980s to only 1.2 percent per year for the 1990–96 period.[23] Once again the rate of population growth exceeds agricultural growth. Is it just a production blip, or a downturn reflecting an erosion in technical capacity or policy commitment?

The debate surrounding agriculture has intensified as Bangladesh struggles to sustain its achievements. Is the downturn in agricultural production policy related, or does it reflect an end to productivity gains? Has the green revolution come to an end? One assessment, by Ibrahim Khalil and David Atwood, argues from recent data that declines in rice production are related to policy and do not reflect any decrease in agricultural productivity. It is disappointing to learn at this writing that the government's food monitoring capacity, about which so much was promised, remains weak. Perhaps donor dependency has a hold on the government's mind. Food aid, though diminished in scope, continues to be important.

Staying power is the issue. Great potential continues to exist for the introduction and expanded use of newer rice and wheat seed, for more irrigation and fertilizer coverage, and for further crop diversification.[24] The government is indeed at a crossroads. It must sustain the pace of its reforms; it cannot stop to savor its successes or allow any donor-funded dilution in effort. The population of Bangladesh has already tripled since the late 1940s, from 40 million to 128 million people. By 2010, if the present rate of increase is not reduced further, the population will reach 150 million.[25]

Market reform principles must be strengthened. Macroeconomic discipline and openness remain paramount, as they do in Indonesia, South Korea, and Thailand. Like the Asian tigers, many of Bangladesh's preconditions for growth and poverty reduction are either in place or are being put in place. Having switched from a philosophy of administering growth to one of fostering growth, Bangladesh must sustain investment. Having once administered trade, government must now oversee competition and legal and financial transparency. Agricultural production primarily, and other, newer sources of growth can draw tens of millions of people across the poverty line.

Bangladesh has tapped only a third of its irrigation potential. Openness and confidence will also attract private investors to agricultural credit, private storage, and international seed networks. The public sector must lead agricultural research. Seed research can only be stressed again and again: "A continuous flow of improved technology remains vital for providing a powerful incentive to sustain growth in production within a socially tolerable price environment."[26] Experts express alarm that financing for research has been reduced and that senior Bangladeshi seed researchers are leaving their own research institute.[27] Even the AID mission in Dhaka has cut its agricultural and general economist positions.

At first it would appear a good thing that Bangladeshi farmers could sell another 1.5 million tons of grain if they had a ready market. This lack of a domestic market could bode ill for the country. Bangladesh must create new sources of demand to sustain and expand its agricultural potential.

Ensuring ever larger harvests underscores the challenge of sustaining food grain price incentives without resorting to budget-busting public procurement. How can this be done?

First, Bangladesh should export grain when harvests permit and prices drop. Bengal's high-quality aromatic rices should be encouraged to find a niche in the international grain market. Their earnings may not be large, but their symbolic significance, as a fine rice with great demand, would be a source of national pride. Donors must support such a step.

Second, beyond rice and wheat, agricultural diversification will better exploit Bangladesh's seasons, soil types, and irrigation potential. New crops will contribute to agricultural exports and create further demand for domestic grain. Diversification should include more fruits, vegetables, cotton, spices, and pulses. In time, some portions of the delta devoted exclusively to rice and wheat can switch production to higher value crops. The private sector must also become the principal impetus for crop diversification.

Third, Bangladesh has already opened its doors to new sources of off-farm growth. The new textile industry, which has become a new source of national growth and employment, creates a new demand for food. The more sources of growth and employment there are, the greater will be the demand for food. Shrimp and leather goods are also new exports and show promise of expanding foreign exchange earnings; perhaps international financial services and computer software design will be next.

Today a science-based agriculture is the foundation of a global economy, and it is the starting point for late-developing countries. Bangladesh proves that it can be done. Now we must learn to initiate and sustain agricultural modernization across late-developing countries.

NOTES

This chapter is based primarily on my tour in Bangladesh from 1972 to 1977. Because of more recent work by AID officers and other experts, I have gained from their reviews of this development effort:

(a) David A. Atwood, A. S. M. Jahangir, Herbie Smith, and Golam Kabir, *History of Food Aid in Bangladesh*, USAID, Dhaka, draft, May 17, 1994, and as published by AID, CDIE, July 25, 1994; also in R. Ahmed et al., 1997 (see d below); which led to my own comment in *Personal Reflections on a USAID, Dhaka Report, History of Food Aid in Bangladesh*, AID, PPC, CDIE, draft, 1994, which served as the basis of this chapter.

(b) Donald G. McClelland, Robert Muscat, Lisa Smith, and Bruce Spake, *United States Food Aid Programs—Bangladesh Case Study*, USAID Impact Evaluation, draft, January 17, 1997. Reprinted as *Food Aid in Bangladesh—A Gradual Shift From Relief to Reform*, USAID, CDIE Impact Evaluation 5, 1997.

(c) Numerous IFPRI studies on Bangladesh food and agriculture.

(d) Raisuddin Ahmed, Steven Haggblade, and Tawfiq-e-Elahi Chowdhury, *Out of the Shadow of Famine: Evolving Food Markets and Food Policy in Bangladesh*, IFPRI, September 30, 1997.

1. The three introductory quotations are from, respectively:

(a) A personal communication with Tom Jannuzi, February 24, 1978, who quotes Gunnar Myrdal. Myrdal was a visitor to the University of Texas at Austin, where Jannuzi was Dean of the Center for Asian Studies.

(b) Secretary of State Henry Kissinger in a 1971 speech, cited in McClelland, 1997, p. 6, and in Ahmed, 1997, p. 32.

(c) W. Paddock and P. Paddock, *Famine 1975!* Boston: Little, Brown, 1967, in which they recommend triage for three-quarters of a billion people in Asia. For a counter proposal, see Jean Mayer and M. A. Islam, *Alternative To*

Triage—Bangladesh—A Case Study, undated draft from the 1970s, pp. 26–27.

2. USAID, Dhaka, *Economic Growth in Bangladesh—The Case For Broad-Based Agricultural Development*, December 1974, which led to my book, *Bangladesh: Equitable Growth?* New York: Pergamon Press, 1979.

3. Stepanek, *Bangladesh*, p. 56.

4. Stepanek, *Estimating Starvation Deaths in Bangladesh*, AID Memo, November 26, 1974.

5. My letter to John Mellor of July 31, 1975, noted that 2.2 million metric tons of food grain valued at $440 million had been used for consumption without benefiting the poor or development.

6. Atwood et al., 1994, p. 27; and USAID, Dhaka, *Open Market Food Grain Sales—Mechanics and Related Aspects of an Integrated Food System*, draft for discussion, April 29, 1976.

7. There were significant leakages in the ration system and in the food-for-works program. McClelland (using an IFPRI study), draft, 1997, p. 10; Atwood et al., 1994, pp. 9 and 25; and Ahmed, 1997, pp. 434 and 547.

8. USAID, Dhaka, *The Title III Open Market Sales Program in Bangladesh: A First Evaluation*, June 1979; and Atwood et al., 1994, pp. 22–23 and 38–39. It was found that 100,000 metric tons of wheat sold via the sales operation had the same price effect as 167,000 metric tons sold via the ration system; see also Raisuddin Ahmed and Andrew Bernard, *Rice Price Fluctuation and an Approach to Price Stabilization in Bangladesh*, IFPRI Research Report 72, February 1989; and Raisuddin Ahmed, *Food Grain Supply, Distribution, and Consumption Policies within a Dual Pricing Mechanism: A Case Study of Bangladesh*, IFPRI Research Report 8, May 1979, p. 12; and in Ahmed, 1997, p. 299.

9. For food aid issues, see Vernon Ruttan, *Why Food Aid?*, Baltimore, MD: Johns Hopkins University Press, 1993.

10. Nurul Islam, *Economic Policy Reforms and the IMF: Bangladesh Experience in the Early 1970s*, IFPRI, 1991, p. 256.

11. Raisuddin Ahmed, *Liberalization of Agricultural Input Markets in Bangladesh: Process, Impact, and Lessons*, IFPRI, and in *Agricultural Economics*, 12, 1995, pp. 115–28; and Roger Poulin, *Assessment of USAID's Fertilizer Market Privatization Program: Bangladesh*, AID, CDIE Working Paper 198, April 1996. The AID project officer, Dean Alter, and the International Fertilizer Development Center of Muscle Shoals, Alabama, established this experiment, in R. Ahmed, 1995, p. 127.

12. R. Ahmed, *Liberalization*, pp. 115–28. Quotation is from David Gisselquist, *Bangladesh Agriculture: A Case Study of the Impact of Policies Associated with Structural Adjustment Programs on Economic Growth*, for the World Bank, July 1995, p. 6.

13. R. Ahmed, 1997, pp. 4 and 508; and Mahabub Hossain, *Nature and Impact of the Green Revolution in Bangladesh*, IFPRI, July 1988, pp. 25–26.

14.   Ibid, pp. 31 and 37; the real price of rice declined 47 percent between 1975 and 1994; also reported in McClelland, draft, 1997, p. 18.

15.   For discussions see: R. Ahmed, *Food Grain Supply*, p. 11; Francesco Goletti, *The Changing Public Role in a Rice Economy Approaching Self-Sufficiency: The Case of Bangladesh*, IFPRI Research Report 98, 1994, p. 53; and Akter U. Ahmed, Haider A. Khan, and Rajan K. Sampath, *Poverty in Bangladesh: Measurement, Decomposition and Intertemporal Comparison*, IFPRI, and in the *Journal of Development Studies*, Vol 27, No 4, July 1991, pp. 44, 48, and 62–63.

16.   Akter U. Ahmed, Haider A. Khan, and Rajan K. Sampath, pp. 55–56; and World Bank, *1998 World Development Indicators*, p. 64.

17.   Raisuddin Ahmed and Mahabub Hossain, *Development Impact of Rural Infrastructure in Bangladesh*, IFPRI Research Report 83, October 1990, p. 12.

18.   Stepanek, 1979. I was not alone in being unduly pessimistic about this aspect of the new seed revolution; notables include Wolf Ladejinsky, Bruce F. Johnston, F. Tomasson Jannuzi, and James T. Peach.

19.   F. Tomasson Jannuzi and James T. Peach. *Report on the Hierarchy of Interests in Land*, Dhaka: AID, September 1977.

20.   Ahmed, R., 1997, pp. 192 and 196.

21.   In 1993, for example, Bangladesh received $12 per capita in aid. Thirty-seven countries received higher amounts of aid per capita. McClelland, 1997, p. iii and note 13.

22.   The White House, *World Hunger and Malnutrition: Improving the U.S. Response*, Spring 1978; AID, *Food Aid and Development, A Policy Discussion Paper*, July 1981, prepared by Donald G. McClelland as based on a draft by Stepanek, *Food for Development: A Food Aid Policy*, July 1979.

23.   World Bank, *1998 World Development Indicators*, p. 176.

24.   Ibrahim Khalil and David A. Atwood, *Rice Self Sufficiency in Bangladesh: Crisis or Opportunity?* draft, AID, Spring 1995.

25.   World Bank, *1998 World Development Indicators*, p. 42.

26.   Raisuddin Ahmed, *Agricultural Price Policy Under Complex Socioeconomic and Natural Constraints: The Case of Bangladesh*, IFPRI Research Report 27, October 1981, Abstract.

27.   John Kruse, Pioneer Hi-Bred International, Inc., IFPRI seminar, November 6, 1997.

5

Creating African Ownership with an Aid Presence

TANZANIANS BUILD THEIR OWN ROADS

Tanzania's roads are a mess. Potholes are seldom repaired by the public roads department but are filled again and again by donors who are willing to rebuild them again and again. Even filling an occasional pothole appears to be out of the question; Tanzania's roads department employees sit by idly, watching their donor-supplied truck fleet rust away. Because their paved roads often have more holes than hard surface, cars and trucks take to the adjacent maize fields for a smoother ride on a dirt track. Badly damaged roads must be rebuilt completely, and only donors have that much money. The World Bank and the major bilateral donors have rebuilt the same roads as many as three times, but the Tanzanian government seems not to care that it repeatedly borrows donor money to rebuild them and to pay for the same foreign construction contractors. Foreign contractors cost twice that of a Tanzanian company, and they leave the country with their profits and their road-building experience. These profits and experience are needed in Tanzania. Because there is little road maintenance by Tanzanians or foreigners, what have become "donor-funded potholes" abound across Tanzania. The cycle of costly failure must be broken.

Why should anyone care whether Tanzania can help itself? It would be cheaper for Tanzanians themselves to maintain their own roads. The AID mission in Dar es Salaam found that a few government officials were just as fed up with the state of their roads as were resident foreigners. The government knew it was in a predicament. A few of its senior roads officials were willing to try an experiment. We put our heads together, believing an AID project could contribute a lasting Tanzanian solution.

Two years later, in 1990, with project implementation well under way, Ambassador Edmund DeJarnette and I visited State House to explain to President Mwinyi that Tanzanians in a public-private partnership were now building and maintaining the rural roads network that served Tanzania's rich agricultural heartland. We thought that he would be delighted and he was. The president exclaimed that he needed "Roads, roads, and more roads!"—that was good to hear—but then he commented, "I don't care who builds the roads." Our hearts sank. Ambassador DeJarnette stood up and turned the conversation over to me. What should I say, I wondered? After some hesitation I challenged the president to see for himself. Weeks later, he did, and we joined him for a day-long tour of roads. At the end of the dusty tour the president spoke from the hood of his Land Rover: "At first the Americans gave us food, then they taught us to grow our own. Now we see that we can build our own roads as well." All in all, this project was a donor-funded process that the Tanzanians owned at the outset. We helped them experiment, which resulted in Tanzanian development at its best and foreign aid at its best. Tanzanian ownership of a donor-funded project deserves a closer look.

For Tanzania of the 1980s and 1990s, potholes have become symbolic of how far a naturally wealthy country can deteriorate. Donor dependency has become deeply ingrained in the government's administrative culture as public planning has held center stage for three decades. Foreigners rebuilt roads time and again as foreign debt grew. But no one cared. Tanzania had lost sight of its own abilities.

DEFINING AID PRESENCE IN DAR ES SALAAM

The AID tradition of placing its staff overseas, its "presence," in seventy countries has a special meaning for AID staff. We live and breath development, and believe in being "over there." Dar es Salaam is where the action is. That is where trust can be built. Staff presence overseas is what creates the results for both the Tanzanian people and for America. The closer we are to Tanzania's potholed roads the better they can be understood and repaired. The closer we are to senior government officials, the quicker we can challenge a deeply rooted dependence on aid. Knowledge gained of culture, language, and country conditions helps create the mutual understanding that is necessary to test ideas, jointly design projects, and effectively implement them. "Being there" means that our counterparts know we are with them; we do not fly in one week and out again the next.

Being there builds the respect, sharpens the differences, speeds the agreements. In these ways we can contribute to poor-world ownership of development. Even a president's mind can be challenged and changed.

Development lessons tried and proven elsewhere could not be handed to the roads ministry in Dar es Salaam, even if they had been proven in nearby Nairobi. Each foreign aid contribution in Africa must be Africa's own if it is to be enduring. Being there makes it easier to identify responsibilities, appreciate subtleties, hold people accountable, and audit the performance and the records. Being there means more, obviously, than just the physical presence of American staff. It means caring enough to stay for at least four and five years; it means making sure that Tanzanians gain the satisfaction of creating their own development, step by step. It means supporting with advice and not being operational; that is, taking charge. It means helping them honor standards that they come to embrace as their own. Finally, presence means being selfless, so that when aid staff depart, Tanzanians own their development.

Aid's usefulness, therefore, cannot be assessed simply by the amount of American dollars, German marks, or Japanese yen, or by the purposes stated in legislation or by the press releases of the World Bank and the United Nations. There is little gained by examining hard-fought legislative battles, dollar levels, or stylized theories of development. An additional perspective—presence—is needed to sort effectiveness from failure.

Critics can question why the billions of aid dollars spent over the last five decades have not resulted in equivalent increases in income and social well-being. The answer may be found, in part, in poor world capitals. Not knowing the workings of development from this perspective is to not know development or donor aid.

Dropping aid gifts "from the air" does not work. Donors used to believe that a gift of a water well, schoolhouse, or road was all that was needed. We now realize that the gift itself raises questions about responsible ownership, maintenance, and ultimate sustainability. We know that we cannot just "do development," as AID once did in many countries. Donor-financed development requires working face to face. High expectations of development cannot be translated into tangible benefits for a poor economy without direct donor involvement. African administrative capacity, weak to begin with, has continued to deteriorate.

Most donors still "do development" for host governments. Most aid-funded projects are built by foreigners on a turnkey basis and then they are turned over to the hosts (with a ceremonial handing over of keys). This does not work. Road projects—all donor projects really—no matter how successful they may at first appear, do not equate to development.

Grant funded aid projects, with presence, can create African ownership and sustained impact. Project gifts may not work, but ironically enough, it was the gift of grant funding by Congress to AID and its predecessor agencies that has made project innovation and staff presence possible. Loans—so-called serious money—were handed to the U.S. Treasury. Soft money, which Washington did not take very seriously at first, was left to the soft heads in AID. Free, donor-funded roads have actually resulted in deep, axle-breaking potholes. But an African capacity to use aid well *does* exist—provided donors are selective and collegial with their counterparts. Grant aid makes innovation and ownership possible.

The AID tradition of placing staff in the field has grown over the decades. AID's predecessor agencies worked directly with the British government under Lend Lease, and with Europeans under the Marshall Plan and Point IV Program. In 1973 Congress directed that foreign assistance focus on the alleviation of poverty; AID had to pay closer attention to impact for people. AID itself, committed to evaluation, has increasingly recognized the importance of establishing and strengthening poor-world capacity and ownership. Without aid administrative presence in Africa, African ownership of its development will remain a myth; aid, a waste.

As a consequence of presence, AID has not only shifted from turnkey projects but has been well positioned to support broader aspects of economic and democratic development. AID now requires much greater attention to host government understanding and initiative, to the private sector, and to nongovernmental institutions. Sharing project responsibilities is one road to ownership and sustainable development. Other donors are also learning these lessons. Aid administration makes or breaks the best intentions of Washington, of European parliaments, and of taxpayers.

A visiting congressional staff delegation noted that: "The value of U.S. foreign aid should not be measured in dollar terms alone. Rather, it should be assessed in the broader context of the influence the United States exercises with host governments in setting and implementing development objectives. In this regard, the United States probably has no peers within the donor community."[1]

GETTING TO PRESENCE—AN AID LIFE OVERSEAS

Getting to Tanzanian roads required first that AID staff get to Tanzania, and to all our other postings around the world. Half the distance between home and work for most westerners is some point on a highway in the

United States or Europe. For most AID staff, "halfway" between home and field work is in a capital city in a distant country—in Dhaka, Jakarta, Nairobi, Dar es Salaam, and Lusaka—in my case. My family moved readily from Washington, D.C. to our next overseas assignment. Excitement filled our Washington home as first a foreign country was named as a possible choice and then approval was formalized, shots endured, and tickets issued.

New faces in a new country behind an airport arrival counter were strange and yet we learned to feel at home quickly—in our fourth AID assignment. Dar es Salaam was hot and humid, the power was out for a while, and the streets were crowded, broken, and dirty. But the AID furniture was familiar and we were grateful for clean sheets, a cold shower, and an American community welcome. The first day seemed like a month and a month later we felt as if we had been at home for years. Warm welcomes greeted us at every encounter. The AID staff of Americans and Tanzanians was glad their new boss had finally arrived. Hundreds of new questions arose. They asked, "Will the AID office stay open?" and "When will we get our salary increase?" I asked, "Are any of our projects working?" My family asked, "Which side of the road do we drive on? What's the currency and the electric current?"

I drove to work at dawn along the Indian Ocean. The sun rose from behind the silhouetted monsoon clouds. It was cool and quiet before the day broke hot and humid. I turned toward town past the president's Zanzibar-style palace, dodging his screaming, iridescent peacocks. Ours was a small community: meetings upon meetings; parties, receptions, and national day celebrations; and squash, tennis, and gossip defined our work-a-day world. The talk drifted easily from the latest project hiccup, to tales of corruption, to school and health problems. For Americans overseas little crises can fester; small losses and thefts can become lifelong bruises—servants who break and steal; picture albums lost forever; poor schools. Illness and divorce are common, and malaria kills as do car accidents and AIDS. Terrorism, gunfire, and evacuations are almost routine. Bombings kill hundreds of people. Our home in Dar, adjacent to the embassy, was badly damaged when the embassy was bombed in 1998. Many AID jobs go vacant in a difficult, high-risk Africa even as thousands of young Americans seek employment in the Foreign Service of the Department of State, USIA, AID, and the Peace Corps.

Still, the benefits of this life can be multiple: travel to wonderful places where people, culture, and geography are unique in time and place. Each trip teases out ever more to learn and explore. The warmth of strangers; the professionalism and dedication of national AID staff. Kennedy-era idealism and Peace Corps experience still fire AID careers.

AID work overseas takes place within our embassies' world. Our ambassadors are responsible for helping to define and implement America's interests and for directing the resident federal agencies of our government. A country team, which meets weekly with the ambassador, consists of the heads of embassy offices such as the political section, and other agencies that implement our interests such as the Peace Corps and USIA. The ambassador reviews and approves all AID plans, projects, budgets, and staff.

The day-to-day embassy and AID work is conducted primarily by our non-American national staff, the Foreign Service Nationals (FSNs). They serve as secretaries, clerks, maintenance staff, accountants, commercial officers, and even as economists. Our FSNs work at an American standard in an American office, keeping our budget and personnel systems in order, our air conditioners and official cars running, and our air and sea freight on schedule. Many of them carry large project responsibilities and negotiate daily with our counterparts.

THE AID PAPER CHASE UNDERWRITES TANZANIAN ROADS

The AID paper chase is endless and seemingly mindless. Paper cycles, and cycles within cycles; meetings that go on forever. Planning, drafting, negotiating, budgeting, accounting, and auditing. The AID guidance, rules, and deadlines are forever changing. But getting to Tanzania's roads requires that we work our way through the paper requirements. This is what it takes to change a president's mind.

The AID paper chase, a laugh to outsiders, has a purpose. It holds all parties accountable for agreed purposes. The AID agreement, with all the negotiation that goes into it, is in fact a manifestation of development itself.

AID missions achieve multiple goals with each dollar agreement (as we saw earlier with food aid shipments). The promise of AID dollars is a source of policy influence with senior government officials, as well as purchasing power when they are actually spent. Dollars, admittedly $25 million of them for a roads grant, helped to win agreement to a change in development policy—such as for a new Tanzanian roads strategy. The strategy encompassed several interrelated policy reforms and project activities. Here a policy experiment is translated into market principles and private road construction. Each dollar spent actually does double and even triple duty for the poor world and for the American taxpayer.

First, the promise of project dollars confirmed the government's use of private Tanzanian companies for road maintenance and construction for the first time in more than twenty years. The policy change covered road repair methods nationwide, not just for one region, as usually occurs with donor projects. The equipment needs were national in scope as well. Because of the economic collapse in the 1970s and 1980s, Caterpillar Corporation (and all other equipment importers) had not been able to buy the dollars they needed to import parts for more than 600 idle pieces of road equipment.

Second, most of the AID dollars were actually spent on Caterpillar and other companies that needed imported American parts for bulldozers and graders. The import component of this project welcomed all companies to import parts from other sources. Some of the dollars were used to jointly develop a new public system to initiate and guide this systemic public-private roads partnership.

Third, the imported parts were not given away, as is often the case with donor aid. The American parts and those from other countries were sold in Tanzania, which generated an equivalent value in Tanzanian shillings to fund road building and maintenance contracts with Tanzanian road contractors. The contracts were bid competitively.

Two years later, with work well under way, Tanzanian farmers, villagers, and truckers were able to use all-weather roads built by Tanzanian companies. Evaluations showed that the new roads system was working. More than 100 contractors were involved at any one time and 500 were registered to bid on contracts. Tanzanian-Asian companies bought equipment under the program and Tanzanian-Asian contractors subcontracted with black-Tanzanian firms. Carefully negotiated contracting guidelines succeeded in opening the door to small firms. Furthermore, the American advisor, Terry Kramer, was replaced by a Tanzanian one. New roads reduced the cost of transportation and become passable during the rainy season when transportation used to stop. The cost of transporting agricultural goods and passengers has declined, and villagers have more assured access to schools, health care, and family planning services. Finally, all-weather roads have opened up old farmlands to new crops, which can be air-freighted to Europe, and have enabled the Tanzanian government to better serve the flood of refugees who fled the bloodshed and hunger of neighboring Burundi and Rwanda.

FURTHER EXAMPLES OF OWNERSHIP

The Tanzanian roads story provides a first look at practical aspects of creating African ownership with donor presence. Three other examples illuminate this: family planning in Tanzania, malaria control on Zanzibar, and health reform in Zambia. For family planning and health, AID joined other donors late in the process. For malaria control, an old AID project required a decision to either continue supporting it or bow out. No handbook guided the AID mission, but hard-learned lessons could be seen at every turn for those who cared to see them.

Tanzanian Family Planning

No greater suspicion existed toward the United States in Tanzania in the late 1980s than in the area of family planning. A few Tanzanians, the central party faithful, thought the United States was in Tanzania with its aid program to control the population level and keep Tanzania poor. Tanzania's population had more than doubled from 11 million people in 1961 at independence, to 24 million in 1987, while the economy and per capita income had collapsed.

One Tanzanian family planning NGO, UMATI, and a handful of government officials knew that AID had worldwide technical experience in family planning and had contributed to many respected programs elsewhere. Throughout the 1970s and 1980s, the Tanzanian government had kept UMATI's efforts alive, but small in scope and at arm's length. With economic reform in the wind in the late 1980s, government leaders recognized that it was time to expand fledgling family planning efforts.

Former President Julius Nyerere led a central party caucus discussion of family planning with Tanzania's religious leaders. I believe he sensed that the country had to face the issue squarely. The religious leaders voiced their reservations, but Nyerere, concluding the national meeting, summarized by stating that he was pleased that there appeared to be consensus that Tanzania supported family planning. He simply overrode the vocal opposition. By doing so he signaled to his health officials and the donors that the matter could now be discussed openly.

Recognizing the extreme sensitivities, nonetheless, I broached the subject of AID support with a senior government official, Peter Ngumbulu. He suggested that it would be useful for AID to meet government and donor representatives. UMATI and other donors also commented that the time was ripe to invite AID into the discussions. The other donors, working behind the scenes with the Ministry of Health, orchestrated an informal welcome, which resulted in an unofficial Tanzanian expression of interest; an invitation was offered and accepted.

We worked carefully and collaboratively to respect Tanzanian views on a range of sensitive family issues. Eighteen months of discussion and negotiation with multidonor, multipartner design teams led to an AID project worth $20 million. We had organized project design teams to work with rural clinics, church and government hospitals, villagers, and the private sector. At first I thought this lengthy design period had been time lost because no project money had been agreed to or spent (a good example of outdated thinking on my part). Washington kept urging us to sign an agreement (or lose the money for it). Only later did I realize that we had gained eighteen months worth of collaborative teamwork and project implementation. The project was, in fact, off to an excellent start well before any large amount of money was spent. This one experience cemented my view that development is about ownership—not money.

Tanzania had Fatma Mrisho, its senior family planning officer, to thank for her determination. A. A. Arkutu, the UNFPA resident representative, was also instrumental in winning collaboration. AID is likewise proud of the early work by its project officers, Paula Tavrow and Dana Vogel.

Paula Tavrow was AID's lead design officer with the Tanzanians and donors at the outset. She had organized small teams that had been meeting for months. Her birthday gave us a good excuse to invite team members to our house for a break, a piece of cake, and to meet each other for the first time. I told Caroline that I thought up to thirty people might come. Two hundred members of Paula's teams showed up.

Five years later Tanzania's family planning acceptance rate had more than doubled, from 10 percent to 24 percent as measured by household surveys. Total fertility was beginning to decline. Unmet demand for family planning counseling and supplies was high. Tanzania's women were doing what they wanted to do; namely practicing birth control, spacing their children, and having smaller families.[2] Donor collaboration behind Tanzanian leadership accounted for this successful beginning, more so than did donor advice and resources. It also taught me another lesson: that development can start quickly for people; it need not take a lifetime, as western experts often counsel.

Zanzibar Malaria Control

In the first two development decades, AID and WHO had mounted massive malaria control campaigns around the world to eradicate the disease. In most countries this top-down effort proved to be a bust, but on the small islands of Zanzibar, such an intensive approach should have worked. The more we looked into the existing project the more we realized we had a mess on our hands. Malaria was returning as a major killer. Why? Primarily because it was a donor's project and not the Zanzibaris'. AID staff were working much too hard to urge achievement of their implementation responsibilities. The Zanzibaris wanted our money, vehicles, and trips to international conferences, but were not able to motivate and sustain an eradication campaign on those small islands. We were also learning that mosquitoes were increasingly resistant to the pesticide DDT and that the malarial parasite was growing increasingly resistant to chloroquine. All the AID-funded experts that I brought in on the decision agreed that the project was a failure and should be terminated; none had the courage to say so in writing. I canceled the project. Presence is a two-way street.

Zambian Health Reform

Health reform in Zambia in the early 1990s was another social sector where donor coordination with the government and new health partners, such as church hospitals, traditional healers, and private health providers promised early results. As in Tanzania, donors welcomed the government's sharing of its health responsibilities with other actors in the health field.

As it had done in Tanzania, AID began to support health care reform late in the game. The Ministry of Health and other donors had already set the agenda and had divided the pie, so to speak, with WHO, UNFPA, Denmark, Sweden, Britain, the Netherlands, and UNICEF as principal donors.

The ministry led the process of determining AID's role. A few donors were more than a little suspicious of our approach. We promised at the outset not work unilaterally and chose to let the ministry and existing donors analyze and justify an AID role in the broader health reform strategy. Barging in at a late date was inappropriate even if AID had the expertise and the funding. AID's project officer, Paul Hartenberger, paved the way for comprehensive and collegial agreement on our role. I also helped to explain this collegial philosophy to a senior Ministry of Health official and asked for his views, but he did not respond at first. He sat stone-faced. Perhaps I had misspoken. Then he said, "Joe, let me collect my thoughts. No donor has ever asked me this before!"

LOOKING TO AFRICANS THEMSELVES

African bureaucracies are not devoid of dedicated professionals. A handful often carry the day for their countries. Ministries have senior staff who make the difference. While some able Tanzanians have fled their country, a few keep the faith and inspire others to do the same. Where others have left for that high-salaried United Nations job, a few remain to guide the hundreds of millions of aid dollars that still flow, forging reform from failure. Tanzanian counterparts of commitment and fortitude carry projects through to completion. It takes but a signature to start a revolution in philosophy.

The ones who stay make donor presence possible. Stars in a graying public filament do seize the opportunity to try a new roads philosophy, a first combined public-private family planning program, and a merit-based scholarship program. Donor presence gives government officials an opportunity to use donor money wisely. Donor residents will go the extra mile for the Tanzanian who goes the extra mile.

AID support for the rail line between Tanzania and Zambia—the Tanzania-Zambia Railway Authority (TAZARA)—let me get to know its chief engineer, Lucas Chogo. Lucas speaks for himself, his family, and his country when he says: "How do I keep going? Why haven't I left for a foreign job? We have to build a new country. I joined TAZARA the day the first track was laid. I was away building it when my children were born. How can I turn my back on TAZARA now? I am building TAZARA for them."

The U.S. Congress Supported AID in Africa

Far from the center of cold war tensions, Africa's development requirements were relatively well represented on Capitol Hill during the 1980s. Aid for Africa had been protected by Congress under a special provision, the Development Fund for Africa (DFA), which gave AID and its Africa missions special flexibility in addressing Africa's problems with fewer congressionally imposed requirements. The DFA granted AID the authority to design programs that addressed African problems, from macroeconomic reform to transportation to health.

AID headquarters was granted this authority, which in turn was granted to the field missions to set priorities, cut poorly performing projects, reprogram money for better uses, and conduct policy discussions with governments and donors. The DFA also granted AID the authority to buy goods and services from sources other than the United States where special conditions made such sources more appropriate to African conditions. The officials in AID and on Capitol Hill who created the DFA, which enhanced America's presence and impact in Africa, can only be faulted for not mandating the same changes for all of AID's work worldwide.[3]

Another factor supporting effective presence is the somewhat reduced pressure on each mission to spend a specific amount of money every year. AID dollars are now more easily reallocated to higher priorities within and often outside the recipient country. This reprogramming flexibility developed as most donor policy-makers began to see the fruitlessness of spending money in no-win situations. Now money not spent one year can be spent the next. Still, pressures on missions to spend persist. Under the DFA in the late 1980s and early 1990s, as much as $200 million a year, out of $800 million made available, was pushed on Africa's AID missions, which in turn were forced to fund low-priority programs.

For these reasons, individual AID missions in Africa have enjoyed some leeway in figuring out what makes development sense within African conditions. This is what makes AID effective. Other donor representatives do not have these types of flexibility. Presence works.

THE DONOR-OWNED PROJECT FALLACY

Donors are gradually learning of the many weaknesses in Africa's development capacity. Failed projects as well as failed plans are beginning to drive reform. Little wonder; donors helped to set up and fund public dominance of African economies, now they are being forced to help dismantle them. Public sector dreams have dissolved in a harsh African reality. "Being there" as donors is one way to help redirect and reverse this collapse of government capacity. Presence is not a perfect administrative vehicle, but it can play a determining role in support of a new policy direction.

Western donors have been slow twice: First, slow to recognize Africa's inability to help itself in the face of a flood of donor money (see Table 5.1); and second, slow to recognize those special circumstances where collegial design and implementation create ownership, sustainability, and impact. (Note the scale of World Bank lending in proportion to that for the bilateral donors, which increased to nearly $200 million the following year.) The Tanzanian roads mess is but one example of success among hundreds of project failures. Not only has public planning failed, but government dominance has slowed and even prevented growth of the private sector, foreign investment, and the nongovernmental community.

Too Many Donors Are Chasing Too Few Quality Projects

The donor world today is very different than it was just a few years ago. There are not only dozens of official donors in Africa, but dozens of foreign NGOs offering to help as well. They all demand the time of a handful of African government officials. Donors compete with each other to fund projects, to keep their career staffs and foreign technicians employed, to place their flag on a bit of poor-world real estate. Their goods and services must be purchased for their projects. There are great pressures

Table 5.1

Donor Aid Levels for Tanzania, Loans and Grants, 1996

Donor	Millions of U.S. Dollars
Canada	9.2
Denmark	91.2
France	3.5
Germany	58.7
Japan	105.7
Netherlands	74.9
Norway	54.4
Sweden	65.2
United Kingdom	7.3
United States	13.0
Other bilateral donors	62.4
The World Bank	120.5
Total	726.0

Source: World Bank, *1998 World Development Indicators*, pp. 348, 352.

to sign up one's money before anyone else does. There are vastly too many separate projects, each requiring separate paper work for governments to effectively implement. Donor priorities and presence can lead to a diffusion of program activities and to great cost. Second and third five-year plans become, inevitably, collections of donor-initiated projects. As a consequence, project quality is poor, African ownership is weak, sustainability is nil. Donors, particularly the Japanese, complain that they cannot find good projects to fund. Small wonder.

Donors have been slow to let go of public approaches to development. We are still tied to public planning priorities because they were once our own. Letting go can take years. Donors invite these pressures on themselves partly because they still view government as the only appropriate recipient of aid. All too much of the assistance from western governments as well as from western NGOs is directed through public channels for public institutions.

Where AID was once alone, there may be as many as two and three dozen separate donor representatives in Tanzania with their own development programs. There are often six to ten donors striving to work in each sector, such as primary education, agricultural research, and rural roads. The government cannot keep track of donor money or donor projects. Its own priorities are seldom observed.

For donors as a group, there is nothing quite like a public subsidy to move the money, reinforce central control and corruption, and, inevitably, slow development. Few donors practice what some are now preaching; namely, effectiveness and ownership, and the channeling of aid resources through commercial and nonprofit institutions. No wonder that private investors in these small economies are kept off balance.

Little Effort Is Made to Create African Ownership

Donors often set up project implementation units within African governments that have sizable foreign staffs, even when there is agreement in principle not to do so. If the government does not have the capacity to administer our money, then we donors set up parallel structures to accomplish our project goals. No African ownership or capacity building there.

Despite a successful AID roads project in rural Tanzania, foreign experts still direct, yard by yard, the maintenance and reconstruction of Tanzania's streets and highways. A Japanese highway expert directs the painting of white lines on Dar es Salaam's newly repaved streets. Never mind that a donor-created parastatal operates at 10 percent of capacity with controlled prices—as long as a donor's largesse and contractors are fully employed. In one case, a European ambassador was ordered by his home office not to terminate a forestry parastatal project because both countries were benefiting from being at the trough together. Public sector turnkey projects remain the rule. I remember being cornered by a Danish parliamentarian at a reception in Dar es Salaam only to be lectured about Tanzanian hopelessness: "We Danes built a factory for them, gave them the keys, and it still doesn't work!"

The reality is a Tanzanian Ministry of Health staffed with eighty-five Danish professionals; and an Institute of Nutrition that is entirely a Swedish creation lock, stock, and barrel. Donor presence, if only to be there to push money, ensures failure.

Talk About Coordination But Avoid Doing It

Donors love to talk about cooperation but few actually cooperate. A few donors, in my experience, actively resist coordination. They know the consequences for their aid; they know they may not find a suitable project for their money; they know they may be pushed out. Annual bilateral consultations to sign up next year's money take place behind closed doors between visiting donor teams and senior African officials. Donors chair but do not lead; hard choices and decisions are seldom made. Coordination of Tanzanian feeder roads remains, even after years, more the exception than the rule. Several donors, led by the World Bank and the European Union, have to disburse money for their turnkey roads, which continue to be built by foreign contractors.

Donor Capitals Rule the Roost

Donor field problems are compounded by their capitals. Donor governments have their own priorities, which can intrude on the African beneficiary. Western foreign policy and commercial interests can intrude subtly on the development process and can cause African development priorities and ownership to be diluted and even set aside. French and Italian aid programs skip the subtlety. African capacity building and effective donor presence are seldom uppermost on the minds of aid donors.

As a consequence of multiple pressures, AID and other donors are often forced to embrace administrative practices that inhibit African ownership and sustainability. Divisive interests can be greater than the nominally legislated or policy-determined directives to coordinate. In reality, donor presence in Africa contributes to heavy-handedness and paternalism, and thereby thwarts Africa's ability to handle its own affairs. Donors are slowly recognizing the need for African ownership and initiative. Donors do not recognize, at least officially, that they are part of the problem. Nice ideas finish last. We have far to go.

United Nations Presence in Africa

For AID overseas, collaborative work with WHO, UNICEF, and particularly UNFPA, has been professional and effective for many years. With UNIDO, and in particular with the parent coordinating body, UNDP, there has been less collaboration. The UNDP will chair but not lead. It talks about host ownership, but does not invite host government officials to its innumerable meetings. The UNDP does not push the frontier of development lessons that have been learned. It looks first for the easiest agreement that keeps their consultants busy flying in and out of Africa with little regard to donor duplication or project effectiveness. In short, the UNDP, the weakest link in the aid business, sums the donors' worst shortcomings.

UNDP shortcomings are made all the more glaring by the very few UNDP resident representatives who struggle to make a difference. When a UNDP resident representative does lead, it excites government officials and donors alike, and gives hope to the broad international civil servant system. The resident representative in Dar es Salaam, Mary Chinery-Hesse, noted upon her departure that unless we donors coordinate, we are all lost.

What the United Nations does contribute to poor-world capitals, as do several donors, is high salaries that raise personal expectations and administrative costs for all in these economies.[4] U.N. salary-seeking behavior is a consequence. African ministers welcome the United Nations because their family members can find employment in U.N. offices. Donor staff members who are resident in the poor world are seen inevitably for their personal well-being, and just as inevitably, African professionals ask themselves "Why not me?" The famed "bright lights effect" works to draw trained African talent out of poor-world governments, NGOs, and even the private sector. So too are Africans often pushed; no one should expect talented people to work under sometimes impossible conditions.

Project issues raise seemingly intractable problems. In 1991 the Swedish ambassador to Tanzania commented to me that, "Maybe it would have been best if we had not been here at all."

As if project problems are not enough, I have to be frank about others. For all the dedicated civil servants I have known, I have sensed hard currents in others. Deep resentment does exist toward the West and the strings it attaches to its aid. It is not unusual to hear, "to hell with your aid." Never mind that free and unconditioned foreign aid is what it has mostly been—unquestioned support of African governmental priorities for more than two decades. It was awkward to tell a Zambian university seminar that students must look to themselves and not to the West for their development. I was once told directly by a senior African church leader that Zambia has a right to AID money as compensation for slavery. To mention dependence to an African audience is to be damned; to suggest African self-reliance is to be damned again.

A few African leaders urge donors to leave; more Africans, in my experience, urge donors to press their governments for reform, and to cut off aid if they do not. Africans, having long been dependent on government, are slow to accept responsibility for themselves. For donors, finding the balance between questioned and unquestioned support, between merely maintaining government consumption and development itself, is a constant challenge.

Donors no longer assume that all other conditions of project success, such as an enabling environment and trained people, are in place. As it has been realized that all development conditions are not in place in Africa, donors have added policy conditions and leverage to foster achievement of mutual expectations. Conditioning and leveraging are awkward tools, and they can be just as inappropriate as turnkey projects, but at least they represent acknowledgment of major problems.

In addition to projects, the bilateral donors have been drawn into supporting the World Bank and the IMF in the effort to support African macroeconomic reform. I mention this additional analytical and resource demand on bilateral donors to illustrate how comprehensive their involvement in Africa has become. Project-focused donors have been drawn, sometimes unwillingly, into macroeconomic analyses and support.

FIELD EXPERIENCE CAN LEAD TO SOLUTIONS

Multiple reforms are needed in development priorities and in donor administration. Market-oriented and human resource priorities must take center stage. Ownership of the aid process must rest in African hands. I offer three prescriptions to foster ownership:

First, presence is justified primarily to win African acceptance of a few worldwide, market-based and human resource principles. It is these principles—as I emphasize in later chapters—that create participation and ownership. Losing sight of a few principles about markets and the preconditions of markets will be to fail Africa once again.

Second, development must involve many partners. The Tanzanian government is now sharing rural roads construction and maintenance with its private sector. The Zambian Ministry of Health now includes traditional healers, condom marketing, and private health services in its national health reform program. Central government is of a new and different kind.

Third, African ownership must be an aid priority. Western capitals still do not demand that their field offices operate in a manner that places project effectiveness first, let alone ownership and sustainability. Personality counts for a lot; it should not. Effective donor coordination does occur by chance, bilateral agreement, and strength of personality, and usually all three. Donor aid works well when donor coordination works. But as often as coordination excites and motivates, it remains the exception.

The Development Assistance Committee, in Paris, reports that other donors appreciate AID's staff presence, possibly because they provide a field balance to pressures from all our capitals—pressures that are more alike than disparate.[5] Creating African ownership requires that ownership, not earmarks and special interests, take priority. Many donor representatives, in my experience, push the frontiers of minimally accepted practice toward what is desirable and ideal. Hard-won lessons that can guide aid administration should be mandated in legislation.

In summary, donors must reform their administrative work as rapidly as they believe Africans should reform their economies. Presence yields development impact and promises sustainability. Legislated directives and strictures, however, hold donor programs in Africa hostage to outdated and conflicting objectives. Idealism cannot be allowed to sink in a sea of realism. How aid is administered will have as much to do with African development responsibility, ownership, and sustainability as will the actual projects that donors fund.

NOTES

Material for this chapter has been drawn from *On the Road with President Ali Hassan Mwinyi*, U.S. Embassy report, July 23, 1990; Kimberly Lucas, Tony Davis, and Ken Rikard, *Agricultural Transport Assistance Program (ATAP), Impact Study*, draft, USAID, Tanzania, December 1995, Executive Summary; Terrence Kramer, personal communications; John W. Koehring, team leader, *A.I.D.'s In-Country Presence—An Assessment*, AID, CDIE, October 1992 (this study includes an assessment of all resident donor programs); and Peter Askin and John W. Koehring, *An Overseas Workforce Allocation System*, AID, 1994.

1.   Stephen E. Biegun and David H. Laufman, U.S. House of Representatives, Committee on Foreign Affairs, staff delegation to Africa, *Trip Memorandum*, January 11, 1991.

2.   Macro International, Inc, Columbia, MD, and the Bureau of Statistics and Planning Commission, Government of Tanzania, *Tanzania—Demographic and Health Survey 1996*, August 1997.

3.   The staffs of the House Appropriations Committee, the Senate Appropriations Committee, and AID's Africa Bureau are to be credited for creating the DFA in the mid-1980s.

4.   AID and DANIDA serve as examples. Their Tanzanian staffs were being paid 30 to 40 percent of the UNDP salary schedule in Dar es Salaam in the late 1980s.

5.   Ray Love, former Deputy Assistant Administrator, AID Bureau for Africa, and DAC Chairman, personal communication, October 25, 1997.

6

Agriculture Is Africa's First Source of Growth

VIEWING AFRICA'S AGRICULTURAL FUTURE THROUGH A TRAIN WINDOW

TAZARA is the Chinese-built rail link between the Zambian copperbelt in the center of southern Africa and the port at Dar es Salaam. It traverses more than 1,000 miles of empty agricultural land. Nearly ninety small rail stations sit idly along the way. Lucas Chogo, TAZARA's chief engineer, and I traveled together several times from Dar es Salaam on the coast, to Mbeya, in the far southwestern corner of the country. As we gazed out the train window at Tanzania passing by, our conversations would inevitably focus on the vast, empty beauty of Tanzania and on the fledgling markets along TAZARA's right-of-way.

Each train stop occasioned a comment on the potential for TAZARA to serve rural communities and vast stretches of arable land. There were few roads, and even fewer trucks, yet Tanzania's agricultural potential seemed boundless. What could this land look like in a few decades, I wondered? Could it become a dynamic engine of growth, in which agricultural processing plants in major towns were linked to world markets? Boxes of air-freighted, high-value crops, such as cut flowers and fruit, could be carried on this rail line and off-loaded as TAZARA passed by Dar es Salaam's international airport. TAZARA's load estimates are today a small fraction of what had been projected in the 1970s. Failed African economies stole TAZARA's prospects.[1] The land remains underutilized while food remains in short supply.

Africa's vistas stick in my mind, from Tanzania and Zambia in eastern and central Africa, to Senegal and Mali in the West. Her natural beauty stretches for thousands of miles in all directions. Africa's vast savannahs and green hills, even her semi-arid zones, hold agricultural potential. Africa's sparsely settled lands can support a modern agricultural future.

Westerners enjoy the African game parks but they may not see the neighboring communities of cultivators and herdsmen. They may see a desolate Timbouctou on the Niger River but not the potential for more efficient irrigation. They may not see the capacity of the Tuareg tribesmen to feed their camels, cultivate a few crops, even on sand dunes, and to replant forests in the nearby Sahel.

Colonialism, war, turmoil, and bad economic policies have kept major portions of Africa undeveloped. Africa can feed itself. Contemplate an Angola, Congo, Sudan, and Mozambique—large areas of Africa—fully at peace and growing. Contemplate roads that are well maintained and agricultural policies that are consistently supportive of openness and growth, decade after decade. Contemplate arable lands opened to new agricultural technologies and to global markets.

Traditional farming methods, overgrazing, deforestation, and poaching—basic survival techniques—can give way to sustainable cultivation, pasture, wildlife management, and forestry practices. Rains and rivers have only recently been tapped for their irrigation and hydroelectric potential. New seed varieties and other modern agricultural practices are only partly known to African cultivators.

Africa's problems are immense; all the more reason that Africans should embrace a broad vision with convincing solutions. Modern agricultural activities exist in Africa but they are few in number and small in area. The green revolution has taken hold in a few countries for a few crops, such as Kitale maize in Kenya. Africa is beginning to air-freight its agricultural bounty to Europe in the form of cut flowers, fruit, vegetables, coloring and medicinal extracts, and spices. Cultivators and investors are responding to economic reform.

Africa has never been given a chance to succeed. Colonial control protected special-interest agriculture, as have newly independent African governments. Only today is Africa opening to market-based national, regional, and global opportunities.

What will it take to get African agriculture moving? I believe it will require a new vision to identify and sort strategic and programmatic priorities. Technical recommendations, even field experiences, yield little in themselves if they are not organized to mobilize Africa's potential.

Africa's problems today are partly of foreign origin; this legacy must be set aside. African governments have neither the resources nor administrative capacity to direct agriculture. Economic control and protection have failed. Opportunity comes from global sources; Africa must be open to the world. Openness and competition must be guiding principles for agriculture ministries. Market-determined prices, not government, must be the starting point for resource decisions. Prices must be free to reflect domestic, regional, and international variations, risks, and opportunities.

My point is not to ignore Africa's many problems but to bring balance to them, and to recognize that Africans, particularly cultivators, have been badly treated for generations. If there is no modern African agriculture, there will be no modern Africa. I believe there is intellectual value in delineating the new from the old because failed public policies and public priorities can sufficiently muddle innovation to blunt the chances for Africa's success. Africa has no margin for error.

FACING THE CHALLENGE: AFRICA'S MOUNTING CRISES

Africa's problems are enormous and will remain so for generations. Population increase is the continent's central problem. Africa's population is projected to grow from nearly 500 million people in 1990 to nearly 890 million in 2010. IFPRI projects that Africa's population will almost double, to 1.12 billion people between 1995 and 2020. By 2075 Africa's population may surpass that of Asia. However projected, an Africa twice the size it is today will create staggering burdens.[2]

More than a third of the population is poor. The World Bank estimates that 250 million Africans exist on less than a dollar a day; that number will increase to 300 million people by 2000. Ninety percent of Africa's rural population is poor.[3]

Because of population growth and bad policies, Africa's per capita food production declined at a rate of more than 2 percent per year from the late 1970s to the early 1990s. Fourteen sub-Saharan countries suffer from declining per capita production levels in comparison to 1964–66.[4]

Africa's children suffer disproportionately. By 2020 Africa will have 40 million malnourished children, a 45 percent increase from 1993.[5] Ninety percent of all children born with AIDS worldwide are Africans; the health burden will be so immense that only a few will receive an acceptable standard of care. Unless African agriculture modernizes, poverty and malnutrition will grow more serious.

These numbers numb us to their consequences. Where will the food and the jobs come from for a population to double? Africa is already a net grain importer. What about education and health care?

My optimism is necessarily balanced by my own personal glimpses of harshness. I am haunted by several impressions. On Java population pressure is forcing rice cultivation higher and higher up the sides of that island's innumerable volcanoes. In Burundi and Rwanda cultivators work the hills to their tops and over, and beyond as far as the eye can see. In Kenya the population has doubled in fewer than twenty-five years. Maize cultivators are being forced to farm poor quality lands that are more drought prone. Their maize-based culture is pushing literally downhill into drier zones; farmers face higher risks of crop loss each year. No empty vistas there. Farming communities are already up against the fences of Kenya's famed national parks.

Civil strife caused by poverty afflicts a third of sub-Saharan Africa and the term *failed state* describes several other countries.[6] Some of Africa's present agricultural activity is unsustainable in every sense. Not just civil strife but inappropriate agricultural policies place Africa at risk. How will Africa's prospect be reversed?

AGRICULTURE'S IMPORTANCE FOR GROWTH

Why is agriculture central to growth? For agricultural experts the answer is obvious. Most Africans live in rural areas; that is where crops and livestock are grown, and that is where work can be found and incomes can be earned. These can be created more cheaply in agriculture than in any other endeavor. Africa is primarily agricultural, that is where growth must start. Agriculture employs 70 percent of the people, generates 40 percent of all exports, and produces a third of the gross domestic product.[7] In this section I examine the "why" of agriculture and, later, the "how" of a new vision for agriculture.

Agriculture is preeminently important because it creates employment, income, and food for the people who need it most—the rural and urban poor. Economic reforms, market openness, and trade benefit small farm holders directly. Food, like air and water, is a daily requirement. Mankind's other necessities can be curtailed and deferred.

Better agriculture is the best way to help women and children to a better life. Women already do most of the work of managing households, raising children, and tending crops in many parts of Africa. Their work accounts for crop yields, grain storage, and marketing; their work in the future will explain better household nutrition, healthier children, even environmentally favorable practices.[8]

Growing food is cheaper than importing it. Imported food does not provide a direct link between agricultural production, income, and household consumption. Agriculture does. Further, food aid is not free if it displaces capacity and effort. Employment in African agriculture is cheaper to create; much cheaper than encouraging migration or creating employment in other sectors, such as manufacturing and services.

Industrial and urban centers cannot go it alone. Their growth depends on agriculture. Historically, factories depended on villages and farms to supply laborers. Furthermore, agriculture has traditionally been the source of revenue for urban development.

Farm production, therefore, feeds cities in several ways. If agriculture did not supply cities, then cities would run short of food and revenue, raw material, and workers, and consequently suffer from mounting shortages and high prices. If cities run short of food, urban wages will rise and ultimately investment will fall.

To ignore agriculture is to invite urban trouble. Food price spikes, which can become a political liability for any government, are as much a function of bad policy and bad roads as are distance and drought. Food price spikes can drive millions of people back into poverty as their purchasing power shrinks.

With modern agriculture, rural demand for industrial goods and services also grows. Industry needs a dynamic agriculture in order to sell to farmers-as-consumers in rural markets. If agriculture is stagnant, then domestic markets may remain stagnant.

In the past, the cultivators' roles were limited. They handed over their surplus food and idle labor as urban needs grew. Agriculture itself was stagnant and unable to contribute to growth. That myth ended in 1964 with the publication of a highly influential book by Theodore Schultz, titled *Transforming Traditional Agriculture.*[9] Schultz explained that rural areas were poor because they were not able to extract any more from meager resources and technologies. Cultivators were poor and hard working, but they were not naive.

The science-based, market-motivated green revolution has made it clear that cultivators respond to opportunity. As the Bangladesh experience makes clear, farmers, tenants, and laborers extract every kernel of cost-reducing benefit they can. The first key to farmer's productivity, according to Schultz, is the introduction of constraint-reducing new technology. With innovation, such as new seed varieties, a cultivator's hard work is rewarded with higher yields. Rising initial crop prices, if combined with new seed, foster production increases year after year, which allows food costs to decline steadily to the benefit of all consumers.

With agricultural development, agriculture's share in a country's overall economy will fall, as will the proportion of food in the national as well as in the household budget. As people earn more and eat better, they spend proportionately less on basic foods. This historic decline in agricultural production as a share of GDP has become one index of development. Downward shifts in agriculture's budget share range from 60 to 70 percent in poor countries to 10 to 20 percent in rapidly developing countries.[10] In absolute terms, of course, modern agriculture becomes many times larger than its traditional self.

Absolute size and relative proportions are important in a different way as well. Very poor people spend almost all their income on basic foods. Their spending matters because spending creates more jobs for others. The payoff for placing food first is the harmony created between growth-enhancing policies and farm, rural nonfarm, and urban job creation, which results in an equitable, poverty-reducing impact. What economists term "growth linkages" work for people. Agriculture must come first.

Agriculture was valuable in the past for what could be taken from it—produce, labor, and taxes. Today agriculture is increasingly seen as a vital part of national growth for its contributing synergy: for its produce and for the purchasing power of people who live on farms and in rural communities.

The spending patterns of poor farmers, when expanded with green revolution advances, have been more robust than was expected. A new maize seed, for example, that boosts rural income by one dollar, has a second-round effect of creating another dollar in income for other workers and businesses.[11] This factor of two is higher than had been previously believed; it is as high in Africa as it is in Asia, in part because of Africa's poverty and the idleness of its resources.

Hope can create reality. Most of the larger African countries can grow most of their own grain competitively, and they can look to household stocks and to regional as well as international markets to augment seasonal and unexpected surpluses and deficits. Good harvests, grain sales, and exports can augment farm income and help support domestic food prices. When food is in short supply, privately held grain stocks and grain supplied from neighboring countries are the first line of defense against shortages and price increases. Open borders, market prices, and new seed varieties, which foster the exploitation of comparative advantage, are beginning to drive crop choices and growth.

The theory supporting African agriculture is robust. Optimism can be well founded, if Africa acts aggressively. Translating agricultural theory into practice is, I believe, Africa's primary hope.

AFRICA'S PAST AGRICULTURAL STRATEGIES

Africa's agricultural prospects are rooted in Africa's colonial past and in the present economic policies of its independent countries. The latter policies are understandably rooted in the former. Both sets of policies have emphasized public control of investment priorities and, therefore, agricultural crop priorities. African cultivators and commercial farmers, who were mostly foreigners in parts of eastern and southern Africa, served these administered decisions. Cultivators did the best they could before the Green Revolution and the days of Schultz.

Decades of public control have resulted in an Africa that is predominately agricultural to this day. Agriculture remains stagnant because of past failures to grow enough food and to improve other sectors of Africa's economy. Partly because of public policy, only 8 percent of Africa's exports take the form of manufactured goods.[12] All other regions of the developing world enjoy a proportionately smaller agriculture because agriculture was given first priority years ago.

With donor support following World War II, African agricultural strategies were modeled after general development theories. Westerners continued to do most of the thinking and the writing about this subject. First, public-sector directed growth was the priority, then growth with equity became the priority, and then more varied strategies were given priority, which encompassed community development, human resources, and environmental sustainability.[13]

For all of Africa's agricultural diversity, the continent's agricultural policies have had numerous common features, according to Christopher Delgado of IFPRI. These include a history of European colonial rule, pan-African independence in the 1960s and long periods of military rule since, cold war–driven donor contributions, and international market and debt shocks in the 1970s. It is not surprising then, that these influences created a homogeneity of strategic thinking toward agriculture. Early post-independence agricultural strategies focused on growing cash crops for export. The principal crops were peanuts, cotton, and cocoa in West Africa; and coffee, tea, and food grains in central and eastern Africa. Export crops, a colonial priority at the beginning of the twentieth century, were grown continuously following World War II and well into the early 1970s.

Export revenues were used first to finance colonial administration and then the governments of newly independent states. Public budgets and donors gradually increased their support for agricultural estate crops. With the growth in African cash crop exports, western countries began to resist the importation of these crops, such as edible oils and sugar, into their markets in order to protect their own producers.

During the years that cash crop strategies prevailed, farmers served as de facto public sector peasantry, or as civil servant farmers, who cultivated cash crops in a world secured by governmental price, marketing, and trade controls. Even corporate and European farms were often outgrowers of state-owned agricultural companies. Zambia used its maize-only policy for three decades to finance a nonviable ministerial structure, with its associated costs, corruption, and ultimate collapse. The failure of African agriculture mirrors the failure of public planning overall. This colonial world, admittedly in decline, survives to this day.[14]

When African countries gained independence in the 1960s, smallholder agriculture began to be treated more favorably in a world formerly reserved for colonial farmers and commercial estates. Rural communities and food crops began to matter to policy-makers. Community development strategies were designed to support rural growth and employment until modern, urban centers could draw rural populations into vibrant economies. For the first time agricultural strategies placed African cultivators first, although as trickle-down beneficiaries of an urban-biased investment environment.

The policy emphasis on community development was overtaken by an unrelenting series of external shocks, including a slump in international commodity prices, another drought in 1973, a global grain price spike in 1975, and then oil price and debt shocks. These jolts sped the decline in public approaches to development. The real prices of Africa's agricultural exports dropped 60 percent over the 1980s, which acted to deflate development arguments on behalf of agriculture.

Nevertheless, the development literature began to recognize that small farm holders were more efficient than large farms and estates. Schultz's assessment was being appreciated; proponents of the small but efficient cultivator eventually prevailed.

Because Africa's declining per capita food trend was plainly evident, the debate intensified over what policies and programs were needed. Proponents of growth-with-equity lined up behind direct and indirect approaches to alleviating malnutrition. Some experts proposed crop and income growth, while others recommended food targeted to the most needy. In retrospect, neither school of thought contributed much to African poverty alleviation or to agricultural production.

Attention to agriculture was overtaken by a belated recognition of the need to stabilize faltering African economies. Economic reform was based primarily on the need to control deficits and inflation and forced the decontrol of fixed foreign exchange rates, prices, and public-sector markets.

The era of public administration of African agriculture was coming to a close. African governments could no longer support agricultural subsidies or their input and marketing parastatals. The debate between market reformers and agriculture specialists, both African and foreign, grew intense. Many experts remained skeptical that Africa's farmers could respond to market opportunities. The debate eventually led to agreement on policy principles.

AFRICA'S AGRICULTURAL VISION

Agricultural growth demands public support of seed research, education, and physical infrastructure. A new public-private-cultivator partnership is beginning to develop. Less government is not the sole prescription for Africa's woes, as all experts agree. A new generation of African policy-makers and experts is coming to power and influence. They have an opportunity to redirect agriculture. Economic reform programs are opening many doors for agriculture to develop through global markets and information. A good deal is known about how economic reform enables cultivators and investors. Asia offers lessons based on the new seed revolution, fertilizer best practices, pest management, efficient irrigation, loss-free storage, and efficient marketing.

Africa's economic reforms may have been forced on unwilling leaders, but opportunities that have been created must not be lost or dissipated. An AID survey of international agricultural lessons documents that countries do not achieve sustained growth without first transforming their agriculture.[15] Africa has started. This transformation must be market-based. Lessons underscore that farmers must have opportunities to make profits. Africa has started. Economic reform means that agriculture enjoys an incentive price structure, open borders, and open access to information, and the freedom to make crop choices. Peace and disease control will open more of Africa to modern agriculture as well.

Africa has lain well beneath its technical possibilities for growth for decades. There should be less talk of trade-offs and more about opportunity and growth. Africa can grow more food and cash crops than it does now. Debating trade-offs, between cash and food crops, for example, or between irrigated and dry lands, or about domestic production and food aid requirements, misses a broad point, which is that the world market with its available technologies, information, and experience can help Africa find solutions to its agricultural potential.

I believe that Africa's primary constraint is neither technical nor budgetary, but lack of vision and the optimism to back it. Africa's leaders are making hard economic decisions. They now need a domestic, regional, and global agricultural vision—a precondition for Africa's growth.

Welcoming the Many Faces of Success

Africa's agricultural vision, and the confidence to sustain it, must be rooted in market-based investment policies, the participation of all agricultural partners and representatives, and political and technical leadership committed to a set of strategies for the long term. Africans must welcome "the many faces of success."[16]

African governments, once the exclusive masters of their agricultural strategies, are now opening up to new African partners. Ministries of agriculture that welcome new partners will make more effective decisions and become confident that private investment contributes to rural growth. These new partners include rural chambers of commerce, domestic and foreign investors, hundreds of rural NGOs, local governments, political parties, and the media. Their interests need to be welcomed into public deliberations as ministries create an agricultural enabling environment. Tension among evolving interest-group coalitions will occur, but increasingly will lead to compromises that foster modern agriculture.

The Ugandan government is experimenting with ways to build a national consensus on agricultural matters that stretch from Kampala, the capital, to the village, in which agricultural stakeholders (but not opposition political parties) are given a voice.[17] President Museveni's "movement politics" directs discussions between ministry officials and lower-level officials, politicians, and business and village leaders. Such a consensus-building process fosters a common vision toward agriculture, based on Uganda's investment and trade reforms. Acceptance of opinions, advice, and expertise from all quarters will, I believe, invigorate and enthuse once-staid bureaucracies.

Ministries of agriculture are looking to private business to invest in fertilizer distribution; in seed adaption, trials, and distribution; and in agricultural extension, irrigation, and even in rural telecommunications. In Kenya, for example, the well-known public maize research center, the Kenya Agricultural Research Institute, is coordinating seed research with private business.

Pushing Africa's Technical Frontier

The global marketplace is Africa's new partner for growth. Experts agree that the continent can achieve a 4 percent rate of agricultural growth and that the rate is within reach.[18]

New varieties of maize cover more than half the maize growing areas of eastern and southern Africa, as well as a substantial proportion of the soybean growing area. In Nigeria 60 percent of the cassava crop in the subtropical zone and 35 percent in the tropical zone are being planted with new varieties; and 90 percent of soybean fields and 75 percent of maize fields in the subtropical zone are also being planted with new varieties. In Sierra Leone 70 percent of the sweet potato growing area is planted with new varieties. Even without such complementary inputs as fertilizer, cultivators are already obtaining 32 to 75 percent increases in yields of cassava, sweet potato, and maize.[19]

Declining per capita food trends, therefore, can be reversed. Africa produces an average of only one ton of maize per hectare, while India produces three tons and China produces four tons. Africa uses 14 kilograms of fertilizer per hectare while East Asia uses 200 kilograms.[20]

Drought-prone sub-Saharan Africa has modest, even minuscule, irrigation coverage in comparison with Asia; only 4 percent of Africa's arable land is irrigated at present (in India, it is 30 percent).[21] Techniques are, however, available to better tap this potential. These differences between Asia and Africa for fertilizer use and yield (but probably not for irrigation) are indicative of Africa's green revolution potential.

Africa's agricultural potential has been constrained not only by bad policies, but by war, civil strife, and diseases. Peace and disease eradication will open low-productivity lands to modern agriculture. Africa's marginal lands may in fact prove to be prosperous for some little-known crop, for no-till or zero tillage agriculture (which conserves topsoil and water), wildlife management, tourism, or mineral exploration. Malaria remains a major source of mortality and morbidity, and trypanosomiasis (sleeping sickness), carried by tsetse flies, robs most of central Africa of its livestock potential. These may yet be conquered. It would be a mistake, therefore, to assume too quickly that poor areas are poor for good, market-based reasons.

Seed—Public-Private Partnerships

Seed research continues its payoff in the world's arable zones.[22] Carl Eicher and Joseph Rusike emphasize that Africa's seed research has focused on traditional export crops, which have been declining in output since the 1960s. Today, western donors and the international research community focus predominately on food crops, partly for reasons of western trade policy. Eicher and Rusike stress, as do some research centers, that research should reach across all crops—cash and food crops, even to spices and flowers.[23]

Africa's green revolution is being primed by privately supplied maize, wheat, cotton, oils, millet, and nontraditional crops such as fruit, vegetables, and cut flowers. In the past the public goal was to control seed quality, which delayed, often as much as six and more years, imported seed from being certified and released for domestic use. Today, African governments must move quickly, as an example, to recognize and enforce intellectual property rights for patents on privately bred crop strains.

It follows that African governments must not only coordinate fully with their private sectors, but that international seed research institutions must collaborate as well as the Kenyans are doing. The Kenya Agricultural Research Institute (KARI) helped a private flower company in the late 1980s set up its own tissue culture laboratory. From this and other private sector collaboration, KARI enhanced its image as a credible, semi-public organization that could deliver quality scientific techniques. Profitable ties with private companies also helped to build confidence with farmers and ensured that research is driven more by demand than by supply.[24]

Most seed centers continue to operate in parallel but apart from private seed companies. For African agriculture, a public-private partnership is needed to foster research cooperation and specialization; to set seed, soil, and micronutrient standards; and to coordinate uses of marginal areas.

African openness must be mirrored by its donors and by international corporations. For new seed to be effectively used across Africa requires a double partnership, between public and private seed research centers, and between domestic and international institutions and corporations. Admittedly, Africa's seed research centers are starved for funding; technical collaboration and corporate support of African and international research centers are needed.

Global Information at the Farm Gate

Agricultural information is increasingly available on the Internet. Large farms and commercial centers have access to international commodity prices, technical information, and transportation rates. Another source of growth and risk reduction will be the ability to make area-specific weather predictions. The day is approaching when the start of the monsoon rains can be predicted, planting dates determined, and crop types selected. This forecasting ability, which is beginning to appear on the World Wide Web, will contribute to risk reduction by indicating whether high- or low-moisture-dependent crops should be planted in drought-prone zones.[25] Market risk is already being reduced for horticultural and floricultural crops in Kenya because crops are planted with European orders in hand.

As with seed and fertilizer, the private sector can be a partner in the delivery of agricultural advisory services. Modern agriculture is evolving too rapidly for public services to stay abreast of relevant seed and extension advice. The open market and not a government ministry will increasingly judge technical relevance, particularly as farmers' technical demands become more specialized. Pilot work has illustrated that farmers will pay fees for extension services, and that higher fees improve the quality of public advice for cultivators.[26]

Africa's High Transportation Costs

The state of Africa's roads is its single most serious physical hindrance to growth. Africa's road network has been an index of Africa's colonial heritage—a few paved roads serve the ports that serve ships bound for Europe. New roads promise more regional trade and market-based food security. Regional road networks and hassle-free borders must become the standard.

Africa's distances are great and its populations are disbursed. Still, high transportation costs also reflect controlled economies, policed borders, and corruption. Transport competition will reduce costs and speed delivery and reliability. To draw from Chris Delgado again, "A 50 percent cut in the unit costs of distribution (that is, transportation) can be as valuable to competi-tiveness as a 50 percent cut in the unit costs of production."[27] Repair, competition, and openness are contributing to regional road networks. But any half-hearted opening of a border by, say, the police but not by customs inspectors, will send mixed signals and will sustain costs and delays.

African integration requires a larger dream. Seckler, Gollin, and Antoine propose a mid-Africa, East-West highway corridor to integrate central Africa.[28] Similarly, an open Congo could link Africa North to South for the first time. Grain price stability would be a beneficiary of domestic trade across regional horizons.

Much of Africa has no roads, even where there is agricultural potential. In western Zambia, beyond the reach of paved highways, oxen-drawn sleds are standard. Up against the Angolan border, rural roads dissolve into sand traps. To be stuck is to know.

Increases in rural earnings come in small steps. The Zambian government, a church, and an NGO helped reestablish ferry service in northwestern Zambia for the first time in twenty years. Ribbon cutting in a driving rain did not dampen local pride. Head loads and canoes were replaced by less costly pickup trucks driven onto a freshly painted ferry, which was pulled across the river by hand, one truck at a time.

Even Zambia's paved highways make a point. Sometimes politically motivated bad policy can get in the way of good development. The dominant party in power, from central and northern Zambia, has little regard for its political opposition based in the eastern and western parts of the country. The main trunk roads to eastern Zambia toward Malawi and Tanzania and to western Zambia toward Angola, Botswana, and Namibia are in terrible shape. Never mind that travelers are inconvenienced by rough roads; allowing roads to deteriorate into seas of potholes has the practical effect of shrinking the market size and growth potential of one's own country. Whether lack of understanding and resources or ill-advised policy, national resources are idled and a potential for growth is lost.

Roads and more roads have remained a standard development prescription for decades around the world. Africa's low population density means that transportation will always remain a challenge; no effort should be spared to improve efficiency.

Opening World Trade for Africa's Benefit

The world economy is changing rapidly. The composition of exports continues to evolve as global markets open and adjust, and as aggressive investors develop new agricultural and industrial product lines in lower cost economies. Today it matters less what African governments want and what donors are willing to finance. The driving issue is whether global opportunities are seized or ignored. Investments are made by competitively determined prices at the farm gate, where opportunity becomes reality.

Historically, poor countries have discriminated against agriculture, and rich ones have protected it. As a consequence, more of the world's food is grown in rich countries than would be the case if the world economy were open. Gradually, budget pressures and energy and water costs are nudging rich-world agriculture southward.[29] Inevitably, changes in this pattern of specialization are being forced by globalization of opportunity as budget pressures force efficiencies on all countries. Rich-world shifts in its cropping patterns are opening opportunities for African agriculture and for value-added processing. Some experts note that developing countries also discriminate against each other.[30]

An IFPRI assessment of this North-South issue confirms a stark picture. While developing countries are liberalizing trade, European countries are not. This North-South asymmetry in trade liberalization reduces export market opportunities for poor countries, primarily in Africa. High-value products, such as beef, sugar, groundnuts, and dairy products are tightly controlled by the rich world, yet late-developing countries are being encouraged by market forces to compete in the production and trade of these same products. To ensure growth and food security in poor countries, future discussions of the World Trade Organization must emphasize the opening of domestic markets in rich countries.[31]

African leaders are beginning to emphasize open regional trade relationships with their neighbors as well as with Europe and the United States. Southern African trade forums are being used for pressing South Africa, for example, to reduce its export subsidies to allow, among other things, for the expansion of grain trade with neighboring countries.

Africa's New Forms of Agricultural Organizations

Despite western trade policies, a counter-seasonal African growing season is supplying Europe with fresh fruit, vegetables, and speciality crops. New opportunities are requiring new support services and new forms of organization. Kenya, Tanzania, Uganda, and Zambia are sponsoring a revolution in the export of dairy and meat products, cut flowers, fruit, vegetables, and spices. This revolution involves as many different contracting forms as the crops themselves.

Domestic and foreign investors are experimenting with new production and marketing systems. They are buying and leasing land for their direct planting operations, and they are working with cooperatives and individual growers, suppliers of inputs, and as collection agents. Zambian and European entrepreneurs are organizing their own small-farm cultivators to produce cut roses for export.

It was exciting to shake the hand of a cultivator of French beans, standing in her field, accepting payment in cash; no wait, no chits, no promises. A mile away I could see the airport from which her beans would leave that night. A Kenyan managing director for a parastatal agency charged with opening opportunities for smallholder horticultural producers and exporters provides another example. While fulfilling his official duties he also grew his own French beans for air-freight export and used his official Mercedes to carry boxes of cut beans to the airport.

Land Tenure and Titles

Land tenure and titles raise as many questions in Africa as they do in Asia. A few socialist regimes in Africa declared that land had no value and outlawed land ownership and markets. Nevertheless a tradition of tribal lands is widespread. Furthermore, Africa's population growth, combined with its high mortality rate, are contributing to high rates of land turnover and fragmentation. Land markets are being gradually reestablished, and governments are privatizing parastatal farms. However, even under the best of circumstances, land uses and sales will go on changing more rapidly than administrative systems can accommodate surveys and registration.

In the case of Bangladesh, and in East and Southeast Asia generally, Green Revolution growth and poverty alleviation occurred with little or no regard for prevailing ownership and tenure practices.[32] Likewise for Africa; experts admit that what is needed, and how to do it, is not clear.

In 1996 an assessment by Don McClelland of AID agricultural programs worldwide concluded that land and tenancy reform are political rather than economic in nature, and are therefore best left to national governments, if they are undertaken at all. Reforms generally do not work because governments do not have the will to do so, the poor cannot pay, and the landed elite do not give up land without full compensation, if they do at all. Also, mechanisms to improve access to land, such as tenancy reform, land surveys, and titling, have been difficult to implement.[33]

Given these factors and lessons from elsewhere, Africa should approach land reform with caution. Central administration of land is not a realistic public objective. It may be prudent for African governments to focus on setting rules for private land ownership and use, but decentralize the administration and adjudication of land issues. Private survey companies should be allowed to operate in order to speed surveying and titling. Legislation should foster the transfer of traditional lands into ownership and lease rights. Recognition of tribal and pastoral rights to land need to be balanced against the needs for new settlements and urbanization, productive land use, sustainable wildlife, and forestry management. Absenteeism and unsustainable productivity should be discouraged by law.

A Budget Constraint on African Agriculture?

Market openness and new partnerships are causing old issues to be seen in a new light. For example, Africa spends 10 percent of its development budget on agriculture, whereas India has spent 23 to 37 percent over a thirty-two-year period. It is improbable that Africa's public budget share for agriculture can reach the levels of India (in part because Africa does not have India's potential for irrigation). The challenge is not to raise the budget share necessarily, but to ensure the effective use of scarce public resources to attract private investment and trade, and therein multiply the impact of public resources and administrative capacity. This multiplier effect should become Africa's new index of an agricultural partnership.

Increasing the budget share for agriculture, about which so much is said among donors and in the development literature, is probably not a primary issue. An African agricultural vision will gain its strength from new proponents, not from budget alone. Private sector voices and votes, mirroring growth and diversity of domestic and foreign investment, should become Africa's new index of success in agriculture.

SOURCES OF POLICY HESITATION: THE CASE OF ZAMBIA

African reality repeatedly tests theory and vision. Southern Africa faced a major famine in 1990 and 1991 as agricultural production fell by 60 percent. Neighboring countries and the major food donors coordinated a relief effort that averted what was predicted to have been a major humanitarian disaster.[34]

A new Zambian government came to power in the midst of this crisis yet acted quickly to liberalize its macroeconomic and agricultural policies. As if to test the new government's resolve, Zambia faced another, albeit less severe, drought in 1994 and 1995. Reforms were sustained and donors helped finance and supply Zambia's food relief program a second time, while striving to reinforce, or at least not undercut, agricultural and marketing reforms. Donors, the government, and NGOs delivered grain to needy people in southern parts of Zambia, while at the same time private traders shipped domestic and regional grain stocks to stabilize Zambia's markets.

With the benefit of hindsight, the Zambian government acted successfully to coordinate market and relief responses to meet market and nonmarket food requirements. At the time, however, policy uncertainty plagued all parties to the food crisis.

The government did not take decisive action in the early months of the 1994–95 drought to assist its own people, aside from pressing the donors for help, nor did it encourage the private sector to take the lead on grain imports as had successfully occurred over the previous two years. Government reform had opened the country to grain trade, but public officials frequently suggested that public intervention was in order.

The major concern of grain traders throughout 1995 remained governmental intentions to import maize. Would government buy grain on its own account and then sell it at a discount? Would donors fund these public purchases? Would grain subsidies be provided? Would the government act to quash private profits? Was border trade open in both directions or only one way? Would all traders obtain trade permits, or only a privileged few? Would government also reverse its decision to stay out of the credit business and fertilizer marketing? Private traders were not convinced that they could import grain profitably. They were not convinced that government actually looked to them as allies in the food crisis. The government's equivocal response to the drought kept farmers, traders, and donors off balance during 1995, into 1996, and even into 1997.

Hesitation made a considerable difference in estimating food aid needs. Were regional traders and regional grain stocks counted in or out of food requirements? Good harvests in Kenya, South Africa, and Tanzania eventually served the grain trade, but the Zambian government's indecision delayed commercial grain imports until after the crisis had subsided. Domestic grain stocks were also held in-country by the private sector awaiting the seasonal return of more favorable prices. The prospects for profit had also drawn a few government officials into the grain trade, which furthered suspicion of government by donors and traders alike. Hesitation meant delay, higher cost, and less food when it was needed, and more when it wasn't. One or two food aid donors, reacting traditionally, imported food aid with little regard to what the private sector was now free to do.

Policy hesitation came from several quarters. Ministers, even the president, would say one thing but allude to another. A few public officials acted to protect their commercial trucking and storage interests. Members of parliament demanded government food security for their constituents. Farmers demanded full adherence to market policies, or to crop subsidies as of old, depending on changing market conditions each day.

The debate over the food crisis and how to meet it raged in the press, among opposition parties, farming groups, and chambers of commerce. Despite all the uncertainty and suspicions of policy hesitation, regional harvests in the hands of private traders became Zambia's primary line of defense.[35] Hints at policy backsliding did not grow into actual Zambian government policy reversals.

American Political Correctness Comes First

The AID mission imported American sorghum for distribution to needy people and also supported the announced Zambian policy of liberalized grain trade. A modest amount of American grain arrived when it was needed.

As the U.S. government met a share of Zambia's estimated food needs, the U.S. mission found that tensions arose from an unexpected quarter. Pressures from the American government to ship food aid were combined explicitly with an American political need to keep pictures of starving Africans off of CNN television.

In August and September of 1995, the National Security Council (NSC) pressed the U.S. ambassador to make sure the United States was directing food to the needy, despite months of reporting that the Zambian government, its NGOs, and food donors were handling the humanitarian crisis and economic reform at the same time.

The AID mission's position of supporting food policy and food relief was unofficially understood—even applauded by AID, the State Department, and the NSC; but officially, Washington was not interested. As if to make sure no good policy effort would go unpunished, AID sent a relief team to Lusaka to look over our shoulder. The team was unhappy that we were months ahead of them and could not bring itself to officially applaud a successful African relief effort defined within a development framework.

Policy hesitation also came from European donors. The European Union shipped its food contribution well after the drought crisis was over and then became desperate to find a group of Zambians hungry enough to eat it, in early 1996. The European Union made a costly spectacle of itself.

Policy hesitation invites higher government costs, and the misuse of donor resources. In a policy environment of hesitation, contradictory high-level signals from government can wipe out growth prospects, which require years to repair. This debate, which started with the new government in 1991, was accentuated by the 1995 food crisis, and continues to this day.

Under Zambia's former president, Kenneth Kaunda, the government had a monopoly on maize. With liberalization of the maize trade in 1991–92, uncertainty prevailed. Were traders still considered smugglers? Did border guards have the responsibility to stop, or let pass, trucks loaded with grain? The official word was seldom clear in towns in 1991, in 1995, and still in 1998.

One foreign diplomat lent a hand to tip the balance toward liberalization. Malawi's maize surplus was being carried to Zambia by bicycle, head load, and pickup truck, even in a driving rain storm. Caroline and I saw a broken down, overloaded truck being pushed by several drenched men up a hill toward Chipata, Zambia's regional market, near the Malawi border. Using an old Colorado climbing rope, we towed the surplus into the bustling market.

AFRICA FACES AFRICAN RISKS

It is one thing to shape a vision; it is quite another to contemplate its risks. Not all African countries have good neighbors. Civil strife plagues several regions. Policy commitment in one country depends on a neighbor's reciprocity: "More than half of the seventeen sub-Saharan countries currently suffering from food emergencies also suffer from civil strife or armed conflict."[36] Underlying ethnic tensions and bloodshed are poverty and natural resource erosion. These severely constrain agricultural growth. Nature itself will continue to test Africa's policy resolve; drought and disease will inevitably retard opportunity.

Inevitably, country and regional food crises will cause all but the bravest governments to revert to old ways. Failed countries have been down this road already. Donors profess support for market based agricultural growth; few place their funding and advice behind it. Nothing suggests that African agriculture should try a public oriented road a second time. International food price hikes will drive millions of people back into poverty. Crises will call for the resurrection of old practices of market, price, and border controls; of vested-interest subsidies; and more food aid.

Food aid is still seldom well managed or targeted. It is generally not appreciated, even by practitioners, that Africa can grow a new crop of food before donors can complete their assessments, order their grain, and deliver it to intended markets and beneficiaries. Ask the Europeans. African policy reversals will compound food crises and slow recovery.

Some African and international institutions still look to food aid first during crises. Africa's food aid needs are projected to double by 2005; 15 million tons of food were shipped in 1996 and this amount is projected to increase to 27 million tons by 2005. Twice this high level would be needed to fulfill minimum nutritional requirements.[37]

This food aid tonnage may not be available. If it is not carefully managed, timed, and delivered, it will not serve a new African vision for agriculture. Growth does not necessarily come from food aid. Africa must look to its own policies and to its own farmers first, just as Bangladesh did.

Lastly, as much as I believe Africa should welcome market openness and the investment possibilities that openness invites, there is a chance that major international investors will focus primarily on exploiting Africa's immense mineral wealth. African governments will welcome this, but major mineral investments, if the past is a guide, can lead to enclave models of extractive and urban development, and thereby leave many Africans looking at growth instead of participating in it. Not only must investment be broad based, but placing agricultural modernization first helps to head off tendencies toward enclave development.

AFRICAN AGRICULTURE IN THE TWENTY-FIRST CENTURY

A small incident speaks of another reason that agriculture is important in Africa. I draw from a visit years ago to the Indonesian island of Sulawesi, where I helped evaluate a small-scale irrigation scheme.

I walked well ahead of others in my party, along a cement irrigation ditch, with a shimmering Java Sea far off in the distance to my right and a verdant bamboo jungle to my left. As I rounded a bend, I saw a farmer tending his fields, the obvious beneficiary of this new irrigation system. We both stopped and stared at each other, and then he started running toward me. I was alarmed. This is the land of the Buginese and the Macass-arese—they are not to be messed with. The farmer ran straight up to me—to shake my hand. As an obvious foreigner, he guessed that I was connected with his new irrigation ditch. He just wanted to say thanks. His reason for a thank you and, I believe, a reason for many cultivators, was not simply the second and third crop that had been made possible by irrigation, but his higher yields and new income. He explained enthusiastically that he could now earn enough income to stay at home with his family all year. He did not need to seek casual employment elsewhere in the off season.

From this incident I have come to believe that African agriculture holds another, unexpected promise: full-time, gainful employment. Africa can foster urbanization around modern farming and agriculturally based market towns. Modern agricultural opportunity will draw many people back to the land. Technologies are changing, as are attitudes. Information availability and communication technologies will soon be everywhere anyone cares to focus an inexpensive solar panel and a satellite dish. Scheduled and chartered flights are within increasingly easy reach. Rural can mean modern and connected. In my vision market towns can be dynamic service centers where varied aspirations will be fulfilled, even for national and international professionals. This is my view of African agriculture, seen through a train window.

NOTES

1. AID supported TAZARA in 1987 with a grant of $46 million for seventeen General Electric locomotives, parts, and technical services. Later, when I was based in Lusaka, I joined AID and Ministry of Agriculture staff to review Zambia's potential use of TAZARA on its side of the agricultural hinterland.

TAZARA's load growth, and hence the need for new locomotives, was projected to increase from 700,000 metric tons per year to 3 million metric tons by the mid-1990s; instead, annual load levels remained flat.

2.   See David Seckler, Doug Gollin, and Pierre Antoine, *Agriculture Potential of Mid-Africa: A Technological Assessment*, Washington, D.C.: Winrock International, July 1992, p. 1; Per Pinstrup-Andersen, Rajul Pandya-Lorch, and Mark W. Rosegrant, *The World Food Situation: Recent Developments, Emerging Issues, and Long-Term Prospects*, IFPRI, 2020 Vision Food Policy Report, December 1997, pp. 9–10; and David Seckler and Michael Rock, *World Population Growth and Food Demand To 2035*, Washington, D.C.: Winrock International, draft, September 1996, p. 10.

3.   See Per Pinstrup-Andersen, *World Food Trends and Future Food Security*, IFPRI, March 1994, pp. 7 and 21; and Christopher L. Delgado, "Agricultural Transformation: The Key to Broad-Based Growth and Poverty Alleviation in Africa," pp. 151–78, in Benno Ndulu, Nicolas van de Walle, and contributors, *Agenda For Africa's Economic Renewal*, The Overseas Development Council, New Brunswick, NJ: Transaction Publishers, 1996, p. 158.

4.   Ousmane Badiane and Christopher L. Delgado, *A 2020 Vision for Food, Agriculture, and the Environment in Sub-Saharan Africa*, IFPRI Discussion Paper 4, June 1995.

5.   Pinstrup-Andersen et al., 1997, p. 8.

6.   Rwandan land pressures caused the civil war and genocide according to at least one study. See Paul Collier and Anke Hoeffler, *On Economic Causes of Civil War*, Centre for the Study of African Economics, Oxford, U.K., November 1997, p. 1. The FAO also identifies civil strife as the primary source of African food insecurity. For a study of pressures on agricultural land in Rwanda, see Joachim von Braun, Hartwig de Haen, and Juergen Blanken, *Commercialization of Agriculture Under Population Pressure, Consumption, and Nutrition in Rwanda*, IFPRI Research Report 85, 1991.

7.   Christopher L. Delgado, *Africa's Changing Agricultural Development Strategies: Past and Present Paradigms as a Guide to the Future*, IFPRI Discussion Paper 3, April 1995, p. 2.

8.   For discussions of the role of women in African agriculture, see Joachim von Braun and Eileen Kennedy, "Conclusions for Agricultural Commercialization Policy," pp. 373–75, in Joachim von Braun and Eileen Kennedy, editors, *Agricultural Commercialization, Economic Development and Nutrition*, Baltimore, MD: Johns Hopkins University Press, 1994; Kevin M. Cleaver and Gotz A. Schreiber, *Reversing the Spiral: The Population, Agriculture, and Environmental Nexus in Sub-Saharan Africa*, World Bank, 1994, pp. 6–8, 73–96, and 146–48; and Rekha Mehra, "Raising Agricultural Productivity: The Role of Women Farmers," in the XXII International Conference of Agricultural Economists, *Agricultural Competitiveness: Market Forces and Policy Choice*, Plenary Papers, Harare, August 22–29, 1994.

9.   Theodore W. Schultz, *Transforming Traditional Agriculture*, New Haven, CT: Yale University Press, 1964.

10.   The World Bank, *1997 World Development Indicators*, pp. 14–17.

11.   Christopher L. Delgado, Jane C. Hopkins, and Valerie A Kelly, *Agricultural Growth Linkages in Sub-Saharan Africa*, IFPRI, draft, June 1994, pp. 1–37.

12.   *Agenda For Africa's Economic Renewal*, p. 180.

13.   For overviews of African agriculture see Delgado, *Africa's Changing Agricultural Development Strategies*, April 1995; and T. S. Jayne and Stephen Jones, "Food Marketing and Pricing Policy In Eastern and Southern Africa: A Survey," *World Development*, 25:9, September 1997, pp. 1505–27.

14.   David Gisselquist, *Note on the Macro-Policies for Agricultural Growth in Zambia*, September 6, 1995.

15.   Donald McClelland, *Investment in Agriculture: A Synthesis of the Evaluation Literature*, AID, draft, July 1996, p. x, reprinted as "Investment in Agriculture: Synthesis and Overview," in Luther G. Tweeten and Donald G. McClelland, *Promoting Third-World Development and Food Security*, Westport, CT: Praeger, 1997. For another view of Africa's agricultural potential, see John H. Sanders, *Developing Technology for Agriculture in Sub-Saharan Africa: Evolution of Ideas, Some Critical Questions, and Future Research*, IFPRI, June 5, 1997.

16.   Steven Jaffee and John Morton, *Marketing Africa's High-Value Foods: Comparative Experiences of an Emergent Private Sector*, Dubuque, IA: Kendall-Hunt Publishing, 1995, p. 319.

17.   David Nygaard, Robert Paarlberg, Jane Sanyu-Mpagi, Ruth Matovu, and Suresh Babu, *The Modernization of Agriculture in Uganda: The Political Challenge of Moving from Adjustment to Investment*, IFPRI, draft, September 1997.

18.   Badiane and Delgado, June 1995, p. 6; and FAO, *African Agriculture: The Next 25 Years, Main Report*, 1986, p. iii.

19.   See Dunstan S. C. Spencer and Ousmane Badiane, "Agriculture and Economic Recovery in African Countries," p. 4, in XXII International Conference of Agricultural Economists, *Agricultural Competitiveness: Market Forces and Policy Choice, Plenary Papers*, Harare, August 22–29, 1994; and "Phenomenal Increase in Maize Production in West and Central Africa," *CGIAR News*, 4:2, April 1997.

20.   Pinstrup-Andersen et al., December 1997, pp. 21 and 25.

21.   For a review of Africa's irrigation potential, see Mark W. Rosegrant and Nicostrato D. Perez, *Water Resources Development in Africa: A Review and Synthesis of Issues, Potentials, and Strategies for the Future*, IFPRI, September 1997, p. 78.

22.   McClelland, July 1996, pp. A-1 and 15–18; Seckler et al., July 1992; and Clive James, CGIAR, *Agricultural Research and Development: The Need for Public-Private Sector Partnerships*, World Bank, December 1996.

23. Carl K. Eicher and Joseph Rusike, "Introduction: Agribusiness in Eastern and Southern Africa," in *African Rural and Urban Studies*, Michigan State University Press, 2:2–3, 1995, p. 17. For further background on research, see James F. Oehmke, *Agricultural Technology Development and Transfer in Africa: Impacts Achieved and Lessons Learned*, East Lansing: Michigan State University, draft, 1997.

24. Cyrus G. Ndiritu, Managing Director, Kenya Agricultural Research Institute, memorandum: *Working With the Private Sector*, June 24, 1998.

25. From the AID-financed Famine Early Warning System (FEWS) project. The FEWS project is concerned primarily with determining risk of food shortages in eastern and southern Africa to enable famine assessment and the planning of assistance accordingly. See also the FEWS web site: www.info. usaid. gov/fews/fews.html.

26. For articles evaluating agricultural extension experience, see the World Bank's *Research Observer*, 12:2, August 1997.

27. Delgado, April 1995, p. 18; and Christopher L. Delgado and Valerie Defrenne, *The Impact of Road Infrastructure on Real Exchange Rates in Sub-Saharan Africa, 1980–1994*, IFPRI, forthcoming, and IFPRI seminar, December 19, 1997.

28. Seckler et al., July 1992, p. 66.

29. See Michel Petit and Suzanne Gnaegy, "Agricultural Competitiveness and Global Trade: Looking at the Future of Agriculture Through a Crystal Ball," pp. 1–2, in XXII International Conference of Agricultural Economists, *Agricultural Competitiveness: Market Forces and Policy Choice, Plenary Papers*, Harare, August 22–29, 1994.

30. J. Michael Finger, "The High Cost of Trade Protectionism to the Third World," in Doug Bandow and Ian Vasquez, editors, *Perpetuating Poverty—The World Bank, the IMF, and the Developing World*, Washington, D.C.: CATO Institute, pp. 317–36.

31. Pinstrup-Andersen et al., December 1997, pp. 27–28; and Sheila Page with Michael Davenport, *World Trade Reform—Do Developing Countries Gain or Lose?* London: Overseas Development Institute, 1994, p. 5.

32. Keijiro Otsuka and Christopher L. Delgado, *New Technologies and the Competitiveness of High and Low Potential Rural Areas in Asia and Africa*, IFPRI, June 15, 1994, p. 2; see also "Growers flourishing on Kenya's natural blessings," *Financial Times*, April 23, 1998.

33. Donald McClelland, *Investment*, findings, July 1996, pp. 32–45. For another study that concludes that tenure is not a major impediment to investment, see Frank Place and Peter Hazell, "Productivity Effects of Indigenous Land Tenure Systems in Sub-Saharan Africa," *American Journal of Agricultural Economics*, 75, February 1993, pp. 10–19.

34. Pinstrup-Andersen et al., December 1997, pp. 22–23; and Badiane and Delgado, June 1995, p. 53 note.

35.   For examples, see "Government to continue controlling maize prices," *The Post*, Lusaka, March 13, 1997, and other *The Post* articles and editorials dated September 18, 1997; December 3 and 11, 1997; and June 12, 1998. Policy hesitation can be said to have the same market effects as civil war, from discussion with Paul Collier, December 4, 1997, IFPRI seminar.

36.   Pinstrup-Andersen et al., December 1997, p. 30; and Ellen Messer, Marc J. Cohen, and Jashinta D'Costa, *Food From Peace: Breaking The Links Between Conflict and Hunger*, IFPRI 2020 Brief No. 50, June 1998.

37.   U.S. Department of Agriculture, *The U.S. Contribution to World Food Security: The U.S. Position Paper Prepared for the World Food Summit*, July, 1996, pp. 1–4.

7

Investment for Africa's Development

BUT FIRST—MOTIVES MOST STRANGE

This chapter is about real-world management of structural adjustment, about whether private investment is encouraged or stalled, and about the motives that speed or slow economic reform.

Structural adjustment means redirecting government economic controls so that open markets determine prices, investments, and trade. In practical terms structural adjustment means living within one's means. No discussion of reform and investment in Africa would be complete without knowing the motives of the major players that foster reform, particularly the IMF and the World Bank. Both institutions have been promoting economic reform in Africa since the western donors began pressing for open markets in the late 1980s. Whether this market-oriented reform process works remains to be seen. A close look at structural adjustment in Zambia and Tanzania explains how it has worked in Africa's late-developing countries.

Just how long it takes Africa to develop depends as much on the donors as it does on Africa itself. I believe donors have multiple and conflicting motives. This explains why there has been little investment or growth so far or much African ownership of the reform process. It also explains the reality of aid dependency and the donor-driven aid process. The western donors are contributing to reform, but also to delay and dependency.

This chapter, therefore, touches on moral hazard—on the concept that donors have become part of Africa's problem. Donor generosity has invited African governments to be lax in their policy commitment and their accounting, and even their efforts to combat corruption. The World Bank and the IMF have been criticized for pressing reforms on poor African countries; I support these reforms but believe only half the story has been told. What donors are actually doing to support Africa, either ignorantly or tacitly, warrants careful scrutiny. To skirt the issues of structural adjustment management and moral hazard is to ensure Africa's continuing failure.

I discuss Zambia because I know it well, and it represents similar problems in two dozen or so other African countries. This discussion may at first appear to be dry stuff, but it has plenty of drama, even a few villains—and the stakes are high. Reader be warned—study this chapter rather than just read it as it contains core arguments for Africa's success.

A Flight of Fancy

Twice a week a Zambia Airways jet took off from Lusaka for a nonstop flight to London. The jet, a DC-10, was the only one in the parastatal airline. Government officials and their relatives flew free even if they were on vacation; a few officials demanded first-class seats from paying customers just to be comfortable. Airline employees also flew free; their families and friends saw the world, compliments of the Zambian government and its donors. At least they used to.

The bill for this public sector consumption created a $60 million loss for the Zambian budget each year. The country's western donors, led by Britain, eventually grew tired of paying the bills and demanded that the government fold the airline or risk cancellation of an aid donors meeting, which was scheduled for December 1994. The government decided to close its premier symbol of national identity.[1] African governments not willing to reform presumes donors and their taxpayers are willing to go on paying the bills. A scant two years after this piece of Zambian structural adjustment was implemented, in 1996, the country had four new private airlines serving Zambia and southern Africa.

ZAMBIA HEADS INTO CRISIS

Zambia was known as a relatively well-off African country at independence in 1963; it was blessed with some of the world's richest copper deposits and enjoyed high social indicators of well-being. Its copper ore remains the richest vein in the world—the deposit's overall magnitude has yet to be defined. Zambia should never have had any need for foreign aid, yet Zambia enjoyed $8.5 billion in donor aid between 1980 and 1993. What policy and management errors, then, could possibly explain Zambia's downgrading by the World Bank from a middle-income to a low-income country in the late 1980s, and to a least-developed country by the United Nations in 1991?

Zambia, like other African countries, embraced African socialism. Zambia's first president, Kenneth Kaunda, was a nationalist and a socialist. He had little knowledge of economics and none of business. World copper prices fell in the late 1970s and Zambia borrowed heavily to maintain governmental standards of living. President Kaunda was advised that these global setbacks would be temporary and that no adjustments would be necessary. Costly World Bank loans, little private investment, and bad management conspired to create $7 billion in debt—nearly double Zambia's GDP.[2]

The Zambian people suffered the largest peacetime fall in well-being of any people in the world. In real terms per capita income fell from $440 in 1970 to $290 in 1992. Infant mortality rose from 80 to 108 per 1,000 births between 1983 and 1993. Malnourishment in children younger than five increased from 41 percent in 1991 to 53 percent in 1995.[3]

Copper production declined from more than 700,000 metric tons (MTs) per year in the 1970s to just over 300,000 MTs today. Copper once provided 42 percent of Zambia's GDP (it is now down to 7.5 percent), and 61 percent of all government revenue (now just 12 percent).[4] The economy gradually imploded; the nationalization of copper and most everything else—urban-centered subsidies, political consolidation, increasing corruption, and donors' unquestioning largesse—gradually but inevitably brought down what the British and nature had provided.

A Zambian minister of finance was sharply critical of this situation, noting that Zambia's performance was among the worst in the world and that Zambia's children had nothing to do with the economic decline, but they were the most direct victims.[5]

The Zambian people had had enough. In 1991 the Movement for Multi-Party Democracy (MMD) ousted Kenneth Kaunda and his twenty-eight years of increasingly authoritarian government. The MMD's *1991 Manifesto* pledged a return to open markets, multiparty democracy, and development. The World Bank, the IMF, and bilateral donors pledged more than a billion dollars to finance the MMD's commitment to reform, and between 1991 and 1993 Zambia did show signs of becoming a model of African democracy and economic reform. For a continent that needed success, a new Zambia was thought to show the way. Zambia attracted new aid pledges to pay off old debts that were due to donors and commercial creditors and privatized more than 200 defunct parastatals. Consumer goods returned to the shelves and long lines of frustrated consumers disappeared entirely. This is what Zambians voted for and that is what they got, at least in the first years.

But the honeymoon did not last long. Reformers within the MMD found opposition from the old guard in the cabinet and within the governmental machinery. Many old-timers, who had become comfortable with large, generously funded portfolios, figured that the old ways were good enough. Reforms were too painful; donor generosity too obviously there for the taking. Too many governmental privileges were to be eliminated. In addition to the national airline, most subsidies, thousands of government jobs, and nearly 300 parastatals, which had kept Zambia's governmental middle class comfortable for two decades, were to be cut. Even the copper mines were to be privatized, and the premier parastatal holding company, the Zambia Industrial and Mining Company, ZIMCO, was to be closed.

The MMD had inherited several failed reform programs and a mountain of debt. The new government had little choice but to accept past agreements and old debts in order to obtain new loans. New loans were inevitably earmarked to pay old debts.

Donors started to recognize that all was not well. Per capita income continued to decline, as did investment. The 1993 donors meeting had been held up until the government ran its rumored drug dealers out of the cabinet. The 1991 Manifesto was increasingly ignored. In a routine Lusaka meeting with donors, the Manifesto was cited by a western ambassador as the basis for the continuing donor partnership. The reply, from a senior minister, came in the form of a loud laugh.

Some reforms slowed, a few were reversed. The promised cuts in government staff did not happen; instead, salaries and benefits increased sharply. Copper production continued to decline. Stories of secret deals and corruption circulated with increasing frequency. A ministerial remark revealed the atmosphere that prevails to this day: "Machiavelli's *The Prince*? Why, strictly an amateur!"

Political reversals occurred as well, starting in 1995 with the cancellation of local elections, the jailing of opposition party members and newspaper editors, and amendments to the constitution, which tightened central government's control. A voter registration contract for $18 million brought howls of outrage from the political opposition and the press. Even the naive could see that the MMD was determined to win a second term.

Crisis to Crisis: The Meridien Bank Scandal

This tragic story starts with the new government's efforts to shore up the failing Meridien Bank.[6] The MMD's willingness to protect the bank, which was failing because its owners were stealing its assets, became the talk of the country. The public soon learned that public money was being used to insure that Meridien's owners and larger depositors, which included MMD leaders, were being protected. This led to a run on the bank; Kaunda-era queues formed and ordinary depositors took the biggest hit.

Meridien should have been liquidated; its assets were never frozen, and a promised investigation never took place. Its funds had been moved offshore. The government's attempt to save Meridien prevented it from meeting its 1995 expenditure targets, to which it had agreed with the IMF in the spring of 1995, and upon which World Bank and bilateral aid was contingent. The targeted reduction in inflation had not been met and the Meridien debacle had immediate consequences for a key IMF agreement and for the donors individually, particularly because it made the use—and uselessness—of donor budget support visible and embarrassing.

Budget difficulties are commonplace in Africa. As a result the World Bank and the IMF have had to develop new agreements (facilities) to accommodate the massive economic failures brought on by African governments. In the IMF the Rights Accumulation Program (RAP) is a formal way to reestablish normal loan relations when a government faces massive debt and interest costs, but it has little or no economic performance. Governments earn rights by meeting good budget and management targets. In essence, an African promise to finally perform is rewarded with a RAP.

Zambia's debt to the IMF of $1.1 billion was costing the country $5 million a month in interest in 1995 (which ultimately totaled an extra $40 million in interest due). A rollover into a less costly, different facility had to be accomplished quickly. The sooner the RAP could be concluded the better it would be for both the new Zambian government and the IMF. The IMF assumed that government would do everything it could to satisfy the outstanding conditions to meet inflation and budget targets by a new date of September 1995.

Complying with RAP conditions meant that Zambia would have solid and consistent financial management of its budget. But it didn't. Saving the Meridien Bank in early 1995 was a budget buster. Agreement on a public expenditure ceiling, to check inflation, had been broken. The delay of the RAP caused the World Bank and the bilateral donors to delay disbursement of their own budget support as well. This compounding of crises nearly bankrupted Zambia as donor money started to dry up. Meridien stands as the MMD's first step toward a continuing crisis—a step of very high cost, questionable motives, and enduring implications.

Despite the beginnings of a continuing crisis with the IMF, the government managed to hold to most of its economic reforms in 1995 and 1996. The decision to close Zambia Airways in early December 1994, just before the 1994 donors meeting, was followed by an equally traumatic decision to close ZIMCO, in March 1995. Losses across almost all parastatals had been intolerably high. The closure of ZIMCO signaled that Zambia was fundamentally committed, however reluctantly, to restructuring its economy. The United Kingdom was credited for understanding the symbolic and budgetary importance of ZIMCO's closure.[7] Zambia's commitment to full privatization as of this writing, however, is seriously flawed by political meddling in the privatization of its copper mines.[8]

A Drought Heightens the Budget Crisis

On top of the Meridien crisis, a drought befell southern Zambia and consumed the attention of the government, NGOs, and donors during much of 1994 and 1995. Because the government did not take decisive action in the early months of the drought, the cost of food relief climbed. Delays in formulating a response also kept the private sector off balance. A de facto policy reversal to import grain on public account would have created a major budget burden, of as much as $20 million to $30 million (on top of the Meridien loss). Policy hesitation arose in part because the government sought revenues from food aid sales. Delays, but no policy reversals, eventually cost the government and its donors roughly $20 million in added food grain costs.

Revenue Enhancing Corruption

The government announced new taxes beginning in September 1995 and insisted that they were being forced to implement them by the IMF. An even larger budget deficit had to be curtailed. Business confidence began to decline. The cost to business and investment of staying in the good graces of the World Bank and the IMF was the high cost of credit, new taxes, and further delay in economic recovery.

To win political favors the government promised civil servants a major salary increase (at a time when spending on education and health was being starved). A defense cost overrun for military aircraft further compounded matters. The government also appeared to be handing out waivers to some foreign investors for dutiable goods, which further upset the local business community. Meanwhile, the copper mines, still government owned, continued to enjoy tax waivers, which further shifted the tax burden to private businesses.

There were also said to be interministerial loans to cover crisis expenditures. The Ministry of Finance raided a public roads trust fund and a privatization fund but did not repay them. In addition, ministries played shell games with routine procurements to raise revenue to pay staff. The Ministry of Defense disguised its purchase of military uniforms to raise revenue.

To compound suspicions political pressures led to the government accepting high-cost bids in order to garner increments for the party as well as for personal gain. Sole-source contracts, unlike competitively bid ones, allow room for extra profit and for profit sharing. These irregularities were found in commercial food imports, in a $700,000 deal for imported military uniforms, and in copper mine procurements. There was talk of irregular public fertilizer imports and a $70 million tender for a World Bank oil import loan. The talk of the town was an $18.6 million deal for a voter registration contract (at a cost three times higher than the next lower bid).

In late 1993 the government announced a public service reform program, which was intended to restructure ministries and reduce civil service employment. By August 1995 no civil servants had been laid off, and no ministries had been restructured, abolished, or merged. Government consumption in its principal form remained sacrosanct. Even in 1998 it is difficult to point to concrete results of this promised downsizing; the public rolls have actually increased. While western governments were reducing their own staffs, the donors in Lusaka were told that the Zambian civil service would not be downsized without full entitlements, which would require donor funding. The government bet that donors would pay these bills as well.

ZAMBIA ACTS, THE DONORS REACT

These interrelated budget crises added cost upon cost. By January 1995 donors had learned of the scale of the Meridien fiasco, and of the military expenditure budget overrun, which were the primary causes for derailing the RAP at an extra total cost, including interest, of $100 million.

Initially, the bilateral donors took a far more serious view of these matters than did either the World Bank or the IMF. The delay in obtaining donor consensus of what to do was costly in itself. Before the bilateral donor representatives could influence the Zambian government, they had to first convince their own governments and the World Bank and IMF governing boards. Not only did this take time, but some western capitals were reluctant to see the poor world through anything other than rose-colored glasses. Promises made face-to-face and at the most senior levels to sustain economic and democratic progress were ignored. A few western representatives at the level of minister were played for fools.

In 1995 Zambia asked several bilateral donors to delink their budget support from the IMF's RAP conditions, and to relink their support to the World Bank's softer conditions (thereby giving de facto blessing to governmental mismanagement). The government was partly successful in doing so; two or three donors disbursed some money to ease the resource squeeze (as they perceived it). The World Bank's governing board in Washington continued to approve loans, releasing $100 million in 1995 and another $90 million in 1996. Zambia's MMD government was inevitably left with the impression that donors would continue to acquiesce to its demands irrespective of its performance.

By November 1995 the Zambian government had met most RAP requirements in time for a late November IMF board meeting. Numerous visiting teams from Washington had finally won the Zambian government's attention regarding the seriousness of these matters.

Paying off Zambia's $1.1 billion IMF debt—the RAP's purpose—was at stake. Until this was done Zambia could not qualify for the IMF's approval, nor for a less expensive IMF loan facility. Once the IMF's board concluded that Zambia had successfully met the RAP's conditions, bilateral donors could then provide Zambia with a bridge loan of $1.1 billion, which Zambia could use to clear its debt with the IMF. The IMF would then approve a $1.2 billion Enhanced Structural Adjustment Facility (ESAF), of which $1.1 billion could be used to pay back the bilateral donors for their loan of $1.1 billion in the first place. Zambia would still owe the IMF $1.1 billion, but this new debt would be on soft, or affordable, terms, not like a RAP debt, which is on near-commercial terms (remember that $40 million in interest payments). This may be confusing (it certainly is to insiders)—but these are the rules of the debt game and they are to be honored.

Except for the continuing debt burden, Zambia believed, with the conclusion of the ESAF, that it was in the best of all possible worlds. The IMF, the World Bank, and the donors would be happy. The "Good Housekeeping Seal of Approval" was to be applied. The transformation of the onerous RAP to a bridge loan, and then to an ESAF would take only a matter of a day or two.

The December 1995 Donors Meeting

The 1995 donors meeting had been scheduled for December in Paris, but airports and trains in France were blocked by a strike. The meeting was rescheduled to take place in Bournemouth, on the cold and rainy southern coast of England. We should have guessed that a switch in venue foretold trouble.

The new soft loan was required by IMF policy to be a three-year, sustainable program, which would lead to financial equilibrium for the Zambian budget. Yet, the initial performance targets were already in question. The IMF had built its RAP analysis of Zambia's likely performance on assumptions and promises. For 1995–96 the IMF assumed real economic growth of 6 percent, up from zero. The inflation rate was assumed to fall to 10 percent, down from 50 percent. Copper production, copper prices, and foreign exchange reserves were assumed to increase.

In reality, foreign exchange reserves were low and falling. The government attempted to steady the exchange rate, but didn't have the resources to do so (and did so contrary to World Bank and IMF agreements). (Local observers had known of this attempt for months, but IMF visitors did not.) Inflation was high and rising. Medium-term commercial loans were unavailable and revenue collections were less than had been projected. The World Bank estimated, to compound matters, that copper mine losses during 1996 would be on the order of $100–$200 million.

Just after the RAP was signed, in early December 1995, word spread that the Zambian numbers used to satisfy the RAP's conditions had been adjusted to secure the agreement. Six of ten agreed performance criteria were breached only weeks after signing. Such games are routine; no one wanted to know what had actually transpired.

Taking various assumptions together, the IMF staff had calculated a relatively rosy future for the Zambian economy during 1995 and 1996. Because of high copper production and prices, an extra $100 million was expected to be earned. Foreign investment was supposed to be on the order of $150 million, not the zero that it was in reality. Aid disbursements were assumed to be $300 million, not the actual $200 million. Differences in optimism allowed Zambia to meet its targets.

Just Water over the Dam—or Throwing Good Money After Bad

Despite the IMF's wild assumptions, the meeting progressed smoothly. The IMF had reported at the Bournemouth meeting that Zambia was essentially "on track." But neither the multilateral donors nor the government knew or cared what kind of mess Zambia was really in. Because of mismanagement and consequent extra costs entailed during 1995, Zambia's multilateral relations would continue to be strained by the appearances of squeaking by with adjusted numbers and the consequent need for more donor cash.

During the December 1995 meeting it began to dawn on delegations that they had been hoodwinked. Gradually it became apparent that the IMF's ESAF benchmarks had been missed. Little new money was pledged during the meeting, which was its primary purpose. Apart from the RAP's wrap-up, Zambia's delegation left empty-handed. A few weeks later World Bank and IMF officials professed surprise that six of ten IMF criteria had not been met. The Bank blamed copper's poor performance and the IMF blamed the Bank. Later, both acknowledged that deeper problems with the Zambian government's management practices were to blame.

Beginning in early 1996 the IMF was forced by poor government performance to accept a shadow program, one that is negotiated when a government is so far from its targets that realistic (lower) ones have to be worked out. Because Zambia could not pass the high school exam (one ambassador's analogy in Lusaka), the IMF decided to let it take the junior high school exam.

Despite all the setbacks, the IMF created newer and lower Zambian performance assumptions to sell to the donors. The IMF told the bilateral donors that Zambia would be back on the growth path by the end of 1998, even though this achievement had been originally projected for 1995. To reach these lower conditions, more donor money was now needed.

Because of Zambia's poor economic performance and because of some questionable political moves during 1995, bilateral budget support essentially dried up during 1996, leaving the World Bank and the IMF to explain Zambia's deteriorating performance to their governing boards. It also gave added priority to loan approvals by the World Bank—and left it to fill in the financial gap by itself.

The real motives behind this fiasco are several. First, all donors have a deeply felt concern to keep Africa's economies stable and multilateral aid programs on track. Second, optimism by the IMF staff stemmed from the need to protect institutional and personal reputations. Third, all parties wanted to keep Zambia's debt repayments flowing to sustain the credibility of the World Bank and the IMF. Because of all of these motives, the Zambian government convinced itself that the donors would continue to support it.

It had been clear for a year that the IMF needed Zambia as much as Zambia needed the IMF in order to clear the costly RAP. The donors agreed to the RAP because they had little choice. But the RAP test is, according to IMF policy, financial sustainability. Even as of this writing, in 1998, Zambia is not on a sustainable financial track. The World Bank and the IMF were forced to move the goal posts of agreed performance, which keeps the aid game expensive and donors off balance.

The Costs of This Drama

The IMF cannot lend new money to countries that are behind on their debt payments. Therefore, it presses countries to meet performance conditions so that new loans can be approved (to pay for old debts). Zambia's debt illustrates Africa's dilemma with the World Bank and the IMF in extra costs to all concerned for government mismanagement, policy hesitation, and public corruption.

In 1993 Zambia owed more to the IMF and the World Bank than the institutions were lending in new loans. This state of affairs describes several country relationships in Africa. The IMF was owed $129 million by Zambia in 1993, the IBRD was owed $72 million, and IDA was owed $6 million, for a total debt of $207 million. But because the World Bank and IMF cannot forgive debt, bilateral donors must provide budget support of more than $207 million if they are also to help finance an enabling environment and development projects.

Zambia also owed the bilateral donors $140 million. Taken together, Zambia owed its official lenders $347 million in 1993. New aid pays these debts. Between 1993 and 1995 donor support for Zambia averaged $250–300 million a year, before disagreements raised the possibility of a funding cut off. Growth and poverty alleviation get lost in the shuffle.

Finale—For Now

The Zambian government, sensing a crisis with the donors, renewed its promise to adhere to the shadow economic reform program and to pledge democratic reforms. A meeting of donors in April 1996 failed to achieve agreement because one donor spoke in favor of maintaining budget support. Because of that announcement, the World Bank declared the meeting inconclusive.

Tensions were growing within the donor community, and even within the World Bank and the IMF, over Zambia's poor performance. Several World Bank and IMF teams visited Lusaka in August 1996, ostensibly to listen to the reasons for donor dissatisfaction. In reality, these teams came to threaten and badger the bilateral donors into line, threatening that they would be blamed for Zambia's collapse. But there was no collapse. Lusaka remained quiet during the period. Few investments require few resources. Despite widely shared concerns that a donor cutoff of budget support would cause a financial crisis, one did not occur.

Past donor generosity has led to carelessness, deception, and dependency. Donors did not discuss the Zambian government's unwillingness to adhere to prior agreements. For the politically correct in the World Bank, sending new money after old was just water over the dam.

Nevertheless, much of this work is successful compared with that of the Kaunda era. Some development had taken place, store shelves were restocked with imported goods, primary schools improved, and Zambia saw the beginnings of health reform. But a good deal more could have been achieved, and the good will of 1991 could have been sustained. The major consequence of this drama is that private investment remains difficult to attract. This is the African dilemma created by aid and debt.

The MMD won a second election in late 1996, which gave it another five-year term. The MMD government was sufficiently entrenched, funded, and confident of the 1996 election outcome to simply ignore donor concerns; the government treated the bilateral representatives in a dismissive manner. The real damage had already been done; Zambia lost its place in the sun. Zambian machinations embarrassed the donor countries that had been providing budget support. Donors had already lowered their expectations and their resource commitments. One or two donors have cut their budget support permanently. Some donors resumed support in mid-1997, although at lower levels because they had little to show their own governments for the money they had spent. By 1997 Zambia had become simply another poor African country.

Damage also occurred among the donors. Trust was strained between donor representatives in Lusaka and their capitals, between western governments and their executive directors on the World Bank and IMF governing boards, and especially between the boards and their own staffs. It was said that many IMF directors came to believe that the Zambia program was approved on the basis of false promises by the Zambian authorities and faulty analysis by the IMF staff. The Swedes provide a succinct summary:

Although the government has come a long way in many regards it does not seem to have got there of its own accord—rather, it has followed the donors. Donors should not continue to lead the reform process in this way. At the same time there is no reason why the current corruption and waste that continues in the government's use of its own resources should be tolerated, nor should the creeping authoritarianism of government's attitude toward opposition. Maybe donors should not force their own views, but neither are they obliged to subsidize the indulgences of others.[9]

TANZANIA PROVIDES ANOTHER LESSON

Tanzania's Minister of Finance, Stephen Kibona, leapt to his feet, lunging for my throat—or so I thought for an instant. Actually, he was anxiously reaching for a cigarette. I had just told him that Tanzanian importers were taking his foreign exchange without paying for it.

In the early 1990s the World Bank had reached agreement with the Tanzanian government to decontrol its foreign exchange system so that the value of the national currency, the *shillingi*, could be market-determined and exchanged freely. To support this reform, the World Bank provided loans to give the government the resources and confidence it needed to take this major step. A nearly worthless currency would be priced accordingly.

The Bank of Tanzania in Dar es Salaam was to sell these World Bank–financed dollars at the going market rate. However, I had learned from business contacts that the government and its central bank had been accepting promises to pay in lieu of actual payment, to the tune of nearly $200 million in shillingi equivalent. In a few cases, traders were putting 5 percent down in shillingi, and scheduling later payments for much later. With 10 percent down, under the table, the remaining payments could be conveniently forgotten. Small wonder that the minister had jumped from his chair. Little revenue was being generated for his budget, nor would there be market-induced investment decisions if resources were being stolen.

But the World Bank had never asked the Tanzanians for an accounting of these funds nor even for an accounting system, let alone for cash payment for all foreign exchange that had been sold. The World Bank then and now (and similarly for the IMF) acts as though all implicit agreements on accounting and transparency will be honored despite decades of experience to the contrary. Citibank Corporation, knowing the problems with the World Bank's lack of accounting requirements, had offered to set up the accounts, but the World Bank turned down the offer. Most donors follow the World Bank's example of providing budget support without requiring accounts. Private and public importers enjoyed the World Bank's and the Tanzanian government's generosity. The government failed to collect nearly $200 million as the World Bank representatives in Dar es Salaam spent months denying that there was a problem.

By 1994 the problem could no longer be ignored. The World Bank feigned outrage at the governmental losses. The World Bank and the IMF

demanded that the government raise even more revenue. Aid was suspended pending resolution of the crisis. But whose crisis? Tanzania was
blamed. Once again, the World Bank and IMF forced higher tax collection
targets and expenditure cuts on an African government in order to balance
its budget and curtail inflation.[10] AID remains the only donor to require, as
a matter of course, full value deposit, accounting, and interest on principal
for all dollar and food aid sales.

There are, in short, two sides to the story of Africa's poor performance.
In 1991 I was promised by a World Bank official that from then on the
Bank would establish accountability controls across Africa. But nothing has
been done. It seems likely that identical revenue fiascos have been played
out in other African countries. Donor overlending, for governmental
overconsumption, goes on. The more examples cited of African failure, the
more we learn about donor motives.

DONOR LENDING INVITES MORAL HAZARD

Donors got into the present economic mess gradually, one step at a
time. A tortured aid process has led to failure, not to success. The World
Bank has been faulted by its many critics for decades for good but
insufficient reason. The conventional criticisms are many but they are not
the whole story. I offer three points for consideration.

First, the World Bank has been driven by the need to meet loan targets
since the late 1970s. As a consequence, Bank staff devote their careers to
the search for acceptable rates of return to justify loan decisions that have
already been taken to support poor governments.[11] The Bank's own
evaluations document declining rates of return for project lending as far
back as the 1960s. Even World Bank staff appraisal reports and project
completion reports have documented weaknesses and low returns for years,
yet these have been routinely ignored by management, as have recommendations for improvement.

Second, the World Bank stopped doing rate-of-return analyses because
policy-based loans, conditioned on macroeconomic reforms, were no longer
based on bankable investments as they are conventionally defined. In
retrospect, project failures can be partly explained by the fact that most
African economies were state-run and overcontrolled.

Third, the World Bank has been sharply criticized for dealing with
African governments in secret. To its credit, the World Bank is taking steps
to open some of its discussions with stakeholders, and to address environmental issues. The IMF and the World Bank were originally set up to

oversee a disciplined international order, but their lending practices have evolved into a miasma of motives and contradictions.

These three points need to be examined more closely. To meet lending targets and the one-percent-of-GNP-rule exhorting aid donors to give more, the World Bank and donor governments have been funding ever larger operations of ever lower quality. This has led to loan defaults, which have compounded Africa's debt burden. Official debt, therefore, has became a major problem for the World Bank, the IMF, for Africa, and for donors with consequences that are not yet fully understood.

Early lending to Africa was on IBRD terms, which are nearly commercial. IMF loans are made on terms at nearly commercial rates as well. Concessional-rate IDA loans are now used exclusively by poor countries, but Africa is so indebted that countries cannot repay these either. This inability to repay has led the World Bank and the IMF to design ever more creative ways to finance failed performance and mounting debt problems.

At first the IMF created the Structural Adjustment Facility (SAF), and then the Enhanced SAF. Then the Bank joined in with its Structural Adjustment Loans (SALs) and Sectoral Structural Adjustment Loans (SECALs). The debt-distressed era of the 1980s witnessed an explosion in new policy-based lending mechanisms (for budget support) to encourage and finance African reforms.

In reality these facilities are primarily designed to shore up first the IMF, and then the World Bank, by making sure, through successive new loans, that countries have the foreign exchange to service their loans. As each new facility has failed, newer mechanisms have had to be invented. If promises to reform don't work, then surely promises to promise at a future date will do the trick. The final link in this preposterous chain is the RAP, which contributed to Zambia's ultimate failure.

It looks like a ponzi scheme. The IMF sustains the hope of being repaid by African governments because the World Bank, and in turn the bilateral donors, are anxious to be seen as alleviating poverty. The bilateral donors can reschedule and forgive official debt, and they use their aid money to pay the World Bank and the IMF. A great deal of aid money is used in this way. There are no public data available, however, to document how much bilateral "aid" to Africa funds a ponzi scheme.

The World Bank has classified the world's most debt-ridden countries as the severely in-debted low-income countries (SILICs). There were thirty-two SILICs in 1997, including major debtors such as Côte d'Ivoire, Ghana, Kenya, Nigeria, Tanzania, Uganda, and Zambia. In recognition that African and other poor countries could not repay the IBRD's near-commercial-term debt, the World Bank established a "fifth dimension," through which

European donors can disburse their aid directly to the Bank in the name of thirteen poor African countries that are unable to pay their debts. The $100 million per year subterfuge remains invisible to all but a very few insiders.[12]

Africa's debt burden may grow larger in the future as soft World Bank loans become due and are rolled over. Debts deferred and rolled over remain unpaid and grow larger with added interest. All parties to these agreements are forced to keep incoming loans and grants higher than the debt service payments.

Despite the special programs that the World Bank and the IMF have created for the most debt-distressed countries, the SILIC countries still face the worst debt overhang, despite buybacks of commercial debt, despite some cancellation of official bilateral debt, despite the restructuring of old concessional debt, and despite new concessional financing. This is the World Bank's conclusion.[13]

The bilateral donors and commercial creditors can, in varying degrees delay, rollover, and forgive such debt. The World Bank and the IMF have not because, they claim, they must maintain international creditworthiness. This assumption must be questioned.

The African debt situation is likely to deteriorate further because most debt relief operations have only deferred debt payment; debt principal and interest, and interest on interest, continue to grow. Africa will enter the new millennium with a mountainous debt, which is but a symptom of larger problems.

Because of generous levels of aid over many years, African governments have come to expect more and more assistance for what has become less and less performance toward agreed goals. More aid appears to have invited less performance. Policy discipline can weaken, with few consequences. According to Inyambo Manawina and Howard White, one or two Nordic countries seem to have concluded that the situation in Africa is so bad, and we are so much to blame, that we should provide more, not less, budget support.[14]

There is justification for foreign assistance, but it has to be defined and administered anew. If aid is to enable governments and poor and destitute people to prosper, how can effort and well-being be improved without inviting government consumption, mismanagement, and corruption? How can governments foster market reforms and investments in people? How do we end the moral hazard of aid dependency that we helped to create? The root of the problem is not debt as such, but the aid-dependent culture we have created.

THE CASE FOR LENDING MORE AND MORE?

The World Bank lends to enable growth and poverty alleviation, yet the case for reform lending is a weak one. Why is this?

Loans function as inducements and rewards for poor world governments. They are bribes to get countries to do the right things. The World Bank argues that private investment is a slow process, hence its money is needed to fill a temporary gap. The World Bank's lending is theoretically designed to fund the lean years until African governments get their houses in order. To argue for gap-filling money is bogus because it slows the very reforms (moral hazard) that are required to attract private investment. Donors tell African governments to think in terms of small and efficient government, while giving them money to remain big and inefficient. The donors stay in business because they finance self-serving advice. Donor financing, not price signals, are to create an enabling environment. Not very likely. Market incentives must be allowed to function. Lending for reform, in practice, crowds out private investment and professed developmental intensions.

In short, the economic case for adjustment lending is a theoretical one with little or no practical experience to back it. It is an inducement for good behavior. Most economists feel uncomfortable justifying adjustment lending on economic grounds. Public consumption and debt have displaced private investment. Donors have helped to drive private investment out of Africa. Africa's economic plight speaks for itself. Aid has created a moral hazard within governments across Africa.

World Bank and IMF Advice Up Close

Development requires macroeconomic stability, openness to market prices and trade, public investments in education and health, independent banking institutions, and law and order. Governments must actively promote human development and opportunity, and foster investment through proper regulations, guidelines, laws, and courts.

Over the years the World Bank and the IMF have come to influence African governments to rely on their advice and their loans, instead of fostering growth through domestic consensus building and resource creation. I offer seven reasons to explain how World Bank and IMF advice have invited hazardous governmental behavior.

First, the World Bank and the IMF encourage public borrowing, which slows development in three ways: One, loans must be paid from domestic tax revenue, or from the printing of money; two, public debt scares away private investment because investors are forced to compete against government for capital; and three, the people of these countries know little of these loans and debts negotiated and used in their name.

Second, the World Bank and the IMF encourage high tax rates because African governments have to raise taxes to pay off loans. African tax rates are far above those for Asia and Latin America. Most experts believe that Africa should implement value-added taxes to raise revenue and reduce overall tax rates on businesses.

Third, to honor World Bank and IMF agreements, African governments exercise tight control of their annual budgeting process, which has the unintended effect of further centralizing budget control in the hands of a few public officials. It therefore becomes easier for officials to choose and interpret which reforms and conditions they tell the public about.

Fourth, World Bank advice discourages financial sophistication. Government borrowing from a domestic bond market, for example, is excluded from the Bank's analysis, which serves to overstate the need for aid. In fact, the World Bank does not promote development of bond and stock markets. Bonds, as Alexander Hamilton wrote in the *Federalist Papers,* force a government to answer to its people; bonds are a manifestation of the fundamental relationship between the governing and the governed. People buy and sell bonds freely, and have a stake in their use.

If interest rates are freely market determined, rather than fixed, then governments cannot print money with impunity. Nor can governments force their citizens to hold bonds at fixed interest rates and prices, unless companies are forced by political pressure to do so, as a form of taxation. A bond market, however, forces governments and private-sector investors to compete in the same market. Furthermore, in the absence of a bond market, investors cannot diversify their risk within their own national economies, but must use foreign currencies to hedge their investment bets and to hold cash. To not foster bond markets is tantamount to not trusting a country's future.

Fifth, the World Bank and the IMF have been slow to support reforms and downsizing of civil service rolls, which is the principal form of government consumption. African governments know that the World Bank will lend them money to do this, even though they can do it without incentives.

Sixth, the World Bank uses policy reform sequencing as a device to keep the need for loans high. Experts disagree over the pace of reforms. One school favors a "big bang" approach; namely, reform everything quickly, while a second school favors phasing the sequence of reforms over a long period. The latter sustains "crowding out" and moral hazard, and requires more IDA loans and more policy guidance by more World Bank experts. I leave it to the reader to guess which approach the Bank favors.

Seventh, World Bank definitions and rules are often bent to help governments meet numerical targets. To compound matters further, donor lending is often treated as part of the domestic resource mobilization target, which reinforces pressures on the bilateral donors to help governments meet conditions to obtain aid.

In summary, the World Bank uses creative techniques to hedge against the very countries it is trying to help. All donors become absorbed in a costly side show; development and poverty alleviation are left to the UNICEF representative to emphasize.

POLICY LENDING IN AFRICA—A REVIEW

Africa is experiencing mounting debt and little growth. The World Bank meets its lending targets, maintains its international credit rating, and its thousands of successful career employees. World Bank economists are professionally compromised. Doubters are forced out, some feel used, most acquiesce.[15]

The World Bank says all the right things, but it does not recognize official debt as a driving force and the debilitating consequences of moral hazard. The bilateral donors are also reinforcing the wrong cultural attributes. According to Gus Ranis, a noted Yale University economist, most judgments about African economic performance are rendered by insiders with strong vested interests in the outcome. With debt burden and career-driven lending targets, "both parties have an incentive to fashion a superficial agreement." The push to lend is "fatigued and unproductive."[16]

Martin Brownbridge concludes for Africa:

The impact of liberalization on growth was disappointing. Of 34 sub-Saharan African countries [that] undertook some form of liberalization, only 8 attained growth rates in excess of 4 percent per annum during 1990–94 and only another 10 recorded growth rates above 2 percent. The response of the private sector to liberalization was weak, with private investment levels being very depressed.[17]

It is not for donors to fill in where governments take away. Enormous sums of money and talent have fled Africa. There is no need to wait for lean years to justify aid. There is no need to phase in economic reforms over a generation. Expatriate Africans watch their home countries closely, and return when they are convinced that a sea change has taken place.

The multiple motives that drive aid generosity require multiple reforms. Donors have not yet acted to welcome African ownership of development and investment. The World Bank claims to understand its internal problems and mounts major public relations campaigns to explain them. The Bank's principal preoccupations have been with matters of organization, training, and particularly public relations, but not reform itself.[18]

Asian contagion has caused western governments, parliaments, and central banks to turn their attention to moral hazard. The U.S. Congress and European Union central bankers have raised questions about the bail-out practices of the IMF that may encourage reckless lending. "The IMF should reevaluate its policies and should question itself on how far its policy generates moral hazard."[19]

A NEW VISION FOR AFRICAN INVESTMENT

The appropriate role for international donors remains undefined. It is time for Africa to take charge of its own house; African policy-makers should see more clearly that poverty is the root cause of instability. Africa's successful countries will be ones that seize investment opportunities created by a willingness to establish market prices, open borders, and welcome talent. Africa's stronger economies, such as Kenya, Nigeria, Senegal, and South Africa, might begin to improve, as might Angola, Mozambique, Namibia, and a new Congo. Donors must speak convincingly of a new vision for development and aid. A younger generation of Africans will join western reformers in a new partnership. But to sustain and strengthen reforms that are now underway, donors must change as well.

Back to Basic Investment Principles

Africa needs a principled vision to guide investment, and a clear understanding of how to help its citizens invest in themselves. Africa also needs debt forgiveness. Official debt of the poorest countries should be written off unilaterally, without condition, now.

Private Investment

The donor community must reestablish the primacy of private investment, according to Robert Myers.[20] Donor support should enable investment, and the policy and regulatory learning needed to establish institutional capability. African policy-makers must expand market reforms that are now underway. Paying RAP prices for what some would call slow-growth advice makes little sense. Success will be measured by return of private investment and return of talent.

African governments must control inflation; keep markets open; keep prices, loans, and foreign currencies based on market conditions; and allow banks and businesses to succeed or fail. Subsidies and safety nets should be judged within the framework of the domestic budget.

The World Bank and the bilateral donors should reintroduce investment criteria in their own grants and loans; they should support learning and experimentation, and discrete project investments that enable, but do not displace, private investment and people. The late Mancur Olson stressed seriousness of "property rights, secure contracts, and sensible economic policies, [which] make all the difference between wealth and poverty."[21]

An enabling environment requires pluralism of financial institutions. Donors should advise and fund organizational innovation; training for financial reform, legal and contractual reform, intellectual property rights, regional and provincial chambers of commerce, and anticorruption commission legislation and administration.

Donors must stop "giving" development to Africa and also stop budget support in any form for government consumption. Donors should not finance turnkey projects by foreign contractors. Let recipients own their own development.

Let financial markets function. African governments should stop borrowing monies from donor institutions for governmental maintenance, and subsidized credit and other resources should never be extended to or through governments to finance the private sector.

Help People Invest in Themselves

Public improvements in the quality of life should focus on health, education, family planning, nutrition, and food security. The Tanzanian family planning program and the Zambian health reform program, as examples, promise full partnership and national coverage. Governments and their donors should fund the costs of these types of programs. Models of African initiative need replication quickly.

Donors and recipient governments are beginning to reexamine the gray area between public and private investment to favor private investors. Even activities thought to be infrastructure, such as power generation and distribution, telecommunications, and transportation can be handed over to private ownership and management. So too can facets of education, health, and family planning. As much as Asia financed primary and secondary education, it left higher-degree education and training largely to the private sector. Western-financed export credit, export insurance, and investment guarantees are expanding dramatically across developing countries in support of infrastructural investments, which have averaged $110 billion a year, or more than double official aid levels during 1990–96.[22]

Unconditional African Debt Forgiveness

African debt relief has to be real, not illusory. The time and talent that currently go into official debt deferrals and rollovers can be better spent. Western donors should write off all official debt to the poorest countries, without delay or condition.

International lending institutions have long accepted the practice of discounting the value of debt for countries that are unable to pay. I recommend that this practice be expanded further. A new concept should be accepted by international institutions: that debt cannot be repaid, and that it *should not* be repaid. The heretofore sacrosanct belief that debt repayment ensures good economic discipline does not bear scrutiny and it feeds moral hazard.

Ever newer loan facilities have been matched over the years by ever newer debt relief proposals. None of these address the central—cultural —issue of using public money to create a private investment environment. Each new proposal for financial support and debt relief presumes the sanctity of African government stability and relegates investment and people to second place.

For all of sub-Saharan Africa, official debts owed the IBRD and IDA amount to $35 billion, and $9 billion is owed to the IMF, or a sum that is about a third of the projected Asian financial bail-out cost of at least $120 billion. Full debt forgiveness may actually bolster the IMF's and the World Bank's credit ratings by making clear to the international banking community that African investment comes first—and that moral hazard has been left behind.

A one-time adjustment would have a manageable cost to donors, no cost to African development, and no cost to African governments. Western governments should accept this write-off as a one-time charge for a permanent cultural change. Trade and investment, which are central to Africa's future, are at stake.

NOTES

1. Vice President Geoffrey Miyanda announced the closure of Zambia Airways on Lusaka public television, December 3, 1995. He used the occasion to

mention former President Kaunda's $42 million refurbishment of his presidential DC-8.

2.   By the mid-1990s Zambia's foreign debt equaled 170 percent of its GDP, or 645 percent of its export earnings. *The Economist* Intelligence Unit, *Zambia—Country Profile 1997–98*, p. 35.

3.   Mark Sterling, UNICEF Representative, statement at the December 1995 Consultative Group Meeting, and various annual World Bank *Atlases*, *World Development Reports*, and UNDP *Human Development Reports*.

4.   Oliver S. Saasa and Jerker Carlsson, *Aid Effectiveness in Africa: The Zambian Experience*, Institute of African Studies, University of Zambia and the Scandinavian Institute of Africa Studies, Uppsala, Sweden, March 1995, p. 18.

5.   Ronald Penza, Minister of Finance, Government of Zambia, at the COMESA meeting, July 25, 1995, and on other public occasions.

6.   Chuck Mohan and Joe Stepanek, *Zambia: Crisis to Crisis Grows More Costly—The Year 1995 in Review*, Lusaka: AID, November 25, 1995. Data and analyses used here are drawn from World Bank and IMF reports, the Government of Zambia, Ministry of Finance, *Macro Economic Indicators*, and numerous telegrams and memos, 1994–96.

7.   Led by Mike Hammond, development counselor, the United Kingdom High Commission, Zambia.

8.   See AID documents on the Zambian Privatization Authority and news reports on privatization by *The Post*, on the World Wide Web as zamnet.zm/zamnet /post/news.

9.   Inyambo Mwanawina and Howard White, *Swedish Balance of Payments Support to Zambia: Draft Final Report*, Lusaka: SIDA, draft, February 1995, p. x.

10.   Conversation with the late Stephen Kibona, Minister of Finance, on May 9, 1990. See Tanzania's *Business Times*, front page, October 25, 1991, "Public Corruption Undercuts Power to Govern," as referenced in Stepanek's *Monograph on Tanzania's Development—Discussion of Issues*, Dar es Salaam: AID, July 24, 1991. The $200 million loss was noted in an embassy telegram dated March 7, 1995.

11.   From David Seckler, *Economic Regimes, Strategic Investments, and Entrepreneurial Decisions: Notes Toward a Theory of Economic Development*, Washington, D.C.: Winrock International, December 1990, p. 3.

12.   European countries funded the World Bank's Fifth Dimension with payments of $96.9 million for thirteen African country debts due the IBRD in fiscal year 1998. Note from a U.S. Treasury official, personal communication, March 24, 1998. See also *The World Bank Annual Report 1997*, p. 207.

13.   World Bank, *World Debt Tables*, Vol I, p. 3; and World Bank, *Heavily Indebted Poor Countries Debt Initiative (The HIPC Debt Initiative)*, 1996. The latest initiative is designed to reduce official debt to "sustainable" levels.

14.   Mwanawina and White, p. 79.

15.   Robert Myers, personal communication, May 23, 1997.

16.   Gustav Ranis, Yale University, *On Fast-Disbursing Policy-Based Loans*, Paper prepared for the CSIS Task Force on Multilateral Development Banks, draft, 1996.

17.   Martin Brownbridge, *Economic Liberalization in Sub-Saharan Africa*, U.N. Conference on Trade and Development, August 1996, pp. 30–31.

18.   "Mr. Wolfensohn's New Clients," *The Economist*, April 20, 1996.

19.   "EU bankers hit at IMF on bail-outs," *The Financial Times*, March 23, 1998.

20.   Robert Myers, *Better Practice for Adjustment Lending*, World Bank memorandum, April 11, 1995, and personal communications, October 3 and February 18, 1997.

21.   "Obituary—Mancur Olson," *The Economist*, March 7, 1998, p. 91.

22.   The World Bank, *Global Development Finance 1998*, p. 58.

8

African Development Requires Democracy

AFRICAN DEMOCRACY
—A NICE IDEA OR A FUNDAMENTAL REQUIREMENT?

Democracy was not mentioned in my Economics 101 course in 1962, nor in any of the development courses I took during ten years in college and graduate school. In retrospect it is apparent that those who live in democratic societies take certain assumptions for granted, and this is reflected in the training that most economists of my generation received.

This has not been an accident or an oversight. Leading development theorists and practioners believed that democracy was a messy business, and that public plans, not markets or votes, showed the developmental way forward. Experts have not treated democracy as a development requirement. Today economists, who are the leading social science proponents of development, are playing catch-up.

For too long most western experts appeared to believe that democracy was a luxury that poor countries could ill afford. Only now is democracy being viewed as a fundamental component of development. This chapter will show just how necessary democracy is to the African people, and how obvious it is that they want it.

African governments have been described by many casual and professional observers as predatory states. This is not an inaccurate description. African leaders have not acted alone however; foreign assistance (and oil riches) have allowed governments to have some distance from their people. African governments have become too dependent on donors, and not sufficiently responsible to their own people.

Few western economists have noted that free markets, private property, and the rule of law define and underwrite democracy. Democratic preconditions have been assumed and ignored by development economists who were caught up in the resources-rush to development. Consequently, the incentives of plan-oriented governments and foreign aid have been wrongly directed for a generation. Aid, not popular support and consensus, has sustained many African governments.

Accepted standards of societal and individual well-being are more comprehensive than they were in the 1950s. For the first time in history, most nation states and most of the world's people aspire to economic, political, and individual principles of universal human rights. More than thirty of the fifty countries in sub-Saharan Africa are struggling with democracy as a right and as a means to development.

Democracy is traditionally defined as the rights and responsibilities that a people give voluntarily to their state. The state, in turn, serves the people and is accountable to them. The people entrust government to serve them well. Regular elections give credence to democracy's maturity and to its continuing credibility. Democracy is defined in law, not by men. It has institutionally prescribed checks and balances. Within government, checks and balances on the executive branch include parliament, the judiciary, and independent commissions, such as for human rights, anticorruption, and electoral processes. Representation of people takes form in a free press, the right of association, recourse to law, and protection of human rights.

That democracy is an imperfect, even awkward, way to organize society is well known. Solutions to problems that are arrived at in common are not always the best. Democracy can be a troublesome work in progress. Democracy resolves, but also can cause, social turmoil. Still, like free markets and capitalism, democracy is proving to be a good idea so far. Alternative philosophies for organizing society's polity have been tried and tested across the world and have been less than enduring; the world is littered with centrally directed, nonrepresentative experiments.

Despite the impression that many westerners have of African democracy as being nascent, and of government as being predatory, the truth, I have observed, is that African democracy is well underway. The issue is not whether democracy exists in Africa as a safe generalization, but its degree of representation, its respects for checks and balances, and its robustness. African civil society, like its informal economy, is vibrant—as life in Lusaka illustrates.

Democracy Is Fundamental to Development

Democratic governments honor universal human rights as values based in law. Democracy is also fundamental to progress because it welcomes initiative, creates ownership, and builds consensus. Democracy is the foundation of development because it defines a process of consensus building and, in turn, ensures that benefits are shared. Centralized control of power, incentives, and distribution is unsustainable.

Today western donors are beginning to help Africa establish and implement democratic principles to ensure broad ownership of development. Development, as we have seen repeatedly, cannot be given to a people. Still, the challenge of development continues to be treated as a resource problem by most practitioners. More recently this challenge has become a management problem as well. The evolution of this book reflects the evolution of my own thinking as well as that of development experts generally. All of us have been slow to appreciate that development concepts have been sidetracked by focusing on the resource gap and management problems that poor countries face. Principles of investment and development of human potential, ownership, and democracy should have been treated as fundamental elements of development from the beginning.

It has been foolish to believe that material development could take place and that democracy could be introduced afterward. Resource decisions demand participation and ownership that only democracy provides. The failure of public planning, that "father knows best," proves that development and democracy must be integrated. What attitudes toward common men and women do experts embrace if they continue to believe that democracy can be introduced to poor people later? If development cannot be embraced by the general population, then we risk believing that development must come from an elite.

Africa is expecting a great deal of itself. Few regions of the world have embarked on political and economic liberalizations at similar periods in their history. Eastern Europe, central Asia, and now Africa have this in common. I examine these twin aspirations that African governments have accepted and the role that donors are playing in these revolutions.

Bilateral donors are supporting, even urging, political experimentation. Donors must sharpen their reasoning and their aid administration in support of democracy. Donors have much to rethink and relearn. They cannot use nonmarket principles to help Africa develop its markets, nor can they use traditional administrative methods to leverage and condition aid support for democratic reform.

THE NEW ZAMBIA: DEMOCRACY BETRAYED IN THE 1990s

Zambia is one of democracy's works in progress. Unlike other countries, such as Kenya, where a few critics claim that democracy is an idea pressed on it by westerners, the Zambian people ousted the long-reigning president, Kenneth Kaunda, from office and voted Frederick Chiluba into office in 1991. The reintroduction of democracy to Zambia was not the result of outside pressures; the Movement for Multi-Party Democracy prevailed in a free and fair election. The Zambian people knew the choice and made it.

The labor union leader, Frederick Chiluba, led the MMD to an election victory in October 1991, with 75 percent of the vote. The election for the Third Republic was deemed by domestic and international observers to be free and fair. The MMD won on a popularist platform of economic and political reform. The Zambian people actually voted for structural adjustment and democracy as promised in the MMD's *1991 Manifesto*. Zambians had grown tired of queuing before empty shelves.[1] The Manifesto also served as the basis for a renewed partnership with donors, and consequently for the return of donor support for the country's development and for relief from Zambia's mounting debt.[2]

Despite wide acceptance of the Manifesto as the basis of a partnership with the Zambian people and the donors, the MMD early on faced the reality of governing. The honeymoon with the donors was short lived. Drug trafficking was said to be occurring within the new government.[3] Just before a December 1993 donors meeting, the MMD government's first, donors suspended aid pledges for budget support and debt relief. The suspension of $150 million prevented the government from paying its debts. Aid dependency had a price. Immediately after the meeting the government asked two of its ministers to step down. The MMD had tasted its first imposition of donor conditionality.

The MMD started to have second thoughts about its Manifesto. Perhaps the drug trafficking incident had prompted some MMD rethinking. Certainly the Kaunda government apparatus was still in place. In a crisis, or simply out of habit, the old timers within the MMD knew they could rely on the Second Republic's police-state–like practices for maintaining control. The MMD government was in fact staffed by United National Independence Party (UNIP) holdovers who knew the mechanics of running an authoritarian state, which kept all the accoutrements for intelligence, surveillance, and control housed in Lusaka's infamous Red Brick Building. The MMD may have thought it was their turn to enjoy donor largesse.

The Zambian people started to wonder about betrayal, as did the press. The younger reform-minded members of the MMD, who wrote the Manifesto at the Garden House Hotel in July 1990, were gradually replaced; some left in disgust, others were pushed out. By late 1996 none of the original Garden House team remained. The old timers, who knew the ways of Kaunda's Second Republic, were in charge.

With the exit of the reformers, tribalism became more apparent. MMD leadership and ministerial appointments increasingly reflected the president's Bemba tribe from northern and central Zambia, at the expense of the Ngoni people in the East (where Kaunda was from) and the Lozi people in the West. The southern people were left out of government altogether.

Other factors also explain the MMD's second thoughts. Kaunda's return to active political life in 1995 gave the MMD great pause, and when he announced his candidacy for the 1996 presidential election, alarm broke out within the MMD. Its political victory over Kaunda in 1991 resurfaced as a nasty and highly personalized vendetta. Observers did not believe there was widespread popular support for the grand old man's return. Nonetheless, Kaunda's public, statesman-like presence in Lusaka partially explained the MMD's volatile behavior.

In 1991 and 1992 the MMD had set the terms for strengthening democracy in Zambia. Much was achieved in short order on both the economic and political fronts. Perhaps because of the high standards set in the Manifesto, and many accomplishments, some letdown was inevitable. Expecting a political elite of old-timers to give away or even share power was expecting too much. What was not expected was the growing frustration and betrayal that was gradually perceived by Zambians.

Although most political and economic reforms achieved during the 1990s remain in place, talk of the Manifesto was heard less frequently. Economic reforms were expanded while the promised democratic reforms were seen as having been betrayed. The MMD aggressively challenged the voices of the recently freed press and of nongovernment, church, and even labor union leaders. Disillusionment and opposition became widespread. The MMD leadership abandoned its Manifesto with a dismissive laugh.

A colonial-holdover Public Order Act was used more frequently and without explanation to suppress opposition assemblies and marches in Lusaka. A human rights commission had been stifled in 1995 and its report was not released for a year. Nor were publicly owned newspapers sold as promised. MMD recommendations for a strengthened and more independent judiciary, drug enforcement agency, and anticorruption commission were delayed. The MMD even proposed (but later reconsidered) the removal of Supreme Court judges for "wrongful interpretation of the law" on the grounds that the MMD-dominated parliament was the state's ultimate authority.

By late 1995 the government was seen as becoming a UNIP-like, one-party state once again. That is how it is seen today by the Zambian opposition, by most political activists, and by African civil and human rights groups. This was neither the mandate nor the government that donors pledged to support in 1991—with nearly $5 billion.

The MMD's Constitutional Review Commission

The principal point of contention during 1995 and 1996 was the successful MMD effort to bar former President Kenneth Kaunda from running in the 1996 presidential election. What had been promised as an open and full debate on a new constitution became instead legal maneuvering to bar Kaunda's candidacy. All manner of debate focused on whether a presidential candidate could serve for more than two terms (Kaunda had served four) and whether he had to be born in Zambia of parents born in Zambia. Debate over Kaunda's birthplace and citizenship (the father of the nation had been born in Malawi) led inevitably to questions of Chiluba's parentage and birthplace (he is said to have been born across a river from Zambia in what was then the Belgian Congo).

Various political steps taken by the MMD government during 1995 and 1996 suggested that retaining political control of the government was their top priority. Each step to question Kaunda's citizenship, to threaten his deportation to Malawi, to control the constitutional amendment process, and to cleanse the party of reformers cast doubt on the MMD's intentions. Kaunda was ultimately barred from running by newly enacted constitutional prohibitions against a president serving more than two terms and not having parents born in Zambia.

The MMD did initially start a formal review of the Second Republic's constitution, as it had promised in 1991. In November 1993 the government appointed a twenty-five-member Constitutional Review Commission, which was charged with recommending a draft constitution that would "guard against the reemergence of a dictatorial form of government." The Commission was to address such issues as the protection of human rights, the rule of law and good government, the independence of the judiciary, and checks and balances among the various organs of government. The Commission was also supposed to recommend whether the constitution should be adopted by the National Assembly, by a constituent assembly, or by some other method.

President Chiluba approved the Commission's terms of reference, and the Commission presented its recommendations publicly on June 16, 1995, following extensive public hearings throughout Zambia. Three days later the recommendations were formally presented to the president. The recommendations called for strengthening the bill of rights, enhancing the independence of the judiciary, strengthening the legislative branch vis à vis the executive branch, establishing an electoral commission and anti-corruption commission independent of the executive branch, and enhancing the professionalism of the civil service. The Commission also recommended that Zambia remain a secular state and that the constitution be adopted by a constituent assembly rather than by the National Assembly.

After the Commission released its draft recommendations, the president castigated the Commission and its chairman for making its recommendations public before the government had an opportunity to comment. The official government response came in late September 1995, when it released a white paper that rejected most of the Commission's recommendations. Any recommendation that strengthened separation of powers and checks and balances or that reduced the power of the presidency was rejected on the grounds that existing arrangements were adequate. A series of recommendations that would have entrenched human rights in the constitution were also rejected. The born-again president prevailed; Zambia became, constitutionally, a Christian nation.

The government initially stifled public debate on the Commission's report and on its white paper through its control of the electronic media and refusal to grant permits to assemble. It later tolerated public discussion, but it did not waver from its position, even in the face of a groundswell of opposition from dozens of civic associations, church groups, labor leaders, and traditional tribal rulers throughout late 1995 and 1996.

The MMD-dominated parliament passed the amendments to Zambia's Constitution on May 22, 1996, and the president signed the changes into law on May 28. Two ministers resigned over the issue.

A New Generation of Zambians Register to Vote

Voter registration blew up into another crisis. Despite promises by the MMD to the Zambian public and donors in late 1994 that voter registration would take place in time for the 1995 local elections, neither the registration nor the elections took place in 1994 or 1995. The local elections were, in fact, cancelled without explanation.

The Nordic countries had been supporting government's capacity to conduct elections. One of their reports urged the government to accept the

National Registration Card in lieu of the costly and time-consuming establishment of voters rolls and a separate voter card, but the MMD rejected that recommendation. The report also recommended proportional parliamentary representation, but that too was rejected.[4]

Voter registration started in early 1996 after much speculation by the public and donor representatives. But what had been merely controversial before the registration process blew up into a scandal when the cost of the registration contract became known. The government had signed an $18.7 million contract with an Israeli firm, NIKUV Computers, Inc., under dubious circumstances. The successful bid was two to four times higher than the average price of the other nine international bidders. NIKUV's extremely high cost for Zambia was never explained, nor was its poor job of doing the same task in neighboring Zimbabwe.

In the meantime more than a third of the 150 elected seats in the National Assembly had become vacant since the 1991 elections because of death, resignation, and expulsion of incumbents. By-elections occasioned by these vacancies were held and were increasingly characterized by election fraud, allegations of vote-buying, MMD use of government resources for campaigning, and violence. The Public Order Act was used repeatedly to constrain opposition campaigning. As a consequence, voter turnout declined to less than 10 percent among those who were eligible to register.

National voter registration had last taken place in Zambia in 1987 and 1988, with some minor updating of the rolls in 1990. Every Zambian citizen who had failed to register by 1990, who turned eighteen after 1990, who changed residence, or who lost his or her voter's certificate was effectively disenfranchised. More than 1.5 million of the 4.1 million citizens older than age eighteen in 1996 fell into these categories.

In 1991 there were 3.4 million Zambians of voting age; 2.9 million of them were registered to vote and 1.3 million actually voted; nearly 46 percent of those eligible to vote did so.

In 1996 there were 4.2 million Zambians of voting age, up from 3.4 million in 1991. The goal was to register all of them for the 1996 election, but only 2.3 million were actually registered by the 1996 election, well below the 2.9 million who had registered for the 1991 election. The record of 87 percent of registered voters in 1991 fell to 55 percent in 1996.

In 1991, 931,000 people had voted for the MMD; in 1996, 750,000 people did so, some 60 percent of the total turnout. Only 30 percent of eligible voters had voted in 1996, or 1.25 million voters. Fifty-four percent of those registered to vote had voted.[5] The voter turnout trend continued downward.

Zambian Voices for Multi-Party Democracy

Tensions were heightened in Lusaka because of the constitutional amendment process, various secret contracts, and then bombings and jailings. The media airwaves and newspapers were filled with debate and accusation. The government's efforts to paint Kaunda as a non-Zambian offended the intelligence of the politically active population as well as the country's traditional tribal leaders.

The government moved aggressively during 1995 and 1996 to reward supporters and to keep the opposition off balance. Fleets of new government cars showed up regularly in Lusaka and members of parliament enjoyed a major salary increase. Rumors flew as observers strived to follow the intricate details of the still-secret NIKUV contract.

Members of opposition parties were jailed on charges that they were responsible for bombings in Lusaka. Rumors circulated that this had been a government set-up. An edition of *The Post* newspaper was banned for printing the Constitutional Review Commission's recommendations and its editor, Fred M'membe, was held for many months without being charged. Other editors and journalists were jailed as well. They were released later but only after many months of lengthy court wranglings.

As senior reformers were driven from the cabinet and even from MMD membership, a few founded opposition parties. None had specific economic platforms other than promises and pledges to return to Manifesto principles. The Zambia Democratic Congress was founded by Derrick Chitala, a former MMD deputy minister; the Liberal Progressive Front party was founded by Rodger Chongwe, another MMD founder and a respected fighter for human rights in Africa. A farmers' party was formed by another former cabinet member, Guy Scott, and Ben Kapita, a farm organizer, but most of the opposition parties were Lusaka-based and Lusaka-limited, despite their claims of wide, regional support.

UNIP promised more of the same in 1996.[6] UNIP's own manifesto showed no sense of the costly economic failure that had been created during Kaunda's twenty-seven-year reign. While most observers believed that Kaunda's candidacy would have caused an even more serious degree of fractiousness during the 1996 election, few believed that Zambians wanted him back.

Several Zambian NGOs were created and a few came back to life during this civil and sometimes uncivil debate. A few NGOs were founded during 1990 and 1991 with the return to democracy and therefore they were well positioned to assess the by-elections and the events leading up to the 1996 elections.

The Zambian Foundation for Democracy Process (FODEP, an NGO) acted to monitor elections, ensure party evenhandedness, and train election observers nationwide in 1991 and thereafter for by-elections and the 1996 elections. Similarly, the Zambia Independent Monitoring Team (ZIMT), led by Alfred Zulu, provided the country electoral assessment, civics education, and objectivity. It too was drawn into the fray; FODEP and ZIMT both received their share of accusations from the MMD for being partisan.

The Committee for a Clean Campaign, founded by Ngande Mwanajiti, published a manifesto spelling out standards for a free and fair election in full-page newspaper advertisements. The Law Association of Zambia directly examined each MMD position and published its assessment. The Zambia Civic Education Association, founded by the late Lucy Sichone, and the Inter-Africa Network for Human Rights and Development (AFRONET) were active in the ongoing debate, as were the NGO Coordinating Committee and Zambia Law Development Commission.

The Catholic Commission for Peace and Justice and several women's organizations had planned a public debate of the government's white paper on the constitutional amendments; the government barred the meeting and detained several of its leaders.

Women began speaking out and organizing across Zambia. Activism was their rule. Women for Change and the Women's Lobby Group advanced womens' and citizens' interests in the midst of the constitutional debate. Too clearly in the past, men dominated in government. Of 150 members of parliament, only 8 were women; of 23 ministers, 2 were women; and of 99 ambassadors, high commissioners, and consuls, only 3 have been women.

All NGOs, whether they were civic or church-related, were accused by the MMD of being donor-sponsored tools and stooges. Neutral associations and observers were often portrayed as being in opposition to the government. Allegations of high-level drug dealing and corruption continued unabated. Even church leaders challenged the constitutional appropriateness of declaring Zambia a Christian nation. Zambians began to see that a belief in the Manifesto's aspirations of 1991 was to be against the ruling MMD in 1996.

There was no lack of information or debate on any issue, and to its credit, government and the MMD did not actually close NGOs or the press. With the 1991 election, six independent newspapers started to publish and three private radio stations came on the air: "The fact that *The Post* continues to publish what it wishes, without successful interference by government, stands to the credit of the Zambian people, and indeed of the government, too."[7]

Private newspapers stood as the most important force for democracy in Zambia during these national debates. The MMD had freed the press and despite all said here and elsewhere, the press remains free. Furthermore, *The Post* went on-line via the World Wide Web to a worldwide readership. The editor acknowledged that this fact helped spring him from MMD detention. *The Post* became a voice for African democracy.[8] In February 1996 the MMD had suppressed *The Post* for a day for printing the Constitutional Review Commission's proposed amendments, which was the first act of censorship of the Internet in Africa. Throughout this period hardly a day passed without there being a political occasion—flap even—that led to *Post* headlines the next morning.

THE WESTERN DONORS REACT TO DEMOCRACY'S BETRAYAL

The bilateral donor resident representatives watched this unfolding betrayal with growing concern. Reports in the local press and rumors heard at the latest national day receptions were reported back to western capitals. Donors had their own parliaments to contend with; they gradually questioned, delayed, and then suspended budget support for the MMD government.

As a consequence the government came to rely heavily on the World Bank for new loans to keep itself afloat and to service its debts. The government's moves against democracy relied explicitly, we were told, on the World Bank's policy not to intervene in political matters. Local donor representatives came to believe that the MMD's political steps—whether they were determined betrayal or tactical hesitation—were measured against IDA loans that were being considered for approval, to sustain the government's budget.

Despite repeated assurances by the MMD to the public that constitutional changes would be agreed to in "a consensual manner," the changes were passed by an MMD-dominated parliament as the president directed. The country and the donors had been assured by the president that a consensus over amendment issues would be worked out with opposition parties. They were not. The amendments were approved on May 22 and the president signed them into law on May 28, 1996. The government had lied to the December 1995 donors meeting and to donor representatives about "consensus." Some donor money was withdrawn. Denmark, Finland, Germany, Japan, the Netherlands, Norway, Sweden, the United Kingdom, and the European Union all suspended budget support.[9]

The government tried to assuage the donors. The MMD voiced repeated arguments that the amendments were the will of the people. One or two expatriate advisers within the government attempted to carry the case for the MMD. One expatriate advisor went so far as to write the government's position paper extolling its democratic reforms and shared it with donors as the government's position, without obtaining approval.

By mid-1996 the impasse between the government and the donors was starting to take its toll. On the one hand the World Bank needed a stable relationship and bilateral donor funds to insure that its debts were paid. It did not preoccupy itself with the larger issues of democracy and betrayal. The bilateral donors, on the other hand, were caught between the obvious importance of sustaining economic reform, and the equally important return to democracy that the Zambian people had voted for in 1991.

The World Bank knew its debt would not be paid by the government unless the bilateral donors contributed their share of overall budget support to close the resource gap; a World Bank representative therefore begged the donors to spell out their concerns about the MMD's democratic reforms. The World Bank repeatedly tried to make democracy's betrayal by the MMD a bilateral donor problem. By addressing the donors' concerns the government could then show (at least to the World Bank's satisfaction) that the MMD was making progress on each element. The World Bank acted divisively toward the bilateral donors by pressing each to express its specific concerns, as if to say that if it weren't for the donors, Zambia would have no democracy problem. A bilateral donors meeting called to assess the situation allowed one European donor to keep the other donors off balance because it voiced support for the MMD. As a consequence the World Bank claimed a lack of donor consensus, and therefore continued its policy of approving loans.

An example of this list of donor concerns, of this step-by-step manipulation by the World Bank of the bilateral donors, was donor pressure for an independent, anticorruption commission as had been promised in the 1991 Manifesto. Observers knew that ministerial-level corruption cases sat on the president's desk in State House. The MMD promised the donors new legislation that would establish an "independent" commission (one staffed with presidential appointees), as evidence of its best intentions. The World Bank claimed this as progress.

In addition to western representations of concern toward the MMD, African governments, the Southern African Development Community, and civic and human rights associations voiced their worries for Zambia's accelerating political direction. Diplomatic representations by Zambia's neighbor countries yielded little from the MMD. In November 1996

Chiluba and the MMD won a second five-year term. The former president and his UNIP party did not participate; several other opposition parties also boycotted the election. The MMD rewrote its 1991 Manifesto, but by then it was neither read nor discussed.

Twelve parties contested 150 parliamentary seats. The MMD won 131 of them with 60 percent of the vote, down from 70 percent in 1991. Just 18 percent of eligible voters returned the party to power.

Tensions in political circles ran high during the election. The amended constitution lacked legitimacy with the public. Demonstrations provoked the use of tear gas, but there were no shootings. The government saw the British as acting to discourage foreign investors. As one consequence the president is said to have rejoiced in the stoning of a British Airways crew bus by university students.[10]

By the time of the November 1996 election damage had been done to the economy and to bilateral relations. Few domestic and no international observers claimed that the MMD's second election had been free and fair. Zambians who were seasoned in the ways of the MMD and its origins commented in 1996 that the MMD had been plotting to consolidate power well before it won in 1991. Kenneth Kaunda's return to the political arena was not the reason for the MMD's betrayal of democracy; he served only as a pretext for a recentralization of political control: "The original MMD ideals were hijacked by a clique. . . . They [the MMD] strategically flushed out all contenders for the presidency. . . . The MMD took in a patriotic elite as well as a parasitic elite and removed the reformers."[11]

Once safely returned to a second term, with IMF and World Bank resources flowing once again, the president is reported to have said that he knew what was right for the Zambian people: "We go through the recommendations and decide what is right for our people because they are not mature enough to grasp these things. So we decide for them."[12]

The opposition disagreed: "The November 18 elections did not solve anything and they [the MMD] could not have, for they were not elections in the strict sense but were contrived as a mere stratagem for President Chiluba and his largely blind and opportunistic supporters to retain power, and the privileges that go with it. "[13]

Domestic NGO election monitoring groups found that the 1996 election did not conform to international standards. For the Zambian people the conclusion was the same: "It would be nice if being poor didn't necessarily mean being oppressed."[14] With the 1996 election just concluded, opposition leaders as well as those within the MMD began plotting campaigns for the 2001 presidential elections.

Well into 1997 and 1998, the MMD continued trying to patch up its international reputation with its neighbors and donors, for which there was still no internal Zambian dialogue or consensus.

Economic and Political Reform Are Intertwined

Major economic and political interests are always intertwined. Chapters 7 and 8 are presented separately, but their issues are joined. The crisis described in chapter 7 was costly but did not represent an MMD betrayal of macroeconomic reforms. The political crisis described here *did* represent a reversal, and therefore donor leverage associated with their budget support became a factor in the donor dialogue.

The bilateral donors were in some measure held hostage to their sense of responsibility for Zambia's stability. Nonetheless, they did start to raise questions about the MMD's commitment to political reform and they did start to suspend budget support. The World Bank and the IMF were also held hostage, in a sense, because of internal pressures from within these institutions to ensure that their debts were paid on schedule. No World Bank representative voiced concerns for democracy, nor even for the self-inflicted budgetary crises described in the previous chapter.

The debt-aid game that has built African dependence on western donors was not played twice—this time. Perhaps the Zambian government had miscalculated, or simply decided to go it alone (with the help of the World Bank and IMF). Donor project aid continued during this period. The United States was not providing Zambia with budget support, partly for the lack of justification, and because of economic and political difficulties with this type of assistance generally, but it had committed project aid for democracy building.

THE U.S. GOVERNMENT AND AFRICAN DEMOCRACY

America has been infamous in the eyes of its critics for overlooking autocratic and corrupt governments and human rights abuses if it involved current friends. Today American ideals are beginning to be matched by formal representations and some resources. The end of the cold war is allowing some shift in policy.

As with our foreign policy, our foreign assistance has been supportive of democratic reform, institutions, and individuals when it suited us. This era may be giving way to a more purposeful and unequivocal commitment. AID's initial authorization, signed by President Kennedy in 1961, directed the agency to "build economic, political and social institutions which will improve the quality of [people's] lives and to help the poor majority . . . to influence decisions that shape their lives." Sections of this law stressed participation and human rights.

Today, nearly forty years later, AID embraces a strategic goal called sustainable democracy. To contribute to democracy, AID has four funding categories: the rule of law and respect for human rights, competitive political processes, a politically active civil society, and more transparent and accountable governmental institutions. In fiscal year 1996, 7.5 percent, or roughly $60 million of the total $800 million AID budget for Africa, was allocated for democracy.

AID's Democracy Projects in Zambia

AID funds democracy building activities in several African countries. A Lusaka-based story, which I tell here, is one example of a new American commitment. Democracy building became a full day's work in Lusaka in 1995 and 1996. Because most donors were funding democracy activities, the subject became complex and fraught with tension for all concerned. The major donors attempted to stay behind the scene as they funded more political activity than most Zambians or outside observers realized.

Take one day, March 27, 1996, for example, two months before the president signed the new constitution into law. The opposition was increasingly speaking out against MMD machinations. Donor representatives sought to confer with each other more regularly. The government tried to close down a donor democracy discussion group; the Swedes were told not to host a meeting, so they looked to AID to do so. We did. Then we learned that a senior government official criticized a foreign advisor for hosting a seminar on Zambia's economic future. That day we also learned that a senior Zambian staff member had been sacked for talking too candidly with donors. MMD pressure mounted on the opposition, the press, and the donors. The western ambassadors and donor representatives met regularly to assess the political scene, but they were not sure how to respond. But the day was not all bad. Two *Post* newspaper editors were released from jail. And we decided, after weeks of deliberation, not to suspend one of our democracy project activities.

Earlier, in 1991 and 1992, donors had been eager to support the MMD's professed commitment to democracy. AID designed one of the first comprehensive projects to support democracy in Africa. AID's first such effort supported NGOs in the 1980s, in South Africa. As with the Zambian economic reform program, the MMD was initially committed to the strengthening of democratic traditions and institutions. MMD reformers welcomed a $15 million AID initiative as well as initiatives from other donors.

In fact, the AID project agreement, which was designed to render public decision-making more accessible and effective, included a statement of the Zambian government's commitment to democratic progress. A bilateral agreement was signed in late 1992 and by 1995 $15 million had been committed to the project's multiple activities. This sum enabled AID to become a lead donor, in both dollar terms as well as in project complexity. It was not only the dollars but the people and the learning curve flexibility this grant provided that contributed to Zambian civic education. The AID democracy advisor, James Polhemus, and Southern University's Chief of Party, Georgia Bowser, translated AID dollars and expertise into support for Zambian civics education, pluralism, and activism. A joint Zambian-AID design team stressed Zambian initiative at the outset. The portfolio was designed and implemented with government, NGO, and opposition party involvement. The project supported the constitutional commission process (together with the Swedes), civic education, media independence, and various steps to improve legislative and cabinet administrative effectiveness.[15]

Most of the NGOs were funded by donors. Zambians nonetheless designed the messages that filled thousands of voter education pamphlets, hundreds of poll monitoring and political party staff training sessions, the air waves with get-out-the-vote slogans, and civic education posters and advertisements.

AID supported Zambia's revision of its middle school civics textbooks on democratic values and practices, which introduced concepts of responsibility and a market economy. We learned that even here aid leverage can be awkward. AID demanded that the new textbooks be written by Zambians, not by American experts, and that they be printed in Zambia. Demanding Zambian ownership seemed like a strange source of frustration. Perhaps ministry officials wanted trips to the United States; more likely, as civil servants, they did not want to risk disagreement over the texts with MMD ideologues. In any event, an admittedly awkward example of a donor-drive-for-Zambian-ownership did lead to a text book written and printed by Zambians.

The Asia Foundation and the Africa America Institute launched a "Global Women in Politics" network in Lusaka, for like-minded women running for public office in Africa. The two AID-supported American NGOs sponsored a workshop and a kick-off dinner. There we learned that womens' political activism was alive across Africa. Assertiveness was not the issue. Dinner speakers were blunt; one speaker described being kept manacled in solitary confinement in Malawi for four years. Another speaker, turning to face a minister, declared: "I want your job." A third woman in the evening's audience told the keynote speaker: "Stop being a man in woman's clothing."

To sustain womens' political activism, the two American organizations used the Internet for the first time to keep African country and regional leaders in touch with each other. The Global Women in Politics Program looked to Zambia's National Women's Lobby Group to serve as the coordinating body for adding country members to the network of like-minded activists.

AID's democracy projects paralleled those sponsored by other agencies of the U.S. government in Lusaka; it was a team effort. Peace Corps volunteers assisted with judicial reform by placing Zambian constitutional and Supreme Court decisions on the Internet. This judicial work was reinforced by visiting USIS-funded Fulbright professionals and USIS-visitor grants for Zambians to the United States.

The Zambia countryside was also alive with political debate. Caroline and I, and Chuck Mohan, the AID economist, had been on a car tour of western Zambia and had promised to visit a rural community to see a "Women For Change" activity, which was funded by AID.

Greeted by traditional song and dance, we were escorted to a grove of mango trees under which the women of the Mangango community had organized the first coming-together of separate democracy village-level discussion groups. We were not sure how the women got the men to come, but they were all there—the village administrative staff, the local police, the MMD, and opposition party representatives. The local leaders, Gertrude Nkunta and Elizabeth Mubiana, plunged right in: "Why should women be in politics? Why vote? Why is civic education needed?" The animated discussion included the role of citizens, their rights and responsibilities, even the advantages and disadvantages of democracy.[16] Caroline won a riotous reaction by insisting that a woman should win State House.

This example from rural Zambia is but one of dozens and dozens. Southern University in Baton Rogue, Louisiana, the contractor for this AID activity, had invited Zambian NGO initiatives from across Zambia to start and expand civics training for villagers. The Southern University office map was filled with multicolored pins representing the various Zambian activities: village-level democracy training, voter civic education, radio drama in seven Zambian languages, fair election and party practices, leadership training meetings, and theater and drama groups.

But political life in Zambia was not all song and dance. We had to get back to Lusaka to face a different kind of music. For every NGO running on its own initiative (even if it had donor financial support), there were a few NGOs that were too glad to take donor money for other-than-transparent purposes. I kept asking one AID-funded NGO about responsibilities for office procedures, plans, and accounts, and ultimate financial sustainability from local sources. My inquiries were not welcomed. There were simply too many donors willing to support NGOs without asking questions about accountability or sustainability. Zambian NGOs can and do raise funding from domestic sources. In reaction to this particular case of NGO donor-dependence, I reduced their funding.[17]

Democracy's Betrayal
—The United States Signals the Zambian Government

The MMD's political shenanigans did not go unnoticed by the U.S. government. We had long since determined that budget support was difficult to justify for Zambia and so we had none to cut. The AID covenant assuring us of government's commitment to democracy had long since been violated. Having spoken clearly and often about democracy in Zambia to the government, the U.S. embassy saw the need to join our donor colleagues in expressing its reservations.

We had long known the AID portfolio of projects—for health, agriculture, as well as for democracy—should be partially "off budget," that is, channeled not only through the government, but through the private sector and nongovernmental institutions. Cutting AID project funding to send a signal to the government proved to be difficult.

A few days after the Zambian parliament passed the constitutional amendments, the president signed the new bill creating an amended constitution, on May 28, 1996. Three days after that a Department of State news release stated:

The United States deeply deplores the decision this week of the Government of Zambia to impose constitutional amendments, on the eve of the first national elections in Zambia's democratic era, that limit the right of the Zambian people to choose their president freely. . . . The United States urges the Government of Zambia to reverse its decision on the constitutional amendments, to renew its commitment to democracy, and to take immediate steps to ensure that this year's elections are free and fair.

That statement was planned in conjunction with project cuts in the U.S. program in Zambia. After reviewing embassy activities and those of the

Peace Corps and of USIS, we agreed within the embassy that the AID democracy portfolio should be used to signal U.S. government concerns.

Two project cuts had occurred earlier. The AID mission had suspended work with the National Assembly because of differences over an agreed work plan; and the National Democratic Institute (NDI) had determined that its work with the political parties was no longer effective and did not wish to be associated with the pending 1996 presidential election.[18] This latter decision was regrettable because NDI had contributed monitoring training and other support during the 1991 election, and was appreciated by political observers and actors in Zambia.

Two additional AID-funded project activities were terminated with the U.S. government announcement on July 16, 1996. One activity supported streamlining cabinet decision procedures and the other supported the independence of a government media training center. Both projects had been moving toward successful completion as democracy activities. But ironically and somewhat sadly, these two activities were all that the U.S. government was financing within the central government. The Zambian political environment had changed. Government-owned media was not being privatized. Further, it was widely rumored that a shadow cabinet of a few people acted for the ministerial cabinet.

Correspondingly, the overall AID budget was cut from $19 million to $17.5 million for fiscal year 1996, and was cut again the following year to $16.6 million. The National Security Council, which had cleared the official statement on Zambia and the related resource decisions, had sought a more significant money reduction.

CREATING DEVELOPMENT OWNERSHIP WITH DEMOCRACY

Despite democracy's betrayal, Zambia's democratic debate remains rich and vibrant. Zambian democracy was not cut down by gunfire and chaos in 1996. Betrayal, yes, but Zambia is not a failed state. Few men as president place national leadership first; power, friends, and allies second. The MMD is committed to a major economic restructuring of its economy, but not to a rebuilding of its democratic institutions.

Some local observers argue that the MMD has invited violent dissent. Bomb threats and actual bombings led to arrests of suspects, and in the absence of formal charges, to releases, in late 1996. During a political rally in August 1997, Kenneth Kaunda and Roger Chongwe were shot, wounded, and hospitalized. Allegations of torture have been reported frequently in the press, and rumors of state-sanctioned murder have circulated. A coup attempt on October 28, 1997 gave the MMD reason to impose emergency rule for nearly five months, and to arrest real and imagined supporters of the coup plotters. Two months later, on Christmas 1997, Kaunda was arrested on charges that he had helped instigate the coup attempt. He was later released but remained under house arrest for five months.

The MMD crackdown has been tempered. As senior opposition members and NGO representatives were arrested, detained, and later released, the Zambian police continued to respect their colonial heritage. Police would return following a sunrise knock on the door after a suspect had had time to dress and have breakfast. One suspect was allowed to take his mobile phone with him, giving new meaning to the term *cell phone*.[19] A human rights commission was finally established, and the independence of the anticorruption commission and the electoral commission were enhanced in 1997. No assessment has been made of their effectiveness. The private Swedish Institute for Democracy and Electoral Assistance was founded to promote political dialogue between the Zambian opposition and the MMD, but little has come of this institute's initiative. NIKUV was hired again to prepare the electoral rolls for the local government elections, which were originally scheduled for 1995, and have now been rescheduled for late 1998.

Assessment of Political Developments

The political events of the 1990s are not the stuff of an enabling environment. The MMD's political leadership is seen with suspicion by ordinary Zambians, investors, donors, and the country's neighbors. Donors have reduced their expectations and their assistance. Governmental checks and balances have been weakened. Parliament is a rubber stamp; the judiciary and the private media remain independent but besieged. A majority of the voting age public has either been disenfranchised or has stayed away from the polls. The MMD's second term has neither the mantle "free and fair" nor the voter turnout to reaffirm its 1991 place in the sun; decisions were not as inclusive as the MMD had promised in 1991.

The Zambian government shows few signs of being committed to representative, transparent government, or to the well-being of its people. According to an economist known for his candor, Robert Klitgaard, "When corruption becomes the norm, its effects are crippling. Such systematic corruption makes establishing and maintaining internationally acceptable rules of the [investment] game impossible, and is one of the principal reasons why the least developed parts of our planet stay that way."[20]

Democracy Issues Facing the Zambian Electorate

These pages make clear that the Zambian debate over democracy-in-the-making is vibrant. With this recent political history as background, it is useful to consider four aspects of this debate: winner take all representation, the relationship of economic and political reform, the role of bilateral donors, and of the World Bank and the IMF.

Winner Take All?

All democracies face the issue of representativeness. Africa's experiment with democracy contains several forms. Anglophone African democracies are often of the Westminster parliamentary variety, with winner-take-all voting, a strong executive, weak parliaments and judiciaries, and a tradition of budgetary secrecy. Further, the premier or president has the primary if not exclusive policy-making authority. On the face of it, this is not a formula for broad-based ownership of development.

Parliamentary winner-take-all voting means that each constituency is represented by the candidate with the most absolute votes. All other parties and their candidates—the losers—are not represented for that election period. African countries with fledgling rules of law and weak democratic traditions do not protect losers of political contests very well. Nor are principles of civil and human recourse well founded.

The alternative is termed *proportional representation*. Winning candidates can represent a cluster of constituencies, in a province, for example. Winning candidates are distributed by the distribution of the vote. Some political experts argue that Africa needs a proportional representation system because it allows minorities to be represented in parliament and in coalition cabinets. If minorities are permanently excluded from parliament and hence from cabinet, they are permanently excluded from the processes of determining development priorities and uses of resources. Experts argue that proportionality reduces tribal factionalism. Furthermore, they argue that Africa must have proportional representation when all other democratic institutions are weak. The Nordic electoral study recommended proportional representation for Zambia. It exists in nearby Namibia, South Africa, and Zimbabwe.

Counterarguments against proportionality carry weight of experience; African tribal and ethnic divisions do not need the formality of democratic institutions to further heighten factionalism and ethnically defined political parties in or out of power. The risk of ethnic conflict is real and yet at the same time, some experts argue that it is a false issue. African justifications for authoritarian rule in the name of sustaining stability over tribal tensions are used most often by those in power to further control. Tanzania is a notable exception. Africa's chiefs are chiefs of homogeneous but small tribal groups, not of multicultural and multiethnic nations. Nonetheless, according to the Department of State, the predominance of the argument and the evidence across Africa is starting to fall on the side of proportional representation.[21]

Some of Zambia's democracy problems are systemic, such as winner-take-all, and will require time to debate and resolve. One of Zambia's leaders adds insight to the problem. "Zambia's present constitution makes him [the president] a dictator."[22] This is one consequence of a first-past-the-goal-post, winner-take-all understanding of democracy. Furthermore, Zambia is, according to another leading politician, a "multiparty democracy with a one-party system."[23] Colonial rules of governance coexisted easily with those of African traditional leaders and later with their one-party states. More than a few observers have commented that President Chiluba believes firmly in the literal meaning of winner take all. Zambians will continue to debate this constitutional issue and may in time amend their constitution to reflect a new consensus on rights to representation.

Do Open Markets Create Democracy?

There is a school of economic thought that believes that markets create democracy; that once the economic genie is out of the bottle, political liberalization follows. To many economic observers and experts, democracy is driven, even created, by market reform. Open markets lead to open opportunity, investments, and competition, which thrive where there is rule of law, respect for property, and recourse to courts.[24] A noted European economist, Fredrick August von Hayek, argues that attempts by government to redistribute income destroy the human spirit as they build dependency.[25]

Open markets do stimulate associations, interest groups, and political organizations. On the contrary, the suppression of markets suppresses the political development of a society. This is the predatory African state. The market-based argument has importance for Africa because market liberalization is sweeping Africa, particularly Zambia. The decontrol of prices, the actual privatization of nearly 300 public firms, including, eventually, Zambia's copper mines, is leading inevitably to new sources of power and vested interests. The MMD may be sufficiently cunning to be committed to the long-term and also to its immediate survival. Perhaps. That the MMD does not have a broad base of economic or political support today is widely recognized. It might regain such support in the future. Lise

Rakner, a Norwegian political scientist, argues that it is because the MMD has had no developmental or political base that it has had to retreat into the ways of the authoritarian UNIP.[26]

The theoretical argument in support of market-driven democracy requires a long view of history—at least for those who may not be serious about development. As much as the authoritarian rule of a Suharto, Museveni, or a Lee Kuan Yew make many western liberals uncomfortable, the evidence is that their economic seriousness can work for growth, for poverty alleviation, and possibly for economic recovery. By extension, development seriousness will ultimately undo centralized control. But the issue of the acceptable time frame remains.

Governments should not be casual about the time frame. De facto laissez-faire capitalism cannot be laid on top of African poverty. Democracy building demands commitment and seriousness.

Should Bilateral Donors Leverage Democracy?

Western donors are helping to advise and fund the democratic experiment across Africa. AID began democratic project activities in 1992 and 1993 in Zambia; other bilateral donors have since followed with their own projects. Many, particularly the United Kingdom and the Scandinavian countries, have active portfolios. But much needs to be assessed to guide this evolutionary process, which must remain an African initiative.

Do donors create, or just enable, democratic deepening? Do donors create or simply support an opposition and a politically oriented NGO community, and to what degree? A few observers agree that donor moral support, in addition to their funding, bolstered opposition voices in Zambia. There are mixed views on these questions.

Some Zambians, certainly those in the MMD, and a few foreigners believed that donors were too closely aligned with the opposition. The 1995–96 era of active opposition was a function in part of donor funding. One expert has suggested that only ten Zambians worked actively in opposition to the MMD during the period.[27] However, I believe most politically active Zambians welcome the donor community, as a source of reformist pressure, possibly more so than is appropriate.

Traditionally, the donors' first concern has been the maintenance of diplomatic good will. Following a strain in relationships, enormous effort goes into reaching new understandings. Zambia's donors have learned to tolerate a constitution that was amended without public discussion or consensus in 1995, and a flawed national election in 1996. However, the donor dialogue with the government is not what it was in 1991, nor are the resource levels. Democracy building, private investment, and poverty alleviation are once again held in abeyance.

Once betrayed, twice shy? Western donors do not appear to be accepting the terms of a new partnership as dictated by the MMD. Donors appear to recognize that, for most African governments, development is "of trifling interest compared with consolidating political power."[28] The issue is not so much what the Zambians think of the donors, but what the Zambian people do to further democracy in their own country. Many observers are critical of Zambian passivity.

Donor support for democracy building can strengthen the argument presented by some African scholars and other critics that donor conditionality is corrosive of democratic values and practices and ultimately undercuts the very processes both parties seek to strengthen. Aid, if not jointly designed and administered, can weaken the legitimacy and credibility for recipient institutions.[29]

What Roles for the World Bank and the IMF?

The western donors face a dual challenge of supporting democracy in Africa and of influencing the several multilateral institutions, particularly the World Bank.[30]

This institution has started to say the right things. "The days are over in Africa . . . when governments can just make secret deals with any-body—including us [the World Bank]—behind the scenes, without informing their people. . . . The ability of governments to actually implement what they have agreed [to] is greatly diminished without public support and understanding."[31] The World Bank continues: "Countries that are fundamentally corrupt should be told that unless they can deal with that they are not getting any more money."[32]

Despite protestations of best intensions, the World Bank and IMF charters bar their involvement in politics. The Articles of Agreement guiding both the IBRD and IDA stipulate that:

The Association and its officers shall not interfere in the political affairs of any member; nor shall they be influenced in their decisions by the political character of the member or members concerned. Only economic considerations shall be relevant to their decisions, and these considerations shall be weighted impartially in order to achieve the purposes stated in this Agreement.[33]

We know how the World Bank staff interpret economic conditions, and now we can see how they treat political issues as well. Perhaps the charters were designed for the immediate postwar recovery period in Europe. Perhaps this wording is designed to win the confidence of dozens of new countries that joined IDA in later years. In any event it is noteworthy that the Articles direct the World Bank to contribute to "an acceleration of economic development" but does so without explicit regard to good governance and democracy.

What is not understood by many is that World Bank credits represent a massive degree of support for African governments and for parties in power. In short, IMF and World Bank resources are massively and fundamentally political. If African commitment to economic and political reform falters, the World Bank has no tradition of its own and little willingness to redirect its assessments or its resource commitments. Democracy is not a priority for World Bank and IMF executive directors or their staffs. They hide behind the word *political*.

World Bank loans allow for no pluralism. IDA loans flow exclusively to governments and therefore the World Bank deals exclusively with governments in power. The exceptions represent less than one percent of IDA, IBRD, and IMF resources.[34] African opposition parties, Africa's private sector, and national and regional NGOs are excluded from the processes and resources that prop up African governments. Opposition parties are closed out of parliaments and out of donor resources. Structural adjustment, as defined by the World Bank and the IMF, and as embraced by the MMD, is the only game in town, and the only source of money. As a consequence, an opposition party can have no alternative economic platform and no voice in parliament.[35]

A continuing governmental monopoly over power and donor resources is no longer the acceptable norm. An African scholar states: "The predatory state in Africa does not reform itself."[36] An American ambassador agrees: "democratic progress is not a luxury but an essential ingredient for real economic reform, especially in Africa."[37]

The bilateral donors may have handed too much of their foreign policy responsibility for Africa to the World Bank and IMF. Both institutions enjoy major resource and policy influence; the bilateral donors less so. Bilateral donor concerns for democracy in Africa are being undercut, blocked even, by the World Bank and IMF. African countries should not be able to seek solace for democracy betrayals, as Zambia has recently done. To observers in Lusaka, the IMF's and World Bank's private signals supported the MMD's betrayal; without their support, the MMD could not have pursued its present course.

CONCLUSIONS AND RECOMMENDATIONS

Zambia could have been on the front ranks of the world's newly democratic nations. Its leaders chose not to take this course. Both what is right and what is disappointing about Zambia in the 1990s have been examined here. Donors share in this disappointment, as they have contributed in some measure to its root causes.

Perhaps Zambia's leaders are out of touch with a younger African generation that is eager for responsibility. An AID colleague, William Pierson, describes for West Africa, the East Africa I know:

African attitudes are changing at the highest levels of government, in regional institutions, and among PVOs and NGOs, and particularly among younger people. New attitudes reflect responsibility for their own development; recognition that Africans must own their development programs; and that African impediments to development can only be addressed by Africans. Africans must stop the economic deterioration they see around them. They realize that deep economic reforms are necessary to achieve progress, and that people must stop looking to the state as the great provider of benefits. Lastly, a new generation of Africans has optimism and the conviction, that with progressive policies, reform of political institutions, and strong leadership, economic and social progress in Africa can be as strong as anywhere else in the world.[38]

African leaders are recognizing the larger challenge they face. Africa must have strong institutions to create the incomes, education, and health needed for younger generations. It is not credible to suggest that these can be achieved without the mobilization of Africans themselves. Open markets and functioning democracies hold this promise.

Africans have found their voice in manifold forms and forums. They deserve western recognition and support. Donors are learning to help Africans open the doors to new generations, new resources, and new talent. An enabling environment cannot rest with one institution, such as a ministry of finance or planning. Donors are beginning to question the commitment of monolithic governments.

However, crises and aid cuts do not necessarily lead to seriousness or to reform of either government or donor behavior. Poor African governments are known for retreating from bad policies at the last minute when faced with the threat of a cutoff in donor aid. Most of the time. The cutoff of budget support by Zambia's bilateral donors over the issue of democracy is but one of many examples of these tensions across Africa. Other cutoffs have included, over the past decade, Cameroon, Kenya, Nigeria, Somalia,

South Africa, Sudan, Tanzania, Uganda, and Zaire. Sadly, parties to these crises pick themselves up and head in the same direction.

Aid cutoffs and wide swings in bilateral relations are damaging to reform, commitment, and good will. Suspensions can only be avoided by clearer understandings of expectations. Donors must express explicit standards as they promote democracy. A nominal stability and donor largesse cannot come first. Africans must appreciate standards required for development, but have independence of action and time to build their own democratic institutions.

To set democracy aside because of claims that it is destabilizing avoids the larger issue of growth and poverty alleviation. Reforming governments do not face angry voters as often as critics claim.[39] Zambia is a case in point. Africans are beginning to see that poverty is the root of instability and, if given the chance, will bear the burdens of reform. Africans are beginning to understand that democratic and market processes, not aid, must bind their interests together.

Democratic Principles As Standards

Donors should provide technical support and funding for democracy building, but should not force the pace with leverage. The West does not have a right to push democracy forward on behalf of others, no matter how noble the cause or great the experience. Africans, on the other hand, should know that donors require African initiative to make western assistance effective. Donors should not stand aside, but donors and their money should stand back.

Western donors have come part way in setting democratic standards, and in being selective of the countries they support; they must move further along this new course. Donor willingness to support democratic expression in Africa must be unequivocal. Donors need to explore new ways of supporting countries, policies, and activities that are committed to democracy. They must also find new ways to signal their unwillingness to subsidize betrayal, failure, and corruption. The technique to use is the sustained expression of standards of democratic representativeness, governmental checks and balances, transparency, and pluralism.

Western donors have moved beyond free and fair election monitoring as the sole index of democratic commitment, to project activism to help build democratic capabilities. The bilateral donors should relax their focus on the daily democracy experiment but continue to demand democratic standards, and adjust and redirect their resource contributions to African governments, associations, parties, and NGOs according to performance.

Donors should not be involved in the details at a policy level nor rely on the leverage of policy conditioning to foster democratic reforms.

Appropriate donor action should be associated with democratic initiative, local talent, and local resource mobilization. Donors should not be the instigators of democratic initiatives or projects, nor fully fund individual democratic activities. Donors will not agree on precise definitions of democratic principles and this is to be expected. But donors can agree that democracy equates to standard principles.

Donors can make a difference in time frame and pluralism by supporting African democratic initiatives from all interests. Viewed in these terms, I am an optimist even in the face of the MMD's betrayal. Zambia's opposition parties, NGOs, women's organizations, rural institutions, and church groups are active, even vociferous.

Pluralism of Access to Donor Resources

Africans are eager to enjoy a deciding vote in the use of donor advice and funding. Donors should support democratic building within government by strengthening the checks and balances of independent legislatures, judiciaries, and commissions. The media, associations, NGOs, and political parties should also have donor-supported opportunities to be heard, and to function as checks and balances on governmental decisions.

Donors can provide checks and balances of their own by funding pluralism directly and selectively. Well-crafted aid can help Africa broaden market pluralism as well as foster institutions of democratic diversity.

For Zambia and for other African countries, however, domestic voices and votes may influence but not determine democracy and development for years to come. Betrayal of democracy is commonplace, but the appropriate role for donors in support of African democratic initiatives should not be in doubt.

The World Bank and the IMF

Africa must come to know that the World Bank and the IMF embrace democratic principles and pluralism of institutional development. The World Bank's charter should be changed or reinterpreted to support democratic principles and institutions. The World Bank and IMF should support democracy as a standard, but not become immersed in its details or make judgments about daily trends.

No donor should attempt to influence the shape of political initiatives and positions of political parties and NGOs. Still, it is a different matter—one the World Bank has yet to recognize—to set democracy principles and to support them credibly.

However sympathetic they are, Africa's proponents must recognize that democracy does not follow automatically from government nor from donors. Nor does democracy in a poor world come necessarily from the free market. Risks of delays and reversals abound. Donors must, nonetheless, set standards for both sets of reforms, and fund and otherwise support African desires to achieve economic and political maturity.

A former senior Zambian politician, Emmanuel Kasonde, speaks to African governments and to westerners when he says:

It is always a great mistake to think that a largely illiterate electorate does not understand. The fact is that people's understanding may not be perfect but they always pick up the essential elements of each policy. If you do not tell them, they do not feel responsible and will not allow you a free hand in the implementation of these policies. If you do not carry the general thinking of the people with you—you may have the most comprehensive policies but you will fail. Public participation is essential. [40]

NOTES

I am indebted to James Polhemus, professor of political science, and resident AID democracy advisor in Lusaka between 1991 and 1997. Mr. Polhemus advised the U.S. mission and the donor community and also managed an AID portfolio of $15 million in democracy activities. Much of the material in this chapter is drawn from his work and our many discussions. See his *Democracy Betrayed: Zambia's Third Republic*, for the Annual Meeting of the African Studies Association of Australia and the Pacific, Canberra, September 25–27, 1997.

I have also benefited from work by Benjamin Hawley, personal communication, July 31, 1997, London; the availability of *The Post,* from Lusaka on the World Wide Web; Lise Rakner's, *Reform as a matter of political survival: Political and economic liberalization in Zambia 1991–1996*, Bergen, Norway: Chr. Michelsens Institute, 1996; and Richard L. Sklar's, "Towards a Theory of Development Democracy," in Adrian Leftwich, editor, *Democracy and Development,* Cambridge, U.K: Polity Press, 1996.

1. For a survey of the 1985–90 era, Kaunda's last years, see Robert H. Bates and Paul Collier, *The Politics and Economics of Policy Reform in Zambia*, Durham, NC: Duke University Program in International Political Economy, Working Paper No. 153, January 22, 1992.

2. Parallels between Frederick Chiluba's *1991 Manifesto* and Julius Nyerere's *Arusha Declaration of 1967* for Tanzania are striking. Although the

Declaration serviced a statist era, both documents served to unite the western donors behind renewed development programs.

3. "Drug barons funded MMD," *The Post*, Lusaka, February 2, 1998.

4. Lars Svasand, Jorgen Elklit, Knut Frigaard, Carl-Goran Gustafsson, and Aanund Hyllan, *Report on Improvement of the Electoral Process in Zambia*, Bergen, Norway: University of Bergen, January 23, 1995.

5. James Polhemus, AID reports, May 24, 1995, October 10, 1995, May 22, 1996, June 1, 1996, and June 7, 1996. Also, James Polhemus, 1997, p. 12.

6. The United National Independence Party, *Manifesto 1996*, May 14, 1996.

7. Theo Bull, "Zambia: Boom, Doom, or Merely Gloom?" *The World Today*, October 1996.

8. Fred M'membe and Bright Mwape, editors, *The Post*.

9. Around $150 million in bilateral budget support was suspended. With the passage of the constitutional amendments Denmark withdrew a parliamentary request for approval of $6.9 million.

10. "Alarming Lack of Humanity," *The Post*, November 22, 1996.

11. Simon Zukas, former MMD minister, *The Post*, July 22, 1996.

12. Letter to the editor by a Zambian, purportedly on the new American ambassador's courtesy call on President Chiluba, *The Post*, January 17, 1997.

13. Editorial comment, *The Post*, February 13, 1997.

14. Father Brian Wallace, personal communication, November 26, 1996.

15. AID, Zambia, Project Grant Agreement for Democracy Governance Project, signed September 28, 1992; Michigan State University, *Zambia Democracy Governance Project—Monitoring and Evaluation Studies*, Mid-Term Review, draft, July 18, 1995; John W. Harbeson, Trip Report, May 22–28, 1995, USAID Nairobi; and Dale Pfeiffer, Neo Simutanyi, and John Holm, *Zambia Democratic Governance Project: Final Evaluation*, AID, Zambia, March 14, 1997.

16. Handwritten notes, Mangango Workshop, July 17, 1996.

17. The Reverend Sakala to the author, August 21, 1995; Stepanek to FODEP, letter of October 16, 1995 reducing AID support; and Paige Hull and Richard Holloway, *Depending on Ourselves: Zambian Experiences in Domestic Fund Mobilization*, PACT, Resource Paper 4, July 1996.

18. Stepanek, memorandum, *The U.S. Mission in Zambia—Discussion of Options and Recommendations*, May 30, 1996; "US Government Cuts Aid to Zambia," *The Post*, July 17, 1996; and USAID letter to the Speaker of the National Assembly, January 17, 1995.

19. Michele Polhemus, personal communication, December 12, 1997.

20. Robert Klitgaard, "International Cooperation Against Corruption," *Finance and Development*, March 1998, p. 4.

21. Department of State, Bureau of Intelligence and Research, *African Democratization: The Need for Workable Political Models*, May 11, 1995.

22. Dean Mung'omba, President of the new Zambia Democratic Congress Party, in a meeting with diplomats, February 2, 1996.

23. Kasuka S. Matukwa, at February 2, 1996 meeting.

24. See Joseph Schumpeter, *Capitalism, Socialism and Democracy*, New York: Harper, 1942; John Rogers Commons, *The Legal Foundations of Capitalism*, New York, Macmillan, 1924; and Francis Fukuyama, "The End of History?" *National Interest,* 16 (Summer), 1989, and his *The End of History and the Last Man,* New York: Free Press, 1992

25. Friedrick August von Hayek, *The Road to Serfdom*, University of Chicago Press, 1944. As shown in chapter 7, the evidence is now conclusive that growth alleviates poverty. Perhaps soon evidence will also document that democracy promotes growth and poverty alleviation as well. For early evidence from the trade union movement, see Thomas I. Paley, AFL-CIO, *The Beneficial Effect of Core Labor Standards on Growth*, Washington, D.C., draft, undated. See also Michael A. Nelson and Ram D. Singh, "Democracy, Economic Freedom, Fiscal Policy, and Growth in LDCs: A Fresh Look," *Economic Development and Cultural Change*, 46:4, July 1998, pp. 677–96.

26. Lise Rakner, p. 28.

27. Thomas Carothers, Carnegie Endowment for International Peace, personal communication, June 4, 1997.

28. Jerry Wolgin, "New Wine, New Bottles: A New Paradigm For African Development," in *USAID Presentations at African Studies Association Meeting*, Toronto, November 3–6, 1994.

29. Lise Rakner, p. 33.

30. Lisa Peterson, *Consolidating Democracy: Lessons We Are Learning from the Results of USAID Democratic Governance Programs in Africa*, Conference in Johannesburg, final report, April 23–25, 1996.

31. Edward Jaycox, World Bank Vice President for Africa, press briefing, June 14, 1995.

32. "Corruption undermines aid, says Wolfensohn," *The Financial Times*, May 7, 1996.

33. World Bank, IDA, *Articles of Agreement*, Section 6 (amended as of September 24, 1960) and the IBRD, Section 10, which contains similar wording.

34. In FY 1998 the World Bank committed $122 million as grants, or 0.6 percent of total IBRD and IDA loan commitments of $19.4 billion. Personal communication, June 23, 1998.

35. Conversation with the late Baldwin Nkumbula, the president of the National Party, and James Polhemus, Lusaka, February 2, 1995.

36. George B. N. Ayittey, *The Wall Street Journal,* March 23, 1994.

37. Letter from Ambassador Edmund DeJarnette to Assistant Secretary of State Hank Cohen, May 4, 1990.

38. Paraphrased from William Pierson, editor, *Concept Paper for a USAID Strategy in West and Central Africa*, Abidjan, Côte d'Ivoire: USAID, December 20, 1996, pp. 6–7.

39. "The rulers, the ruled and the African reality," *The Economist*, September 20, 1997, p. 49.

40.   From "Structural Adjustment in Sub-Saharan Africa: Research and Policy Issues," *Poverty and Development—Analysis and Policy,* Ministry of Foreign Affairs, The Netherlands, September 1994, p. 99.

ANNEX

Managing Decentralization—Sustainable Wildlife Use: An Example from Zambia

African countries are working to integrate support for wildlife preservation with local community interests so that rural residents find that wildlife preservation and economic reward go together. Several countries have community-based conservation programs. The Zambian government is implementing a form of political and economic decentralization in support of wildlife, not unlike the decentralization of the Tanzanian roads program and the Zambian health reform program.

Environmentalists have learned that communities bordering national parks and forests must have a stake in the sustainable development of these resources. Zambia is testing a model of devolution for sustainable resource management, which may prove to be good economics and good politics.

Zambia has nineteen national parks that cover 8 percent of the country's area. These in turn are surrounded by thirty-three game management areas (GMAs) for an added 22 percent of the country—which protect the parks as buffer zones. There are villages in these GMAs but not in the parks. By tradition and law, game may be hunted in the GMAs but not in the parks. A third of the country, covering 1.1 million people, has protected status.

The GMA program, Administrative Management Design for Game Management Areas (ADMADE), comes under the Ministry of Tourism, Department of National Parks and Wildlife Services. During an earlier time government had unquestioned authority and capability to administer national parks and other lands held in trust.

Concern for good park management arose because of widespread poaching, which has led in turn to better understandings of the motives behind village-level and large-scale poaching and to local communities and their interests. Today, ADMADE focuses on the preservation of wildlife for viewing and for sustainable hunting. Fees for hunting, some of which are earned from international trophy hunting, are shared with GMA communities, and can be used for locally determined infrastructure projects such as roads, bridges, schools, and clinics.

Hunting licenses and trophy fees can be considerable: for a leopard, cheetah, or lion, they can be $1,500 each; for a giraffe they can cost $2,500. (Elephants cannot be hunted legally in Zambia.) Furthermore, it is important to recognize that individual GMAs set trophy limits on the basis of sustainable yields for trophy-quality hunting. ADMADE therefore links up-scale hunting, local hunting for village food, and general tourism with the interests of the community. Thirty-five percent of gross revenue from fees are shared with communities in the GMAs, and an additional 40 percent supports a system of village game scouts.

Comanagement, revenue sharing, and local ownership are at the heart of this successful model-in-the-making. Because of governmental policy seriousness and the inclusion and training of traditional leaders and game scouts, wildlife management responsibility is beginning to rest with the community where it belongs by statute. Technical and community training takes place at the Nyamaluma Research and Training Center, located on the banks of the remote Luangwa River, in the wilds of eastern Zambia. Village leaders and scouts are trained there and initial recommendations are made on animal quotas. With the encouragement of the National Parks Department, Nyamaluma, under the local leadership of Dale Lewis and his wife Julia Nagata, has grown into a regionally recognized training and research center.

Sources: Jim Billings, *Suitable Community-Based Wildlife Management Mechanism*, a report to USAID and The Ministry of Tourism's Department of National Parks and Wildlife Services, October 17, 1994; Irving Rosenthal and Frederick W. Sowers, *Natural Resources Management Project—Zambia Component of Southern Africa Regional Project*, August 23, 1995; Dale Lewis and Nick Carter, *Voices From Africa—Local Perspectives on Conservation*, Washington, D.C.: World Wildlife Fund, 1993; and Guy Scott, *An Evaluation of the ADMADE Programme*, January–February 1998, Lusaka: Mano Consultancy Services.

9

Master of Their Own House: African Training and Western Advice

MANPOWER IN THE PROMISED LAND
—RETHINKING TRAINING IN TANZANIA

Imagine an educational philosophy that stops children from going on to high school. Or a development philosophy that stops the growth of a middle class. Or a national policy that is predicated on a foreign minority handling the so-called dirty business of business. These policies are all unthinkable today, but they were central to Tanzania's socialist promise in the 1960s and 1970s.

Tanzania was to be run by planners according to plan priorities. To fill a handful of planning positions, only a few children would need training beyond primary school. All other children would grow to adulthood in cooperative villages, or *ujama* communities. As for Tanzania's work-a-day world of business—the dirty work of trading, importing, wholesaling, and retailing—that would be done by Tanzanian Asians.

That was the socialist dream of *mwalimu* Julius Nyerere, Tanzania's founder. (*Mwalimu* is an honorific Kiswahili word for teacher.) It did not all happen this way, of course, but Nyerere implemented portions of his vision and they define Tanzania today.

What was once an experiment caused ruin for a generation. Secondary school enrollment in Tanzania remains the lowest in the world—at 5 percent of the relevant age group as recently as 1993.[1] Now Tanzania is too poor to catch up; an ironic—even bitter—legacy for a state that was committed to the well-being of its people.

Africa's training objectives have not been achieved for a variety of reasons, partly in the name of equality and a philosophical bias against advanced degree training for individuals. Late-developing countries have assumed all along that they could train their own people. There was no lack of dedicated people willing to work for government. But all of the overseas and in-country training failed to create the cadre of people who were deemed necessary for designing and implementing publicly directed development. Today we see the cost of this failure.

In the 1990s few donor-funded projects function without a long-term foreign advisor to manage and protect the donor's interest. African governments gradually have come to rely on foreign advisors to help achieve promised plans, and they find, as with financial assistance, that they have become dependent on foreigners. African governments have come to rely on upward of 50,000 to 60,000 expatriates.[2] Most ministries function because of foreigners who come to advise and stay to manage.

Foreign training and foreign advisors were seen much like foreign aid generally—as a temporary measure, filling a talent gap, if you will, until Africa could get on its feet. In reality, western training and advice failed. My penultimate chapter is about the late-developing world's efforts to train its people—to be masters of their own houses. Ownership of development requires millions of trained people—all with primary schooling, most with secondary schooling, and many with advanced degrees. As with my previous chapters, I examine successes and failures, and conclude that there is still much to be done. Again we find lessons to learn, accept, and apply.

Defining Western Technical Assistance and Training

The phrase *technical assistance* has been used throughout the fifty-year development era. It includes all forms of technical transfers from the developed world to the developing world. Technical assistance encompasses scientific and technical subjects; the social sciences; legal, administrative, and management matters; and communications and infrastructure. Much of the advice and training is scientific and technical, but a growing portion is about democratic values and procedures.

Technical assistance is provided by westerners through universities, companies, and meetings, and through all forms of personal and electronic communication. Western training and advice is designed to train people and strengthen institutions. Training and advice can enlarge poor-world capacity and ownership.

Under President Harry S Truman's Point Four Program in 1949, American technical assistance became a major contributor to development. It was an age of high idealism. American advice and training could meet obvious needs. For many countries it worked well. All donors today, including the World Bank and many NGOs, provide training and advice to serve multiple development objectives. As we shall see, it is nearly impossible for a developing country to make use of outside advice without there being an educated public to accept it.

THE TRAINED AND MOTIVATED INDIVIDUAL —ONE KEY TO DEVELOPMENT

It is striking how little attention has been paid by development theorists and policy-makers to the role of the individual. Yet development experts have known all along from evaluations and experience that a handful of poor-world officials play major roles in creating development successes. A few case studies illustrate this point.

Education was an important contribution to development in East and Southeast Asia. In the early 1950s the noted economist Simon Kuznets pointed out that input-output analysis, an economist's methodological mainstay, did not explain America's record of growth. The iron and steel revolution did not explain very much. How did America grow? We now know that our growth is explained largely by our investments in human resources, such as education, skills, knowledge, organization, and drive.[3] In 1961 Theodore W. Schultz, a noted American economist, wrote about the primacy of education for development:

Economists have long known that people are an important part of the wealth of nations . . . the productive capacity of human beings is now vastly larger than all other forms of wealth taken together. What economists have not stressed is the simple truth that people invest in themselves and that these investments are very large. By investing in themselves, people can enlarge the range of choice available to them. The notion of labor . . . as manual work only . . . was wrong in the classical period and it is patently wrong now. Laborers have become capitalists not from a diffusion of the ownership of corporation stocks, but from the acquisition of knowledge and skill that have economic value. It simply is not possible to have the fruits of a modern agriculture and the abundance of modern industry without making large investments in human beings.[4]

True then, and true today. In the developing world primary education continues to be the number one investment priority.[5] This investment is being made in almost all countries; primary education is nearly universal. The payoff of education in developing countries is high: studies document a return of 27 percent for primary education and 16 percent for secondary education.[6]

Education has been further appreciated for its contribution to the well-being of women. Women with some primary education have fewer births and take better care of their children, their nutrition, and their health. Women with an education take better care of their fields and seed stock. Their unpaid contributions to child-rearing, carrying of firewood and water, food preparation, and health care helps keep poor families—and countries—functioning.

The returns on investment in women's education is higher for secondary schooling than they are for men. This is because of women's heretofore unrecognized household and farm contributions, and because of educational underinvestment in the past. In Asia women receive only 60 percent of the education that men receive. In Africa women receive even less than that, but when they leave home to go to school or to work elsewhere, the household and farm can suffer. The noted French economist, René Dumont, saw this for Africa: "If your sister goes to school, you won't have anything to eat."[7]

An East African comparative educational assessment—in Kenya and Tanzania—by John Knight and Richard Sabot, sheds light on contrasting educational philosophies.[8] As one would expect, the social returns from primary and secondary schooling were found to be high in both countries. With a closer look, however, sharp differences become apparent. Tanzania directed its educational system to train and assign only a few students to meet public manpower requirements. The government did this in order to reduce elitism and the tendency for schooling to promote inequality and class formation.

Kenya's educational philosophy was more responsive to parental and societal demands. Kenya practiced an expansive educational policy rather than a public-sector directed manpower policy. Restraining secondary school enrollment, Knight and Sabot found, actually contributed to social class stratification in Tanzania. Furthermore, and contrary to Tanzania's policy intention, the poor and uneducated in Kenya had easier access to education. A policy of equity led to extreme inequality in Tanzania; in Kenya, a commitment to primary and secondary schooling led to growth and equality. Many of Tanzania's present problems are attributable to Julius Nyerere's decision to constrain public education.

The Entrepreneurial Individual

In the decades-long debate over the value of markets versus public planning, mainstream theorists and practioners gave some attention to education generally, but little to the individual entrepreneur and his motivation.

Who actually does the enabling once there is an enabling environment? How do individuals choose what they do in society, in the market place, even in government? Does motivation explain development?

Social anthropologists and sociologists know a good deal about entrepreneurial spirit.[9] Some theorists place entrepreneurship at the door of society at large. Cultures forge individuals into being risk-, work-, or savings-oriented. Other theorists believe that parents shape their childrens' aspirations, particularly in education, and economic and social achievement. For Asian and European cultures, both the individual and society are seen as being work- and savings-oriented. For Latin America and possibly Africa, colonial, landed, and tribal enclaves and cultures are seen as less given to an individual work ethic to achieve material gain throughout society and across generations.

Although entrepreneurial talent is present in all societies, it actually occurs in relatively few people. Whether in the rich West or in the poor world, it takes only a few among us—one in a thousand, perhaps fewer—to be entrepreneurial, to translate motivation into business and employment impact. This behavior in most societies is what enables markets to function. The rest of us find private employment in a world that is created largely by entrepreneurs. Individuals must have an enabling environment in which to work. If we jeopardize the work-a-day world for a few, we place economies at risk.

Advanced training, and individual motivation and its effect on achievement have largely been ignored by development economists, aid practioners, and recipient governments. I can speculate as to the reasons for this.

First, economists appear to have ignored entrepreneurial behavior because the subject is analyzed and prescribed by other social and behavioral scientists, and also because economists believe intuitively that getting prices right will free talent in any event (and over the long term). The sociologist, Max Weber, wrote of capitalism and the Protestant work ethic in the 1930s. Joseph Schumpeter was one of the first economists (and one of but a few) to write about the human spirit as the motivator of capital accumulation.[10] Most economists assume the existence of entrepreneurial behavior and so ignore it; they believe the real issue is whether markets are free or controlled. Perhaps economists have believed that business could not be entrepreneurial within controlled economies. Only recently have economists talked about enabling in Africa.

The second reason is that donors themselves have been biased on this issue. Advanced-degree training smacks of entrepreneurial and professional elitism. Donor-funded degree training has helped many people but the cost has been high and the rewards to society have been viewed as too low and too distant. The world's poor need to be helped immediately.

Also, many foreign students stay in their host countries or find jobs with international organizations. Entrepreneurs and trained people might understandably argue that they have been driven away from their home countries because their governments have not been committed to professionalism, national budgets have been strapped for decades, and salaries and conditions of their civil services have deteriorated year after year.

Third, all countries have entrepreneurs, most of whom are, by definition, minorities. They vitalize economic life but are blamed for being excessively successful and reclusive. Each developing country has its own unique experience in this regard. All African countries have minority groups, such as the ethnic Indians, Greeks, Lebanese, Europeans, and other Africans (who are not always in power). These groups continue to face discriminatory practices and laws that prevent their being active investors and political participants. Development openness and ownership should embrace these minorities as it does the majority.

REVIEW OF AMERICAN TRAINING FOR ASIA AND AFRICA

America offered training to Asian and Latin American countries, whereas Africa was almost entirely ignored. Asia and Latin America are masters of their own houses. But it is not too late for Tanzania to learn that it takes bright individuals and a vibrant middle class to create jobs for Tanzania's younger generation of job-seekers.

The Fulbright Scholarship Program celebrated its fiftieth year in 1997 and the lesser known Agricultural Development Council (ADC), founded by David Rockefeller, has served Asian agriculture.

Ninety-thousand Fulbright scholars from the United States have lived and studied in 140 countries, and 120,000 foreign national Fulbright scholars have come to the United States to study and teach. Senator William Fulbright was convinced that by such exchanges all nationalities would see that there are equally valid ways of looking at the world. He also sought to train future leaders: "The Senator often emphasized that his scholarship program was openly and blatantly designed for an intelligent elite. He wanted the most alert, energetic, potential leaders in all disciplines and walks of life to experience the development and expansion of mind that one cannot avoid when studying in another culture."[11]

American Training for Asians

David Rockefeller, on a trip to Asia in the early 1950s, concluded that the recovery from World War II needed dynamic agriculture and family planning, and so founded the ADC and the Population Council. The Rockefeller Foundation funded masters and doctoral training for a generation of Asian scientists starting in the 1960s. Abe Weisblat, who guided training for ADC for twenty-seven years, was asked to assess the training that Asians had received courtesy of the Rockefeller and Ford Foundations, the International Development Research Centre of Canada, and AID. Weisblat studied 944 Asian men and women who had studied in the United States and Canada. Fifty-five percent had been trained in economics, 12 percent in sociology, and the remainder had studied other social sciences. Eighty to 95 percent had returned home, 56 percent said they worked in colleges and universities, 16 percent said they worked in research institutions, and 15 percent worked in government service. Their titles revealed their impact: presidents of countries; and presidents, rectors, and deans of universities and institutes. More than 80 percent said that their training had been valuable or extremely valuable. The proportion of women in ADC programs had increased from 12 percent before 1970 to 19 percent in 1985. All of the Asian employers of the ADC graduates agreed that the advanced degrees were very useful; there was no other way to obtain these numbers of higher degrees. American training, according to Weisblat, helped strengthen educational and research institutions in several Asian countries and helped found their green and health revolutions. A grandfatherly Abe Weisblat summed up this historic training experience by saying, "These ADC graduates run Asia now. Children do grow up, they know more than we do, they get together and work jointly."[12]

Rice and a New Vietnam Story

Vietnam's leaders are experimenting with economic liberalization. They are reentering Asian markets and are leading off with the country's rice exports. This story, new in the 1990s, describes an example of the continuing tradition of effective technical assistance.

IFPRI is acting as advisor, analyst, and trainer for Vietnam's senior policy-makers and junior analytical staff. IFPRI was asked by the Vietnamese government, with funding from the Asian Development Bank, to help the government to quantify domestic and trade options and priorities in order to enhance rice export earnings.

Joint analyses by IFPRI and Vietnamese experts revealed large potential increases for domestic production and export expansion as well as welfare benefits. Options costed out by government staff with the help of IFPRI analysts yielded social savings and positive social benefits far greater than had been anticipated. Each option proposed held positive implications for the country's gradual liberalization of its agricultural, marketing, and trade sectors. The government has already liberalized the internal rice trade, decentralized rice exports, and opened competition between state exporters and provincial enterprises. This example of jointly conducted policy learning illustrates the continuing relevance of advisory services in late-developing countries. IFPRI's analytical rigor and focus on food security issues, combined with its cultural and collegial sensitivity, ensured that the Vietnamese would own their project at the outset. Vietnam's junior staff were trained in theory, modeling, and computer applications, which enabled them to knowledgeably discuss issues with senior staff.[13]

The story of western training could be extended to Latin America, which would help to explain the gradual liberalization of their protected economies.[14] But as I have already taken the reader on too many meanderings, we return to Africa to stay.

Kenya and the "Kennedy Airlift"

The only memorable American training program in Africa was the "Kennedy Airlift" of the late 1950s and early 1960s. When Kenya was about to become independent in 1963, Tom Mboya, Kenya's brightest political star and Secretary General of the Kenya Federation of Labour, saw the need for trained people. Mboya traveled frequently to the United States, and won then-Senator John Kennedy's support for a training program that soon carried the Kennedy name. The Kennedy Airlift brought 300 young Kenyans and a few Tanzanian and Ugandan students to the United States. American businessmen paid for the Kennedy Airlift tickets; American universities donated the scholarships.

At the time, Makerere University College near Kampala, Uganda, was the only university in East Africa, and only one of ten in all of sub-Saharan Africa. Of all foreign students in the United States during the period 1948 through 1958, only 1.2 percent were Africans. In the decade leading up to the Airlift, American university grants to Africans numbered 206—in total!

Senator Kennedy gave personal support and later Kennedy Foundation money. The Aga Khan contributed, and Mrs. Ralph Bunche, Harry Belfonte, Sidney Poitier, and Jackie Robinson were fund-raisers. The student list from the time now reads like a *Who's Who* of today's prominent Kenyans.[15]

Western Technical Assistance for Africa
—a Disaster for Decades

Dozens of experts and evaluations document that western training and technical assistance for Africa has been a major waste of money and talent. State planning might explain Africa's inability to mobilize and use her people as effectively as did Asia. Even the World Bank has come to view technical assistance in Africa as a failure. Edward Jaycox, retired vice-president for the Bank's Africa operations, states flatly:

Donors and African governments together have undermined capacity in Africa; they are undermining it faster than they are building it, or at least as fast. . . . African governments, in many cases, have pushed away professional talent that was trained at very, very high cost. . . . There's been an amazing brain drain from Africa. . . . Ethnicity has also gotten in the way of professionalism in Africa. People have been excluded; people have been thrown away . . . when political power has been monopolized . . . there is no room for professional growth. . . . On the donor side, they tend to use expatriate resident technical assistance to solve all kinds of problems . . . this is a systematic, destructive force [that] is undermining the development capacity in Africa . . . expatriate management substituting for domestic management.[16]

Elliot Berg, a development economist, noted that western technical assistance in Africa has been nearly a third of aid overall, and that it has been ineffectively utilized. The total spent for technical assistance in all forms was $3.2 billion to as much as $4 billion *a year* during the late 1980s and early 1990s.[17]

Berg identifies, as have many others, the arguments on both sides of a heated debate. African governments believe this form of aid is costly, which it is, and that it is a condition of a donor's overall assistance, which is often the case. African government officials justifiably grumble: Just give us the money and we'll hire our own advisors. You are paying yourselves often as much as $300,000 per year per consultant, ten times what our ministers make. Your overhead costs can run a startlingly 240 percent of direct project costs and we do not see a dime of it. You keep your own people employed and your offices open at our expense. You come to advise and stay on as managers, often for years, displacing our own people who were assigned to work with you. It is no wonder our new Ph.D.'s stay away.

Explaining by use of an African analogy, an African minister of health relates a tale of an old woman who tells her granddaughter of a marriage between an African woman and a foreign advisor:

Grandma, tell me about the joy of partnership and self-reliance the granddaughter asks. She replies: He will ask for your hand, he will speak of real collaboration, but then he will insist that to find out how compatible you really are, he will ask how many men (other donor collaborators) you have had in the past. He will impregnate you by artificial insemination with a possibly malnourished sperm and hope you bear his baby out of wedlock. He will leave you to attend antenatal clinics, but he won't drive you there. During your pregnancy he will start looking for another collaborator, probably from a newly independent or democratic country, like South Africa. And at the Men's Club where he drinks—they call it the Paris Club—he will discuss you in bad taste and praise highly the idea of his new collaborator. If you are lucky, you will deliver something he can appreciate, but if you deliver a disabled child, it will be all your fault and he will say you have a problem of absorption capacity.[18]

The reality of high cost and low effectiveness of technical assistance is amply described in the following letter. It is so harsh that I disguise its origins. An African minister appeals to his president:

The project we contracted with them out of the donor grant was not well executed . . . and I am certainly technically competent enough to judge that they have no experience or expertise. We seek value for money . . . our people are dying . . . while they have been making big bucks out of money intended to help build local capacity for prevention. I do not accept the "second chance" argument (from the western contractor) because our people do not get a second chance because we fail to reach them. It is scandalous that we could even allow them to come and lobby you, sir, for an extension given their track record.[19]

Donors, in turn, claim that African governments cannot manage projects well or account for aid funding or materials. Africans, they say, only want the cash, the overseas trips, and the new vehicles. To get anything done, donors believe they have to be on the ground. How can Africans ever own and run these projects if they will not help themselves, the donors wonder. They have our money for aid advisors, but will not hire their own able staff people. Many government staff are in fact ghost workers; someone else higher up collects their salary. Donors know that African governments often hire foreigners because they do not trust their own professionals (who may be from the wrong tribe). All these problems are complicated by the Kenyan government (or Tanzanian or Zambian) policy of hiring every university graduate.

Conflicts can become heated. Kenyan economists finally revolted in the 1980s. Their senior officers and economists met with the Principal Secretary of the Ministry of Finance to discuss grievances over reliance on foreign economists:

The foreigners get the most interesting tasks, the Kenyans are treated as junior staff and there is little or no opportunity for advancement within the government. Twenty-five hundred expatriates are in Kenya. Twenty-five or so play very senior roles within the Office of the President, Treasury, and Ministry of Agriculture. They do all the important drafting of options, analyses, and policies. A wall has been built around the seniormost Kenyan officials that prevents the Kenyan staff from getting close to their own Principal Secretary. Kenyan counterparts are mere clerks.[20]

Western advisors are often protected by their positions, which are well hidden within African government structures, where they are famed for helping to manage, in a few notable cases, the authoritarian African state. They are so well protected by their positions that their own evaluations do not pick up on internal tensions. Contract renewals come first. They protect their turf and go so far as to call (privately that is) their own evaluations a whitewash.[21]

"I believe," says a UNICEF expert quoted in Berg's study, "that the vast bulk of technical experts and expertise at present provided by the United Nations and donors have outlived their usefulness." For Tanzania in 1988 (and as remains true today), a DANIDA study estimated that $300 million was spent for 1,000 or so consultants, of which $200 million was for their western salaries and per diems, housing, air travel, and education allowances. Tanzania saw none of this $200 million, and gained little from the other $100 million spent in Tanzania. Most of this aid was financed by the Scandinavian countries and they in turn are harsh on all parties in their evaluations.[22]

The same general criticism can be leveled at the World Bank's operations in Africa (as noted in the DANIDA study). Only one quarter of the Bank's institution-building projects have had their intended impact. For other loans exclusively for technical assistance, 42 percent have had negligible impact.

Donors must be candid yet balanced about their commitment to African ownership of African development. Much of the West's advisory assistance is designed to police project implementation schedules and to account for money and materials, and yet these requirements become self-defeating. Africa is weak in its design and implementation of development projects, yet donors press Africa with more money for less government. Civil service reform—smaller and leaner government—is expected to accomplish the impossible.[23] How can African governments and donors move beyond this standoff?

GRAPPLING WITH SOLUTIONS FOR AFRICA

A senior Kenyan civil servant, Harris Mule, speaks for Africa:

First, Africa must ensure good governance practices that emphasize transparency and accountability, and demonstrate commitment to comprehensive political reform. Then we must professionalize and depolitize the civil service. Nevertheless there is a gap between the declared aims of the World Bank in Africa on capacity building, and results on the ground. Instead of transferring expertise, this approach has created a dependency upon foreign experts. The Bank must develop a corporate culture that is not dominated by . . . hierarchy, control, and the imposition of conditions. . . . The Bank must abandon a corporate culture that commends the rapid approval of loans, and which is overly concerned with the volume of lending.[24]

Mule's advice applies to all donors. It is in this contentious environment that Africa is struggling to implement economic reform and experiment with democracy. To help Africa develop, portions of donor contributions, such as training and advice, necessarily presume that all other portions—the economic, the democratic, agriculture, and health—are developing as well.

Donors Struggle Once Again to Be Effective

Donors are learning how to provide training to Africans. Here I offer AID-funded success stories. Actually, these are partial successes; only time will prove their relevance and sustainability. Donors must be optimistic but not naive.

In the late 1980s donors returned to Tanzania to support its economic reform program, which it agreed to with the IMF and the World Bank. AID reopened its office. Reform created an opportunity for some educational experimentation for the individual, for merit-based training, and for official recognition of a de facto middle class. While the government, Scandinavian countries, and the United Nations still promoted manpower plans, a few donors started to select and train individuals on the basis of merit and ambition. By the early 1990s it was clear to a few experts in and out of government that able people were needed in large numbers to run the country.

Tanzania relied on AID and other donors to train the manpower of the Tanzanian public sector in the 1960s and 1970s. AID trained staff people in the ministries of agriculture and finance and the Central Bank of Tanzania. But in time we found that training everyone in the public structure did not work very well. AID had been training masters and doctoral candidates for years, many of whom had been waiting for years for that chance to earn their advanced degrees.

Neither domestic nor foreign training worked well. The Tanzania economy in the 1970s and 1980s was deteriorating; few foreign-trained professionals returned to their assigned responsibilities. Many manpower boxes stayed empty—or at least empty of seriousness.

The newly reopened AID mission to Tanzania thought of a different way to spend scarce training money. By the 1990s an American Ph.D. cost upward of $250,000 for a four-year program. This expense is difficult to justify even when successful candidates return home. Ability, not position, became our guide. We thought we knew of a way to ensure that able students would return home.

When AID announced its merit-based, competitive scholarship program in Tanzania, we upset the manpower approach to training more than we realized. The Tanzanian government selected candidates for advanced degree training according to a person's existing position and influence within the system. Ability and performance were often of secondary importance. For the few women who earned advanced degrees overseas, sexual favors were often demanded of them by the controlling officers in the government.

When word got around that AID was changing its training philosophy, the training officers of the Ministry of Finance and the Bank of Tanzania came to see me within a week of each other to voice their official protest and disappointment. Each woman gave me the official arguments for maintaining the old ways—but upon leaving my office, each in turn whispered, "Thank you!"

Boulder's Economics Institute Creates Opportunity for Tanzanians

AID was determined to make sure that able Tanzanians returned to Tanzania to work. The Tanzanian-AID scholarship program had its roots in Boulder, Colorado, thirty years ago.

The Economics Institute was founded in 1958, in Madison, Wisconsin, by Professor Wyn F. Owen of the University of Colorado's Department of Economics. A year later the Institute was moved to Boulder, with the support of the American Economics Association and the University of Colorado. The seminal idea was to offer summer refresher courses for incoming foreign students who were beginning masters and doctoral programs in economics, agricultural economics, and business administration. Refresher courses in English, economics, statistics, and math seemed like the right idea. With a summer's worth of individually tailored refresher training based on a battery of individual tests, new students would be better prepared for graduate training. Besides, a summer of American hospitality in Boulder would help the adjustment to student life.

From modest beginnings, the Institute grew into a full-year program offering a range of specialized courses for mid-career professionals from around the world as well as preparatory courses, of up to a year, and placement for incoming students.

In any one year the Economics Institute has 700 or so students and professionals from forty countries or more in intensive course work. By the late 1990s the Institute had welcomed more than 12,000 students from 160 countries who went on to earn advanced degrees in more than 100 American and Canadian universities. Almost all of these graduates returned to serve their countries. The Institute remains unique for its individually tailored course work.

To reach more students and to reduce cost, the Institute has offered refresher courses in Indonesia, Malaysia, Mongolia, South Korea, Venezuela, and Vietnam. These have been supported in part by host governments that see the payoff in the form of professionalism. A mini Economics Institute remains in the planning stage for Africa.

In addition to the obvious benefit of refresher training, the Institute began to provide more subtle contributions as it gained experience. Selecting the right candidate is the first key to training success. One lesson the Institute has learned is to select candidates from among those who are already employed in their home country. Having a job back home indicates motivation, ability, and relevance. It also fosters the competitive spirit needed to succeed in graduate school. Also, because a sponsoring institution is usually stuck with a returnee, they also have a major interest in the person's success.

The Institute's summer program cost is high, around $6,000 for a ten-week course, but this can be justified. Institute graduates earn their advanced degrees in less time than other incoming foreign students who have not received refresher courses. Also, Institute courses enable many incoming students to win exemption from basic courses once they are in graduate school. The Institute supports its students throughout their graduate work after leaving Boulder, which ensures a greater chance of success. Failing students are dissuaded from further studies and are sent home at an early date with a certificate of achievement. The Institute has been able to accept students without onward graduate school placement, and to place them in top-rank schools.

The most valuable lesson of all has to do with selection criteria. The Institute has learned that English proficiency, while desirable, is not necessarily a good proxy for ability. Because governments, universities, and donors have historically accepted candidates from the developing world who spoke English or French, there has been a built-in bias in favor of upper-class backgrounds. English ability should be but one of several selection criteria, not the primary one.

The Institute's best test of this thesis came with the Mexican government's commitment to send 600 of its young professionals to the Institute for preparatory course work and graduate degrees in American universities. Mexico sought to turn its new-found oil revenues in the mid-1970s into wealth of a lasting kind. The Institute pledged to train and place these students, provided that their scholastic aptitude and selection were not based heavily on English ability. Students with poor English but who otherwise showed promise were accepted. At the end of this experiment, the Mexican students as a group performed as well as incoming Japanese students, although they required extra time at the Institute.

English and subject matter deficits can be made up in time provided that high-potential students are selected in the first place. Twenty to thirty weeks of intensive training can earn a bachelors degree, even with a language handicap at the outset.[25]

A Scholarship Program for Tanzanians

Tanzania had turned its back on the West for nearly twenty years. There was plenty of lingering suspicion of the United States, at least among the older socialist diehards. Few Tanzanians would admit to it, but their country was starved for ideas and professional contacts of all kinds.

Manpower training was out; there was already enough of it within other AID projects. Upon arriving in Dar es Salaam in 1987, I found that there were too many stories circulating about nonperformers receiving costly training, of Tanzanians not returning home, and of women being denied training altogether.

How were we supposed to identify those Tanzanians who would make the most of further training? Providing Africans with exposure to the United States was admittedly one motive. We decided to offer advanced degree training in the United States to Tanzanians in specified development fields. We would trade manpower studies and government positions for able individuals who were working in Tanzania. We would select them without regard to present position or future assignment in Tanzania. We assumed that well-motivated individuals, with additional training, would find their own way to contribute to Tanzania's development.

The AID mission was determined to keep candidate selection out of the hands of government, as is the case for all donor-funded projects. Wyn Owen suggested that we just advertise scholarships in Tanzania's newspapers, and so we did. Large ads appeared in the newspapers across Tanzania in early 1989. They became the talk in the tea shops, particularly for the phrase: "Women are strongly encouraged to apply."

I had obtained an approval signature for this experiment from Peter Ngumbulu, Deputy Principal Secretary in the Ministry of Finance, Economic Affairs, and Planning (and a graduate of the Economics Institute and Williams College). AID established topic priorities for training, selection criteria, and a selection committee, and then published the ads nationwide. We expected 300 to 400 responses, which, given the budget, would have to be pruned sharply to just a handful of successful applicants. A few weeks later, in June of 1989, our mailroom was flooded with 4,500 responses from all twenty regions of Tanzania.

To ensure fairness the selection committee of six consisted of men and women from public and private backgrounds, and from the AID mission. Candidate applications were assessed using points, and finalists were assessed again during face-to-face interviews. At the end of the candidate selection process we found that half of the awardees for scholarships were women, even though their applications had not been weighted.

We had the fortuitous flexibility to raise the budget to $3 million by the beginning of the second year. We also were able to employ the administrative procedures of existing worldwide AID training programs, and remodeled them to suit a Tanzanian purpose.[26]

Risk-taking paid off. We learned how biases against training women could be set aside. We learned that Tanzania's best people can be selected, that their commitment to their country's development can be assessed, and that they do return home to continue their work. We also learned that able women are eager for further training. They, not AID or the government, determined their best career path.

Because of the nature and cost of long-term training, it is too early to say whether returnees will indeed contribute to Tanzania's development. Some returnees appear to be joining the seminar and foreign conference "industry" instead of employing their new skills. Perhaps they could not find challenging and remunerative work. Graduates are returning to a still-troubled economy and workplace. Perhaps Tanzania's enabling environment is not enabling its citizens fast enough.

This scholarship pilot did win one Tanzanian supporter in private business. A leading businessman, Mustafar Jaffar, a Tanzanian Asian, sought to train six of his own employees in industrialization, finance, and international export marketing at the Economics Institute. When he expanded his training offer to the Tanzanian public; more than sixty applied. However, this parallel effort did not win government approval.

Zambian Small Business Training

As in Tanzania, years of state control in Zambia had taken their toll on private enterprise. Partially because of a stagnant formal sector and nearly 300 stagnant state companies and firms, the informal sector had come to life out of necessity as Zambians sought income in any manner to put food on the table.

More so than in Tanzania, educated Zambians had fled their country. Justifying AID funding for advanced training in the United States would be an uphill battle. My Lusaka staff said, "No way, José." Besides, they already had an idea for training Zambians in Zambia.

Manufacturing had declined but trade was picking up. Some bank credit was becoming available. Most price controls on business had been removed. Open-air markets were busy and the informal sector and the grain trade started to boom. Informal retail outlets for fresh food and used clothing sprang up across Zambia; private transporters and retailers operated everywhere. New economic policies were being kept in place. A bustling informal sector gave hope that the formal sector would start to move as well.

The AID mission sought to be supportive of private enterprise, the smaller the better. Again the mission tried a pilot project, this time for short courses in Zambia on modern business practices. Again we advertised, as we had done in Tanzania. If no one responded to an offer of business training, that would be a clear enough signal that it wasn't needed. Through newspaper ads we encouraged small and medium-size business owners to apply for one- and two-week courses in accounting, management planning, marketing, business contracting, and quality and cost control. The demand for short business courses far surpassed our expectations. Andrews Hotel near Lusaka became a bustling training center.

On field trips I kept meeting men and women who had had a week or two of AID-supported training. One trainee was able to land two major international tenders because of the preparation and planning techniques he learned at an Andrews Hotel course. Another trainee, the owner of the

Northwestern Bee Products Company, started exporting natural honey and beeswax.

A closed economy was opening up even for small businesses. Some of this expansion was made possible by getting informal businesspeople to face bankers and win loan approvals from commercial banks. Facing an actual bank official in an Andrews Hotel session took the mystery out of bank loans.

AID offered an international tender to assess this small business training. A local firm, M and N Associates, run by a former AID partici-pant, won the bid. Their evaluation was reassuring: Between 1991 and 1993 the training courses had reached 572 enterprising people, more than half of whom were women. From 1993 to 1996 half again as many sought training, and again half were women. Hundreds and possibly thousands of Zambians were anxious to learn the basics of standard business practice. Eighty-five percent of course participants said that their businesses had improved because of the training. Seventy-five percent said that their gross revenue had increased after the training.[27]

This AID-funded project was coordinated with the Zambia Association of Chambers of Commerce and Industry (founded in 1938); the Ministry of Commerce, Trade, and Industry; and with Clark Atlanta University, which acted as the contractor for course material development and project administration.[28]

Early success had as much to do with the state of the Zambian economy as it did with donor training. People were starved for business advice and ideas. Most of them were new to business and realized that they needed help to survive. They knew their state-controlled world had been thrown on its head. Governmental safety nets were rapidly disappearing for many who had depended on controlled prices and for those who had been on the public payroll. Business owners and managers demanded this training and, from the evaluation results, were clearly in a position to apply it effectively in their small companies. They were the bosses; lessons accepted were quickly applied.

By 1995 it became apparent that the high cost of the project would have to change. Besides, it had to be a Zambian initiative; it wasn't at the outset. We sought to Zambianize project design and administrative work, and so started moving it away from the United States toward a Zambian institu-tion. Our contractor, Clark Atlanta University, supported this decision and agreed to shift its project into Zambian hands.

America's International Executive Service Corps (IESC), already at work in Zambia, became a partner in this process. IESC was founded in 1964 by David Rockefeller to accelerate growth of market economies and democracy by transferring the technical and managerial talents of American business retirees to the developing world. Since its beginnings, IESC has assisted 20,000 companies and organizations in 120 countries through its headquarters in Stamford, Connecticut, and sixty offices in more than fifty countries.[29] By providing its volunteer services on demand, IESC ensures sustainability. No expert travels without a request in hand.

The Lusaka office of IESC agreed to help coordinate and support a Chamber of Commerce business development and support center so that AID trainees could be offered specialized training. IESC volunteer experts also provided start-up training to business groups that met under the auspices of Zambia's nine provincial business associations.

Other donors and foreign NGOs contribute to informal sector training in Zambia, such as the British Executive Service Overseas (BESO), the German government's Technical Assistance (GTZ), the Friedrich Ebert Stiftung Foundation of Germany, and the International Chamber of Commerce. AID also works with (and around) UNDP and UNIDO.

Each donor claims to improve coordination and reduce duplication, but each prefers to stake its flag on its project. For now, the demand for informal sector training is so great that there is room for all donors. In time, coordination and the offering of training-on-demand will improve. Zambian business associations and donors have only reached 1,000 or 2,000 firms in the informal sector out of an estimated 500,000 small and medium-size businesses.

RECOMMENDATIONS FOR AFRICAN EDUCATION

Africa's failure to use western training and technical assistance explains a continuing crisis. Asia's successful use of trained people and technical assistance is a fact rooted in public decisions that were made decades ago. Asia continues to demand American training, while the numbers of Africans being trained overseas remains modest if not insignificant, far beneath requirements. What is remarkable is the scale of Asia's investment in American education, which has been sustained long after donors have left the stage.

During the academic year 1995–96, 454,000 foreign students studied in the United States; 20,700 were from Africa, less than 5 percent of the total.[30] Asian countries sent more than 260,000 students to American universities—more than half of all foreign students in 1996–97; most were from Japan (45,000), China (39,000), South Korea (37,000), Thailand (13,000), and Indonesia (11,000).[31]

With the advantage of hindsight, it appears that higher-degree training planted a seed that may have split development thinking and practice between the wholly owned development that is occurring in many East and Southeast Asian countries, and in an aid-dependent Africa.

Why is this? Is Africa poor, and therefore has become aid dependent? Or, perhaps, Africa has allowed itself to become aid dependent, and therefore remains poor? These pages allow for consideration of these questions, but on balance, I suggest that dependency explains the failure of training and particularly of advisory services. Perhaps Africa's talent base has been artificially constrained by ideological priorities and donor interests. Africa is changing because of economic reform and a willingness to experiment with democracy and pluralism. Doors are being opened to African talent that heretofore had been shut.

There are several sources of reinvigoration: Because donors fund such a high proportion of African training and advisory services, it is for donors to rethink the ways in which they help Africans deepen African capacity. This is beginning. Donors must not attempt to fix what is profoundly broken; namely, African public planning. The DANIDA assessment of technical assistance, as damning as it is, recommends more of the same. To recommend the "need to strengthen manpower planning" is not the answer. Hiring African talent is part of the answer, but not for statist economies that are dominated by public projects.[32]

Finland's aid program is striving to at least share project ownership: "Aid recipients are permitted a greater role in the formulation and management of Finnish-funded projects."[33] The Finnish prescription for ownership is guided by six "ownership principles," which are designed to share responsibility for the management of Finnish aid funds with partner agencies in developing countries. Like the DANIDA assessment, the Finnish study says little of an African enabling environment or of African responsibility.

Sharing may not be enough. An AID officer explains:

At this stage of Africa's development we need to recognize that this continent is changing and that a significant cadre of well-trained Africans is now available in public and private African institutions, firms, and organizations. Most importantly, there is an increased desire to face and address the development challenges from an African perspective. We (AID) need to develop new approaches and models of cooperation that really expand and accelerate what Africans, who are committed to their own development, would like to do.[34]

Donors must embrace this African commitment.

Migration across Africa is also opening opportunities for talent. West Africa's major cities are populated with citizens from neighboring countries. Abidjan, the capital of Côte d'Ivoire, is filled with tens of thousands of Europeans, Asians, and Americans, and hundreds of thousands of other Africans, mostly from Burkina Faso, Guinea, Mali, and Niger.[35] This commercially oriented multinationalism is becoming a feature of the major cities of eastern and southern Africa as well.

Formal Education

African governments must expand their continuing commitment to primary schooling and must ensure high-quality public education as well. Declines in literacy must be reversed. Able students must be ensured secondary schooling.

Improving the quality of colleges and universities in the developing world remains a perplexing challenge, even in Asia.[36] Perhaps Boulder's Economics Institute offers one avenue out of this crisis. African governments should establish their own African-based economics institutes, and refresher courses and first degrees for onward training to the masters and doctoral levels in the United States, Europe, India, and Japan. A goal should be set to train tens of thousands of Africans in the next decade. Western donors and African governments should design such programs to attract students from private industry and NGOs.

Furthermore, African governments should attract and retain career civil servants at competitive salaries. There is no escaping this reality. Salaries should be raised dramatically as civil servant rolls and benefit packages are reduced. Well-trained and motivated professionals are needed to delineate a new governmental partnership in pluralistic economies. Attractive salaries, smaller governments, and new governmental cultures are needed to mobilize African talent.[37]

Reforming Technical Assistance

Donors are dealing with increasingly well-trained and technically sophisticated counterparts.[38] No donor would question who is in charge in an Asian ministry. The foreign advisor who has come to stay in Africa should be sent home. Foreign advisory services are best provided on a short-term basis only. Governments must hire their own professionals first.

The exceptional long-term advisor must represent the best that presence, as I have defined it in an earlier chapter, has to offer. It is for Africans to be selective, to ensure that advisory services represent the best available. Africans must be willing to reject expensive foreigners who simply fill donor-funded manpower slots.

Quality must come first for higher degree training and for advisory services. People must be enabled to invest in themselves. There is no conceptual difference among green revolution farmers, merit-based scholars, businesspeople demanding training and advice, entrepreneurial behavior generally, and the careful selection of long-term advisors. Development sustainability depends upon all of these people—upon the quality of their own investment.[39]

Some of these prescriptions have been commonplace for years, and have been ignored by donors and governments alike for years because, primarily, expecting African governments to perform slows the flow of donor interest, donor money, and the placement of foreign advisors.

African governments can now pick and choose donor-funded, high-quality advice from more sources. There are now far more sources of donor advice and training, as well as voluntary and commercial sources, than there were in the 1960s and 1970s. Where poor governments once had little choice on whom to rely, today an aggressive African government minister or corporate official can and does shop for the most effective advisory assistance and training. Zambia's privatization program advertised worldwide for its chief executive, only to find the best candidate at home.

Donors cannot talk convincingly about openness, ownership, and competitiveness if they continue to tie Africa to second best—to aid-funded contractual sources that cannot compete on their own or even explain their overheads.

The growth of African talent will open Africa to world lessons, technologies, and investment. Domestic and foreign investments will be drawn to a trained labor force, which in turn, will enable Africans to grow into higher skill and professional levels.

Whichever way one may turn, the conclusion remains inescapable: People come first. In these pages I have illustrated the importance of people to their late-developing countries, as consumers, as farmers, as participants in economic and political society; as being eager to invest in themselves, their families, and their countries.

NOTES

1. World Bank, *World Development Indicators 1998*, p. 78. The educational issue may not be simply an ideological one. The founders of independent Tanzania and Zambia were concerned with the control of dissent, as had been their British colonial predecessors. It is reported that Julius Nyerere and Kenneth Kaunda,

socialist comrades who met frequently in the late 1960s, agreed that "poor and uneducated people were easier to govern." Source: Personal communications with Emanuel Kasonda, former UNIP Minister of Finance, May 21, 1996; and Guy Scott, former MMD Minister of Agriculture, March 14, 1996.

2.   There are no current estimates for the numbers of donor-funded advisors resident in Africa for the 1990s. This estimate, based on guesstimates from the 1960s, is drawn from Elliot J. Berg, *Rethinking Technical Cooperation: Reforms for Capacity Building in Africa*, New York: UNDP, 1993, p. 72. Forss and colleagues estimate that there are 80,000 advisors working in the public and parastatal sectors in sub-Saharan Africa; in Kim Forss, John Carlsen, Egil Froyland, Taini Sitari, and Knud Vilby, *Evaluation of the Effectiveness of Technical Assistance Personnel Financed by the Nordic Countries*, Copenhagen: DANIDA, 1990, p. 1.

3.   From T. Paul Schultz, *Human Capital in Women and Men: Macro and Micro Evidence of Economic Return*, San Francisco, CA: International Center For Economic Growth, 1994.

4.   Theodore W. Schultz, "Investment in Human Capital," *American Economic Review*, 51:1, March 1961, pp. 2, 3, 16; A. Sen, "Editorial: Human Capital and Human Capability," *World Development*, 25:12, December 1997, pp.1959–61; and S. Munde, "Financing Human Resource Development in the Advanced Asian Economies," *World Development*, 26:4, April 1998, pp. 657–742.

5.   George Psacharopoulos, *Returns to Investment in Education—A Global Update*, World Bank, January 1993, p. 25; and for the general case for primary education and a literature review, see Marlaine E. Lockheed and Adriaan M. Verspoor and others, "Improving Primary Education in Developing Countries: A Review of Policy Options," Education Conference, Bangkok, March 5–9, 1990.

6.   John B. Knight and Richard H. Sabot, *Education, Productivity, and Inequality—The East African Natural Experiment*, New York: Oxford University Press, 1990, p. 41.

7.   René Dumont, *False Start in Africa*, Westport, CT: Praeger Publishers, 1966, p. 88.

8.   Knight and Sabot, pp. 41–48.

9.   David C. McClelland, *The Achieving Society*, New York: Van Nostrand, 1961; David C. McClelland and David G. Winter, *Motivating Economic Achievement*, New York: Free Press, 1971; Everett E. Hagen, "The Process of Economic Development," in *Economic Development and Culture Change*, April 1957; and Lawrence E. Harrison, *The Pan-American Dream: Do Latin American Cultural Values Discourage True Partnership with The United States and Canada?* New York: Basic Books, 1996.

10.   Max Weber, *The Protestant Ethic and the Spirit of Capitalism*, First printed in English in 1930, London: Routledge; and Joseph A. Schumpeter, *The Theory of Economic Development—An Inquiry into Profits, Capital, Credit, Interest, and the Business Cycle*, New York: Oxford University Press, 1961.

11.   Harriet Mayor Fulbright, address to Fulbright recipients, March 22, 1996.

214   WRINGING SUCCESS FROM FAILURE

12.   Abe Weisblat and Bryant Kearl, *Building National Capacity in the Social Sciences: Insights from Experience in Asia*, Washington, D.C.: Winrock International, April 1989; and Weisblat letter to author, December 12, 1996.

13.   Francesco Goletti and Nicholas Minot, *Rice Monitoring and Policy Options Study*, IFPRI, December 1996.

14.   Eric Zallman, AID Memorandum, April 8, 1994; *Caribbean and Latin American Scholarship Program: Eighth Annual Report*, Arlington, VA: Aguirre International, March 1994; and Arnold C. Harberger, "Secrets of Success: A Handful of Heroes." *The American Economic Review, Papers and Proceedings*, 83:2, May 1993, pp. 343–50.

15.   Department of State telegrams from Nairobi, March 29, 1985 and October 9, 1985; a paper titled *Thirst For Education*. March 21, 1986, author not known—perhaps Mansfield Smith, the unofficial historian of these pioneering efforts; and "The Time That Was: Airlift Remembered," in Nairobi's *Daily Nation*, July 3, 1986. Tom Mboya was assassinated in Nairobi on a street across from the AID office; his death was never explained.

16.   Edward V. K. Jaycox, *Capacity Building: The Missing Link in African Development*, World Bank, May 20, 1993.

17.   Berg, pp. vi and 245.

18.   Katele Kalumba, *Better Health for Whom?*, a health conference, Stockholm, July 1995.

19.   Formal letter from a minister to a president, May 16, 1996.

20.   Joe Stepanek, *Kenyan Economists' Waiting Room*, Memorandum to the file, June 1, 1985.

21.   Ibid.

22.   Forss et al.

23.   Oliver S. Saasa and Jerker Carlsson, *Aid Effectiveness in Africa: The Zambian Experience*, University of Zambia and Uppsala, March 1995, p. 114.

24.   Harris Mule, chairman, *Partnership for Capacity Building in Africa: A Report of the Working Party on The Impact of Bank Policies, Instruments and Operational Practices on Capacity Building in Africa*, World Bank. October 1996.

25.   Letters to Stepanek from Wyn F. Owen, January 27 and April 22, 1983; Wyn F. Owen, *Recommendations and Comments Regarding The USAID Training Goals and Strategies for Tanzania*, Director, Economics Institute, November 28, 1988; and Anne Gilsdorf Bliss, *The Effects of Intensive Pre-graduate Instruction on International Students: A Study of Economics Institute Traineers*, University of Colorado Ph.D. dissertation, 1993.

26.   Several AID officers created this program: Miki Mdoe, Paula Tavrow, Z. Kristos Minja, Christine Hjelt, and Flora Majebelle. Wyn F. Owen and Elizabeth J. Kawambwa of the Bank of Tanzania supported us, as did the AID Washington-based African Training for Leadership and Skills (ATLAS) Program, and the Human Resources Development Assistance (HRDA) Program.

27.   David T. Musona and Gertrude Ngenda, *USAID Zambia Human Resources Development Project Impact Evaluation*, M and N Associates Ltd., Lusaka, First Interim Report, June 8, 1995 and Final Report, September 15, 1995.

28. AID enterprise training work was initiated by Asina Sibetta, Bessie Thornicroft, Susan Gale, Max Sichula, Wilbur Jones, and Earl Picard of Clark Atlanta University.

29. International Executive Service Corps, *Annual Reports*, Stamford, CT.

30. *Open Doors—Report on International Educational Exchange 1995–1996*, New York: Institute for International Education (IIE), February 1998.

31. "Asian crisis to hit US universities," *Financial Times*, January 23, 1998.

32. Forss et al., p. 43.

33. Finland Ministry of Foreign Affairs, *Ownership in the Finnish Aid Programme*, 1996.

34. Souleymane Barry, AID, Abidjan, memorandum, March 28, 1996.

35. James Rupert, "A City That's Working Its Way Up in the World," *The Washington Post*, December 4, 1996.

36. An Indonesian government commitment to excellence arose from recognition of its own educational shortcomings and the unsuccessful use of foreign advisors to strengthen its own universities. AID, the World Bank, and the Ford and Rockefeller Foundations had supported Indonesia's universities but with little effect; perhaps the cultural and language differences were too great. Letter to author from Wyn F. Owen, January 27, 1983; see also a mention of the paucity and weaknesses of African universities, in Berg, p. 64. For assessments of agricultural economics training in African universities, see C. Ackello-Ogutu and W. M. Mwangi, "Train-ing of Agricultural Economists in Eastern and Southern Africa"; and Josue Dione, "Human Capital Investment for Agricultural Competitiveness in West Africa," in XXII International Conference of Agricultural Economists, *Agricultural Competitiveness: Market Forces and Policy Choice, Plenary Papers*, Harare: August 22–29, 1994.

37. Ian Lienert, "Civil Service Reform in Africa—Mixed Results After 10 Years," *Finance and Development*, June 1998, pp. 42–45.

38. Elena Brineman, *Technical Managers: Roles and Responsibilities*, AID, 1992 and 1994; and Norm Nicholson, *Report on Field Survey of Demand for Technical Assistance from AID*, AID, 1992.

39. I am grateful to Liz Loughran for this insight.

10

Endorsing Development in the Poor World

FACING THE WORLD'S DEVELOPMENT PROSPECTS

I have now shared my development experiences from Asia and Africa and therefore must bring this adventure to a close. It is time to reflect on the distance traveled. We have covered a lot of ground together. If you have been with me all along the way, I am grateful.

My recommendations center on Africa and have relevance for the few poor countries on other continents as well. Africa has been left behind. Its population is doubling, its food availability has declined, its new jobs are few, and its instability is dramatized weekly. What of Africa's future with twice the population?

An older generation of African leaders, long in power and dependent on donors, shy away from—even appear afraid of— openness, competition, and trade. Mismanagement, corruption, and aid dependency have instead taken hold of many African minds. Western donor countries, in the name of development during the cold war, have given Africa bad advice and have supported bad governance for several decades. Those donors that continue to think in terms of stability for an elite either do not understand or do not wish to understand the reality of their foreign policy compromises or of their actual aid-giving practices.

First a colonial legacy then a cold war legacy belie the poor world's potential for growth. But economic and even political reforms are underway. A new generation of leaders is coming to power and influence in the poor world. The West must reform its own policies and practices toward them; Africa and other poor countries deserve support, but only of a special kind.

Conquering poverty in a competitive world is a daunting task, but poor countries can compete. Their people, labor forces, and agricultural and mineral wealth remain largely untapped. Peace and stability within dozens of reforming countries and the return of failed states to normalcy will open broad opportunities for growth. Public sector dominance is being redirected; agriculture, business, and the informal sector are being given room to grow.

According to Jeffrey Garten, Dean of the Yale University School of Business, global competition is upon us with implications that reach every society, rich and poor. In the next decade 1.5 billion young people from across the world will be entering the labor force—nearly a quarter of the world's population. These young people will be educated, energetic, and anxious to advance. Garten notes that young professionals will use western technologies and western management techniques. They will work for $5–$10 a day in the developing world while American workers will work for $100 a day. Young foreign workers will be 85 percent as productive as American workers. Worldwide competition is becoming brutal. Brazil, China, India, Indonesia, Mexico, Poland, South Africa, and Turkey are active members of the global market. Products and services will be increasingly turned out with nearly the same efficiency in these new market economies as in the West, but at far less cost.

To remain competitive, Garten emphasizes, western-based corporations will continue to move to countries with lower labor costs, and they will continue to seek broader, expanding markets. The downward pressures on western wages will grow and western corporations based in the West will continue to downsize.[1] Developing countries (as well as rich ones) that have enabling environments and educated, motivated people, will compete and prosper. Poor countries must join this world to survive and prosper.

REFLECTIONS ON NINE CHAPTERS

The book has been more serious in tone and intention and more complicated than I originally envisioned. Unexpected consequences of bad development advice have intruded at every turn. I just wanted to tell a story. Inevitably, personal assessments of my own past work have cut into the sense of satisfaction I enjoyed during my AID career. Program and project successes, in isolation from macro seriousness, may not amount to very much. I found as I wrote that I addressed myself as much to a poor-world audience as to a rich one. Still, I have been lucky that personal experiences have enabled me to write a story that holds together.

I was compelled to address mismanagement, corruption, and aid dependency; factors that traditionally are minimized in the development literature as well as in practice. I have also had to introduce some theoretical background and analytical frameworks to clarify and justify my recommendations. In short, I have had to continue learning about development and aid and to reconsider and reformulate lessons and recommendations I thought I had learned years ago.

Why has Africa's development been so difficult to achieve? Why is the case for foreign assistance so daunting? What reflections are warranted?

At first I did not appreciate the scale of the differences between Asia's commitment to development and Africa's unintended but deeply rooted dependence on western aid. Nor did I appreciate the difference between Asia's evident capacity to help itself and Africa's self-serving elites and donors.

Historians and development experts flag the delineation of Europe's colonial interests in Africa at the Congress of Berlin in 1885 as contributing to her present fractious predicament. It is edifying to consider recent western contributions, such as the several decades of cold-war competition and the related growth in dependence on western aid. Are these legacies any less damaging to Africa's prospects for stability and growth?

We know that Africa's debt problem is serious, but I did not expect to find a debt-driven, donor-aid culture at the very heart of western operations in that continent. (A generalization about African aid dependency is less true of poor countries in Latin America and Asia.) Also, Africa's deep-seated government corruption is probably more serious than I have described. Correspondingly, the corruption of the donor development vision and their interests is more deeply rooted and widespread than I originally thought. The two forms of corruption are integrally intertwined.

Keith Richburg of the *Washington Post* notes that "Black African leaders talk about foreign aid as if they are entitled to it—it's something that is due to Africa, with no strings attached." So, "you're left with black people wallowing in a safety net of dependency."[2] Cold war competition in Africa will not be over until the dependency culture it spawned dies.

I have avoided the temptation to compare and contrast the poor world with the rich, North with South, or to emphasize how modern markets and democracies face perplexing challenges. These pages were drafted before the Asian economic collapse occurred and western markets faced their own sharp adjustments; sadly, little accommodation in my analyses or recommendations in recognition of these events have been needed. With few exceptions I have not engaged in matters of blame, paternalism, or racism. Many able critics precede me in these topics.

This book was to have been a positive, even convincing, case for foreign assistance for late-developing countries. By assessing development history, its strengths and weakness, I had hoped to build a case for foreign aid in coming decades. I had hoped that the reader would conclude in the end, that foreign aid, with modest adjustments here and there perhaps, was a good idea that warranted support into the next century. Now I am less certain of this positive conclusion than I was at the outset. My book's title could well have been *Wringing Development from Aid,* which in turn, hints at my lasting preference for a title drawn from Abraham Lincoln's second inaugural address. . . *Sweat of Other Men's Faces.*

What I have found, and the reader has presumably found as well, is that the case for foreign aid is hard to make. There have been successes along the way, but the actual contributions of foreign assistance, project by project, given the scale of western advice and generosity over fifty years, does not show up in the lives of poor states and poor people for whom these contributions have been made. Development is not about little projects, however successful they are, momentarily, in themselves. Our foreign policy, ideology, and special interests have come first; the world's poor people have come second, if at all. *The prayers of both could not be answered.*

American liberals express concern for poor people in the U.S. and overseas, or at least are anxious to be seen as caring; classic liberals, caring less for poor people, embrace market principles that draw millions of poor people into gainful employment. European socialism, as with American liberalism, as manifested in aid programs, remains caught in a costly and ineffectual paternalism. It is jobs, not intentions, that matter.

I started this adventure believing that donor money was not the answer to poverty alleviation, and that I would not be putting forward arguments in favor of aid dollar increases. I am now more confirmed in this view than before. Rules that guide the effective use of foreign aid, such as those proposed here, are more demanding than I had originally believed.

Documentation has been a problem throughout this story. Although there are comments here and there throughout the development literature, official data do not document waste, loss, mismanagement, aid dependency, and governmental corruption. Tables full of official data tell a story of poverty but not of its causes. Many experts do not see a problem unless it is cast in numerical terms; most economists do not wade through rice paddies, donor evaluations, or make the tough decisions.

In time, causally oriented data sets may be taken for granted. Transparency International, a German NGO, is documenting corruption worldwide. A few NGOs are quantifying democracy's advance.

I have alluded to the need for casually revealing data in these chapters. New data sets are required on routine donor matters to enhance visibility: on the value of all aid given but lost in conversion to poor governments and poor recipients, on donors that require full value deposit and accounting for all cash and commodities, on aid as a percentage of poor world development and operational budgets, on aid and debt flows disaggregated by recipient country, on donor contract overhead costs and rules governing competitive contracting, and on percentages of donor resources shared with various types of nongovernmental institutions. Such evidence, I believe, would stun the reader by revealing overwhelming magnitudes of donor waste and self-interest, even before recipient government centralization, mismanagement, and corruption set in.

LESSONS LEARNED AND APPLIED

All of the chapters, focused as they are on difficulties facing the poorest countries, have detracted from an appreciation of economic and social accomplishments worldwide. This was not my intention. In the fifty years since the end of World War II, the state of the world has improved markedly. The glass is much more than half full. The independence and growth of most of the world's 190 nation states has been dynamic. The world's population is stabilizing at an undreamed-of eight billion people. These successes make it clear that a few dozen poor countries have successful models to emulate.

It remains in the interests of rich countries to help poor ones. Expanding commerce depends on poor-world growth. Political crises, refugees, and poor-world food demands place strains on international relations, commerce, and budgets. Because all countries face risks from illegal drugs, terrorism, disease, environmental degradation, and global warming, we have a common interest in international agreement and action. A more widely shared prosperity enhances this promise.

I believe the missing ingredient in the poor world is not aid, but the policies and traditions of ownership that bind people, talents, and resources with the interests of their nation state. Markets foster integration and democracy builds consensus—these are the ties that bind even poor nation states together with their people. Ownership is the unifying theme I have pursued in these pages. I am satisfied that this theme proves robust; I trust that the reader is satisfied as well.

Bilateral and multilateral donors began serving a poor world after World War II. Multiple motives served multiple foreign policy objectives during a protracted cold war. Less development was accomplished than had been mandated, although western foreign policy experts would argue that most rich-world objectives were achieved. Experts would also argue that much of the growth and development witnessed around the world comes from forces and factors other than deliberate programs of foreign largesse.

Most poor countries have only started on the path to reform; so too, have donors only started. Both are disappointed that development promises have not been kept. Few reform programs have been implemented on schedule; most have yielded the promised funding but not the promised pace of reform. Citizens of both the rich and the poor countries have been cheated.

If foreign assistance is to be effective in the future, it needs to be rethought and rejustified to warrant support by rich-world taxpayers. Development and aid-giving lessons are clear; it is less clear that our congresses and parliaments will focus their deliberative energies on a single-minded goal.

The formulae for economic growth in a poor world, assessed in chapter 3, are available from developing Asia, if Asia continues on a course of market and democracy deepening. Cronyism should not be tried a second time.

Many countries have been developing rapidly and appear to have done so despite aid, not because of it. It is Africa that has not been able to surmount the tempting effects of aid offered to governing elites. Asia has been largely open, and invested heavily in education, health, and family planning. Preconditions for Asia's growth were being put in place long before development experts paid Asia much attention. For Africa, preconditions are only now being considered.

In retrospect, developing Asia mirrored the West's own market-based philosophy but did not rely on its funding; Africa took the West's funding and, ironically, its statist, planning-oriented advice (advice that the West taught and gave freely, but did not, with few exceptions, practice). Consequently, East, South, and Southeast Asian countries are growing and are reducing poverty; Africa is achieving neither. The hurdles in Africa's path are major indeed. The price of cold war aid has become deeply rooted in patterns of mismanagement, corruption, debt, and aid dependency. Nevertheless, we must remain optimistic. African citizens have not been given a chance to participate in an enabling environment in the several decades since the end of colonialism, the beginning of African independence, and the cold war era. Colonial dominance of administration and markets gave way at independence to a no-less-centralized governmental dominance throughout the continent. Cold war donor aid reinforced these traditions primarily in Africa, but elsewhere as well.

The tragedy of Asia's financial crisis is not that market principles have been deemed ill-founded, but that millions of Asia's professional, skilled, and semi-skilled workers, who benefited from growth over these last four decades, now face certain unemployment of uncertain duration. To cut this tragedy short, Asia's markets must be reinforced by the checks and balances of independent, democratic institutions, and transparency of decision-making. Africa should be confident that a commitment to growth works. Although Asian lessons are by no means complete, Asia's recent crisis underscores the importance of growth-oriented and people-oriented principles. This crisis may yet prove that democracy is also a precondition for sustainable growth.

It remains to be seen whether western and African experts and policy-makers will see that Asia's market-based development principles must be embraced by all developing countries, or whether Asian economic bail-outs will serve to bail out their thinking and their lack of courage.

Agriculture comes first as a precondition to overall growth. Asia's success, and now Africa's, must be rooted first in food. Asia was caught in the race between population and food, now Africa is. As we saw for Bangladesh, open markets and publicly supplied new seed created agricultural growth and alleviated poverty. The race between people and food is like riding a tiger—however, there is no getting off. Bangladesh's green revolution success remains achievable but its sustainability appears elusive.

Agriculture can provide an early and enduring boost to the incomes of poor people. Development success has to be measured by per capita incomes that grow by three percent and more every year; such rates of growth provide well-being and create choice. There can be no diminution in the attention to food and population fundamentals by government or donors if Bangladesh's early success is to be sustained. For Africa, too, people and food must come first and remain foremost in policy priority.

The western donors' Development Assistance Committee, based in Paris, estimates that cutting poverty in half by 2015 among the world's poorest countries will require a per capita income growth rate of 3.5 percent each year over the next two decades. Over the *last* two decades, the average has been a mere 0.5 percent.[3] This task may seem to be of impossible proportions—as was once claimed of Bangladesh.

My expectations for African agriculture, and for Africa and the rest of the poor world generally, is deliberately optimistic, but I hope not naive.

What has been achieved elsewhere must be achieved in Africa. If Bangladesh can embrace a green revolution under seemingly insurmountable handicaps, so can other food-poor countries. As with growth and poverty alleviation generally, the lessons are clear: agriculture requires open markets, public policy, and infrastructure support, and the willingness to embrace global markets and information. Stagnation—even hunger—await those countries that do not implement policies in proven directions.

In chapters 4 and 5 I discussed donor staffs at work in Asia and Africa. The Bangladesh example illustrated what can be achieved by donor presence. A resident capacity to learn, design, and implement with counterparts counts for a great deal in explaining and testing ownership, impact, and sustainability. Project successes are few but hold promise for all donors, provided donor support takes place in, and contributes to, an enabling environment. Entirely too much bilateral and multilateral aid is loaned and granted for governmental maintenance, while not enough is collegially designed and administered to enable investment and systemic enhancement of education and health.

Chapters 7 and 8 used Zambia to dramatize the difficulties donors face in promoting economic and democratic reform. Both chapters detail how best intentions by donors, in the face of different and determined African priorities, can create disasters with multiyear consequences and costs. The Zambian government's attempt to protect a private bank in 1995 derailed an IMF program of structural reform, and therein made donor dependency and the aid-debt game visible for all to see. The Zambian people voted in a democratically elected government in 1991, which then progressively acted to betray its mandate.

Both chapters 7 and 8 force visibility of tough questions. The World Bank, the IMF, as well as the bilateral donors, by striving to support seemingly fragile African governments, sustain government consumption and consequent traditions of mismanagement, corruption, and, ultimately, further aid dependence.

Africa is reforming, but donors must extinguish the idea that they must entice, badger, bribe, and otherwise coerce Africa into doing the right thing. Donors cannot demand that African governments be smaller by expecting them to spend more. Western donors cannot negotiate loans and grants with African governments knowing that the agreed terms will not be honored, and then blame African governments for nonperformance. This money-driven culture creates a moral hazard—wherein African governments are told to do one thing—with a wink—and then are signaled that the money will flow nonetheless. The dependency culture created by moral hazard contributes to public corruption and further acceptance of public loans and public debt, simply to finance a nominal stability.

Because donors have long delivered their resources into a few African hands at the top of government, other Africans outside of government have withdrawn their talents and resources. Donors cannot claim lack of governmental capacity when western aid sustains public cultures that drive private resources and talented people from investment and out of Africa. Donor aid cannot continue to be the substitute for development it has become. Donors cannot fill in where others take away. These cycles must be broken.

Zambia could have been a model for African democracy. Instead, it was able to hide behind the World Bank and the IMF as it betrayed its own people. Although the bilateral donors suspended budget support, in reaction to democracy's betrayal, the World Bank continued its loan releases, which had the effect of allowing the government to believe that it had the IMF and World Bank in its pocket.

Aid for Africa has allowed most African governments to escape representation of and responsibility to their own people. (Oil functions much the same way.) Opposition party leaders know this. African leaders in power know it even better. Democracy is needed to break the monopoly over public decisions and public resources. Africa cannot ignore its potential for participation and productivity and also expect to foster national unity, growth, and poverty alleviation. Donor practices that have historically ignored the involvement of the African people are slowly being redesigned to enable their contributions and their eventual ownership.

A Kenyan woman from the Kennedy Airlift of the 1960s, who spoke her mind at a White House conference, also speaks of my own conclusions:

Five hundred years is a long time to struggle against oppression. The task ahead is enormous because the battles of five centuries have left Africans weakened culturally, economically, and politically. But above all it has left us without visionary leaders. The crisis we have in Africa is a crisis of leadership. It is important to emphasize that it is not the tribes who want to fight; rather, it is the leaders who are using tribes to arouse ethnic nationalism. The truth is that Africans, like all other human beings, want justice, equity, transparency, responsibility, and accountability. Power sharing in South Africa offers an interesting alternative. The political culture of the winner takes all was forfeited for national unity. [4]

Many experts believe that democracy is a nice idea whose time has come for Africa; I am convinced that Africa's growth depends fundamentally on democracy and all of its principal attributes. Donors who talk about democracy and pluralism but cynically fund central governments keep African development at bay.

Open markets and democracy as idealized systems contain many shortcomings. But for African governments with little market experience, and less democracy experience, there is no escaping the importance of getting started. Africans, not foreigners, must struggle with and shape these principles in their image and in their own institutions.

Market openness and economic growth have been proven to alleviate poverty. It remains to be determined whether democracy in the world's poorest countries promotes ownership, pluralism, and, ultimately, stability. I believe that it will. One half of the development equation has been proven.

Chapters 4 and 9 described major American contributions to the developing world. Asia took our technical assistance, training, and the seeds of the green revolution and made them their own. Africa, sadly, has not had the vision, leadership, or technical ability to embrace what has been offered free for two generations. Donor advisors went to Africa to advise, and stayed to manage. Perhaps, too, food aid went to stay.

Donors have been partly responsible for this major disappointment. Training and advisory successes are possible, but few in number. Africa needs its own economics and private business institutes to create tens of thousands of first-degree holders, and to prepare students for advanced-degree training. Today Asia supports 300,000 students in American and Canadian universities every year; Africa, 20,000. It is noteworthy that a developing Asia demands North American training.

Africa's problems cannot be ignored, nor will they disappear. If the Western countries were to fund only 10 percent of an African country's development effort, as has been typically the case in Asia or Latin America, these dependency and debt issues would not be significant. I write precisely because concessional funds finance most development in Africa. The choice is clear. I do not believe there is an alternative to tough recommendations. Lessons learned can ensure promises kept.

WHY IS AMERICA'S PRESTIGE NEEDED?

On the fiftieth anniversary of the Marshall Plan in 1997, nothing was said of the poor-world's plight. There was no call for Africa's development nor for an appreciation of continuing development challenges elsewhere. Understandably, the focus of that celebration was exclusively on Europe.

George C. Marshall saw Europe's war-torn requirements and imagined a plan to match that scale. Today it is sad commentary on America's foreign aid program that we make its case to Congress and to the American people on the basis of how much of it we spend on ourselves.

America once championed development aspirations for the poor world; it should do so again. America can set new standards for development for remaining poor countries. America has much to build on to reestablish its leadership in development fora. Secretary of State Madeleine Albright reaffirmed at the outset of her cabinet appointment that the United States has "no permanent enemies, only permanent principles—respect for law, human dignity, and freedom."[5] President Clinton's trip to Africa in 1998 placed trade ahead of aid for the first time. This pronouncement must prove to be an historic opening. These several principles can serve as the basis for a renewal of America's leadership.

Only America, of all western interests in Africa, has the congruence of values, aspirations, interests, and influence to support Africa's nascent belief in its own development prospects. America, more than most countries, strives to keep its borders and its society open to all talents and ideas; America flags the domestic riches of its ethnic and cultural diversity.

Only the U.S. government can lead a sea change in the way western trade and aid are understood, justified, and administered. Only the U.S. government has the grasp and influence to combine trade, investment, debt, and aid into coherent and compatible principles to redirect international aid-giving fora and institutions. Only the United States can redirect and reenergize western governments, the World Bank, and the IMF to serve development.

America understands that development is in America's national interest because development promotes poor-world understanding of global issues. Development ensures that global issues are embraced and acted upon by an expanding number of robust nation states.

We need a new foreign assistance articulation for an additional reason: Congress' fractious micromanagement of foreign affairs will continue unabated until there is a new bipartisan foreign assistance understanding. Market and democratic principles, manifested by trade, investment, debt forgiveness, and development must be combined and integrated.

TOUGH CONCLUSIONS, TOUGHER RECOMMENDATIONS

Recommendations offered here will enable poor countries to grow, to share growth, and to join the world economy. These recommendations are directed at sub-Saharan Africa and to the few remaining poor countries in Asia and Latin America. My purpose in offering recommendations is to ensure poverty-reducing growth, ensure that growth creates employment, that the aid dependency culture comes to an end, and shift development responsibility and ownership to the poor world.

Economic Openness and Growth

Market openness is the sine qua non for development. Growth reduces poverty: the first goal defines and delivers the second. Even during the time that I have been writing, further analyses strengthen this conclusion. For sixty-five countries assessed in a Harvard University study, poor populations shared proportionately in national growth in all countries but two. The good economic news for poor people is inescapable.[6]

Modern agriculture must receive sustained emphasis. Cultivators on large and small farms and landless laborers all can grow the food and create the rural linkages that ignite widespread growth processes. Agriculture is the first place to expand and sustain governments' commitment to widely shared growth.

Help People Invest in Themselves

Enabling markets presume that governments will enable people to learn and invest. Primary and secondary education, good health, family planning, nutrition, and food security remain mandatory, but not exclusively, public responsibilities. Africa must also train large numbers of its public and private professionals to the advanced-degree level on the basis of merit. Asia is investing aggressively in its future by sending, mostly at its own expense, vast numbers of people to American and Canadian universities.

Educated people require productive environments. For people to invest their own talents and resources, governments must respect individual and property rights, secure contracts, and sustain sensible economic policies.[7] As many theorists argue that markets invite—even cause—democracy, so too will global education.

Let Africans Shape Africa's Future

Democracy is a value in its own right and, I believe, is a prerequisite for Africa's growth. Market openness will eventually enable and demand pluralization of institutions and the rule of law. But poor governments should not simply rely on market pressures to create a pluralism of voices and institutions.

The monolithic control of donor resources that African governments presently enjoy must be broken. It is for this new reason, this lack of a preexisting but necessary condition, that I have come to believe that African democracy is mandatory for its development. It is regrettable that the Asian economic crisis has come without there having been a debate about democracy's importance to Asian growth.

Although there is no proof as yet of democracy's centrality to development, such as now exists for market openness, Africa (and its donors) will make a grave mistake if they continue to believe that corrupt or even benign leaders know best. African governments that sustain their monopolies over donor resources invite further rounds of failure. Democracy is a high-risk experiment, but the principle is inviolable.

Democracy—for its pluralism of public and private institutions—is needed in Africa to create ownership of development and to open and pluralize African access to investment and donor resources. African individuals and institutions must be encouraged to flourish. Overseas African talent and capital look to democracy at home as one factor that invites return.

Donors Must Enable Investment

The multilateral and bilateral aid donors should focus their policies and funding priorities on advice and training to help Africa establish and define environments for investment, trade, and talent; and for programs that systematically expand education, health, and family planning.

In essence, donors are back to the world of Marshall Plan Europe. The western donors must now help Africa implement the preconditions for growth that were safely ignored during Europe's economic recovery. According to Theodore Schultz, Europe's postwar prospects for recovery were greatly underestimated, and for the poor world, greatly overestimated, because of the lack of understanding of the preexisting, mostly human, condition.[8]

Donors should promote learning with counterparts; policy and technical learning should become the new paradigm. Instead of giving aid as a done deal for poor people, all aid must help people help themselves. If project aid does not have learning as a central tenet, it should be redesigned. Grant money, the so-called soft money, must be treated, as AID often does, as 20 percent money—that is, as being precious. It must be used for leading-edge studies, advice, pilots, and reform.

Donors should not fund African governments, support their budgets or their promises to perform, or support public and private consumption and maintenance. Governments, even poor ones, must be rooted in their own people and in their own resources. Donors cannot continue to sustain the consumption levels for poor governments and believe that they are contributing to the well-being of poor people. Donors must insist on hard-nosed accountability and transparency of resource use. To do the opposite keeps paternalism in place.

Donors Must Fund Africa Selectively

Western donors should stand by governments that are committed to the types of principles defined here and terminate assistance to those that are not. Western donors should not agonize over those countries and ministries that demonstrate a lack of commitment to reform. Some countries and many ministries do not understand what it is to support policies and programs for the well-being of the people they serve. A few African countries might choose to go their own way without donors. Most late-developing countries already understand that policy seriousness equates with growth and poverty reduction. For those that do not, a radical change in donor culture, a requirement in its own right, might facilitate their understanding.

Donors should be clear that they do no harm. Doing nothing, or spending less, is better than pushing money that sustains a costly and destructive donor-dependent culture. It is not acceptable to support governments with cash in the name of eventual reform, with all of reform's attendant mismanagement and corruption. Nor is it useful to pretend that donor projects, in hostile enabling environments, help investment and people. Donors cannot have it both ways. Enabling environments and appropriate policies, not individual, ameliorative projects, count.

Official Debt Must Be Forgiven Unconditionally

There is no wider gulf in Africa today than between the theory and practice of official debt, that is, the debt created by World Bank and IMF loans. Theory would have us believe that reforming African governments will grow their way out of their debt problems by economic recovery and ultimate debt repayment.

I am convinced that the risks are simply too great that African debt repayments, primarily to the World Bank and the IMF, will be purchased at the price of continuing stagnation, donor dependency, and centralized and secretive rule. My field experience tells me that theory will not prevail. The debt trap is a dependency trap. Escape is unlikely.

My argument for debt forgiveness is based on a pervasive culture. African governments have learned that they continue to win World Bank and IMF loan approvals on the basis of less-than-agreed performance.

Beware of moral hazard. African governments know that the primary, albeit unwritten, priorities of the multilateral and bilateral donors are governmental stability and the repayment of outstanding World Bank and IMF debt. The World Bank and IMF operational staff wink; African policy-makers wink back. More poverty attracts more aid to sustain African governments. Western bilateral donors foolishly pay the difference; the African people suffer the difference. Africa, with few margins for error, will not find moral hazard and dependency foundations for growth and poverty alleviation.

These debts cannot be repaid—*nor should they be repaid*. Furthermore, I believe my Zambian-based argument has applicability for other debt-distressed poor countries. I do not believe it is the debt per se that keeps African governments from spending scarce public resources for health and education; it is the donor-dependent culture that this debt represents, which sustains public elitism and consumption. Debt is a proxy for the larger and more deleterious dependency culture that has a grip on the African continent, and on the bureaucratic mind. Similarly, converting aid loans to grants, seemingly a step in the right direction, must also be accompanied by a recommitment to investment as defined in these pages.

Ever newer Bank and IMF loan facilities, with ever-newer debt proposals, like switching loans to grants, miss the main point. It is the dependency-debt culture itself that must be set aside in favor of a return to investment. Furthermore, to demand ever-newer conditions (originally agreed to years before) for new loans is to sustain the present failed culture. Each time there is an African crisis and donor aid is suspended (which happens frequently), the western donors pick themselves up and head in the same direction and obey the same money-pushing rules. Donors must get off the treadmill of failure.

Western governments should be magnanimous in writing off official debt for the world's poorest countries. A one-time write-off is in order. Its full forgiveness may even reaffirm investor confidence in Africa and in the World Bank and the IMF if debt write-off is linked to credible investment criteria.

Furthermore, official debt forgiveness should be enacted unilaterally; that is, without performance conditions being leveled on African governments. My recommendations regarding investment, people, and donor aid are conditions enough as stated.

In conclusion, these six recommendations must be taken as a whole. Specifically, debt forgiveness by itself will not address the central challenge of focusing donor resources exclusively on investment and people. All donors should make this case to their congresses and parliaments.

RENEWING AMERICAN ASSISTANCE—BUILDING FROM EXPERIENCE

The U.S. government does not have a development model for sustaining reform in Africa for the twenty-first century. The Development Fund for Africa (DFA) successfully guided AID's development assistance thinking through an initial economic reform era of the 1980s and early 1990s, but by itself the DFA did not reflect the full strength of an integrated mandate directed at Africa's predicament.

AID's present sustainable development strategy includes economic growth, health, the environment, and, for the first time, democracy. These worldwide priorities take AID beyond the DFA toward a comprehensive contribution to African development, but they are not strategic in their implementation. They are not accepted by the U.S. government as a central tenet of its foreign policy toward Africa, or by other development institutions. Furthermore, U.S. policy toward Africa falls short of calling for a coordinated and consistent development policy for multilateral and bilateral donor institutions. Trade with Africa and agricultural growth may be back on the presidential and congressional agendas.[9] Debt forgiveness is being considered, but these are modest and disjointed efforts. A robust, integrated agenda is needed.

U.S. foreign policy does not as yet, as a matter of strategic interest, state that development can and does reduce the manifold risks of divisiveness and instability, or that development enhances commerce worldwide, or that development helps each country address global issues. Or that late-developing countries require special attention.

The answer to our foreign policy and foreign aid predicament lies in creating a new understanding of the divisive tensions and forces that are loose around the world and in forging a new balance between U.S. military and commercial interests and our developmental ones. The latter needs to be treated, for the first time, as a strategic interest, with the leadership and consensus that the former have historically enjoyed. The central concern is not "What role for AID?" but a Department of State, U.S. Treasury, and AID authorized to focus uniformly and firmly on long-term, global, and country-based development issues.

AID has much to be proud of; its managers could have told a remarkable story. AID has had strategic and sectoral impacts of historic proportions in many countries; it can again. AID's elements of success—professional staff, an institutional ability to learn, overseas presence, the flexibility of grant funding, and collegiality—are all proven. AID can contribute aggregate impact for the poor world. What is missing is the very seriousness we demand of our poor-world counterparts.

The flexible operational authorities tested under the DFA should serve as the model for AID worldwide and should include authorized attention to macromanagement and reform, trade, and debt forgiveness. AID administrative practices, proven for enhancing ownership, sustainability, and impact, should also become authorized objectives. Congress must allow AID to embrace the experience it has earned: "The agency seems to be forever shooting itself in the foot by discovering incredible things about itself and presenting the information as a grave problem. This report [*AID's In-Country Presence—An Assessment*] should be good news—aid has an advantage by having in-country presence!"[10]

AID approves few grants to poor governments for their maintenance; such budget support is becoming a thing of the past. AID is primarily a technical assistance and training agency. This should be welcomed, even mandated. The agency must also reestablish its macroeconomic and strategic capacities.

Welcoming competition in technical excellence would strengthen AID and serve the United States well. AID should act as a referral service for other centers of American excellence. I believe that if AID were directed to be competitively excellent, its expenditures would continue to rebound to American contractors and universities, and would probably grow. Witness Asia's demand for our training. Instead, a congressionally earmarked AID is forced to be expensive, uncompetitive, and possibly second best.

AID needs a clean authorization bill that creates some measure of institutional independence. Perhaps American foreign assistance should be established in a direct relationship to the president. Perhaps it is unrealistic for foreign policy institutions charged with long- and short-term responsibilities to be combined. AID should not be accidentally effective on behalf of the world's poor when other U.S. government objectives and special interests do not intrude. Security assistance should be reauthorized to the State and Defense Departments as nondevelopmental interests dictate. America cannot expect Africa to own its development if our security, trade, and aid interests are circumscribed by the political truths at home.

With declining staff and resources, AID and the State Department are not able to maintain their presence overseas as they have in the past, to the detriment of our foreign policy. Furthermore, it is worrisome that the U.S. government may not see Africa as requiring development policy unity or additional interagency commitment, preferring instead to hand even more policy and resource responsibility to the World Bank and the IMF.

The World Bank and the IMF

The World Bank and the IMF have become the primary sources of development direction and funding for Africa, displacing public plans, private investment, and the bilateral donors. The United States as well as other western donors have yielded too much of their African development dialogue, resource commitment, and even their foreign policy to the World Bank and the IMF, and have done so in a manner that may be exacerbating the continent's development problems. The bilateral donors have sought as a first priority the stability of African governments; this priority, which appears to guide the World Bank and the IMF, must be reconsidered and redefined.

In addition to economic matters, there is a grave risk that the World Bank and the IMF act to negate bilateral support for democracy and pluralism in Africa. Zambia should not be able to hide behind these twin institutions as it did when it betrayed its own people. The World Bank and IMF should be directed by western countries to support and reinforce democratic principles and projects in the poor world. World Bank and IMF charters should be revisited and reinterpreted accordingly.

AID is advised by its own proponents to look to the World Bank and the IMF for macroeconomic advice and reform. This is a very serious mistake. Their advice is more self-serving than growth oriented; more centralized and big than devolved and pluralistic; more given to moral hazard than openness and transparency.

The U.S. government should act to reintroduce investment, human resource, and debt principles outlined here through the executive directors of the World Bank and the IMF; the World Bank's Special Program for Africa; the OECD's Development Assistance Committee; and the many developing-world, debt, and trade fora. A mandate to reform aid must be shared with our European donor colleagues.

LAST THOUGHTS

I have argued here that a handful of market and democratic principles can create a new basis for development understanding and integration for the world's one poor continent, and for western interests there. The same principles—universal values actually—have wide acceptance and applicability for other poverty-related struggles elsewhere—in the world's mega-cities, in the Middle East, and in central Asia. The reader may have gained an impression that I promote these principles with such unqualified enthusiasm that global and consumer homogenization are the inevitable outcome. That is by no means the intention—but it is a risk. Better that the poor world faces these risks—ones founded, for the first time, on their full participation—than face a historic but ruinous continuation of patronizing aid prescribed by others. Poor countries must sort economic, political, and cultural priorities for themselves.

Africa must look to itself. Africa must embrace democracy; passivity and dependence do not work. The bilateral donors are most unlikely to reform themselves; the World Bank is presently on an expansionary path as the poor-world's lender of first resort. The demand for domestic institutional robustness in Africa is greater than I have suggested earlier. Growth, openness, and opportunity invite global disruption, risk, and uncertainty. All countries require institutional robustness at home to deal with international shocks. As I explained many times in these pages, macroeconomic reform, even "free and fair" elections, do not in themselves represent the degree of robustness required. Dani Rodrik argues that continuing education, credible and effective governance, transparent and independent judiciaries, pluralism in representation, and social safety nets are all obligatory for survival in a rapidly globalizing world economy.[11]

America's present foreign policy and foreign aid course, for all of its wondrous idealism, is increasingly fraught with inconsistencies and will continue to invite misunderstanding and tension. Critics of capitalism believe that economic imperialism brings cultural imperialism as well. There is a subtle but vital difference between embracing and practicing a few universal values, and believing that these values, thought by many elites to be inherently western, will ultimately dominate all other belief systems. They must not. The world's cultural diversity is here to stay, if development is universal; the sincere practice of principled values should enhance these riches.

What is the alternative? Who knows best? Can development be predicated on the sweat of other men's faces? A handful of market and democratic principles have applicability for all of us—these jewels from the sea of human experience.

NOTES

1.   Jeffrey E. Garten, "What Should Global Business Leaders Know?" *Yale Alumni Magazine*, May 1997, pp. 22–23.

2.   Keith B. Richburg, *Out Of America—A Black Man Confronts Africa*, New York: Basic Books, 1997, p. 180.

3.   Organization for Economic Cooperation and Development, Development Assistance Committee, *Development Co-operation: Efforts and Policies of the Members of the Development Assistance Committee, 1997.* Paris, p. 3.

4.   Ms. Wangari Maathai (a Kennedy Airlift student), Statement for The White House Conference on Africa, June 26–27, 1994.

5.   "Ambassador Albright on the Hill," *Washington Post* editorial, January 9, 1997.

6.   Michael Roemer and Mary Kay Gugerty, *Does Economic Growth Reduce Poverty?* Harvard Institute for International Development, April 1997.

7.   Mancur Olson, "Obituary," *The Economist*, March 7, 1998, p. 91.

8.   Theodore W. Schultz, *Transforming Traditional Agriculture*, New Haven, CT: Yale University Press, 1964, pp. 184–86.

9.   An *Africa Growth and Opportunity Act* (for trade) and an *Africa: Seeds of Hope Act* (for agriculture) were before Congress in 1998.

10.   Charles W. Johnson, Memorandum to Bradshaw Langmaid, AID. December 28, 1992, p. 2.

11.   Dani Rodrik, "Globalisation, Social Conflict and Economic Growth," *The World Economy*, 21:2, March 1998, pp. 143–58.

Bibliography

Ahmed, Raisuddin, Steven Haggblade, and Tawfiq-e-Elahi Chowdhury. *Out of the Shadow of Famine—Evolving Food Markets and Food Policy in Bangladesh*. Washington, D.C.: International Food Policy Research Institute, September 30, 1987.

Atwood, David A., A.S.M. Jahangir, Herbie Smith, and Golam Kabir. "History of Food Aid in Bangladesh." Dhaka: USAID, draft, May 17, 1994.

Badiane, Ousmane and Christopher L. Delgado. *A 2020 Vision for Food, Agriculture, and the Environment in Sub-Saharan Africa*. Washington, D.C.: International Food Policy Research Institute, Discussion Paper No. 4, June 1995.

Bates, Robert H. and Paul Collier. *The Politics and Economics of Policy Reform in Zambia*. Duke University Program in International Political Economy, Working Paper No. 153, Durham, NC: January 22, 1992.

Berg, Elliot J., coordinator for AID, UNDP, and DAI Inc. *Rethinking Technical Cooperation—Reforms for Capacity Building in Africa*. New York: UNDP, 1993.

Burnside, Craig and David Dollar. "Aid Spurs Growth—in a Sound Policy Environment." *Finance and Development*. Washington, D.C.: World Bank, December 1997.

Catling, David. *Rice in Deep Water*. London: MacMillan Press, 1992.

Delgado, Christopher L. *Africa's Changing Agricultural Development Strategies—Past and Present Paradigms as a Guide to the Future*. International Food Policy Research Institute, Discussion Paper 3, April 1995.

Forss, Kim, John Carlsen, Egil Froyland, Taini Sitari, and Knud Vilby. *Evaluation of the Effectiveness of Technical Assistance Personnel Financed by the Nordic Countries*. Copenhagen: Danish International Development Agency, 1990.

Fox, James W. *What Do We Know About World Poverty?* USAID, CDIE, Evaluation Special Study Report 74, May 1995.

Garten, Jeffrey E. "What Should Global Business Leaders Know?" *Yale Alumni Magazine*, May 1997.

Grant, James P. "Development: The End of Trickle Down?" *Foreign Policy*, No. 12, Fall 1973.

Hunter, Robert E., James P. Grant, and William Rich. *A New Development Strategy? Greater Equity, Faster Growth, and Smaller Families*. Washington, D.C.: Overseas Development Council, October 1972.

Jaffee, Steven and John Morton, editors. *Marketing Africa's High-Value Foods—Comparative Experiences of an Emergent Private Sector*, Dubuque, IA: Kendall, Hunt Publishing, 1995.

Jannuzi, F. Tomasson and James T. Peach. *Report on the Hierarchy of Interests in Land*. Dhaka: AID, September 1977.

Johnston, Bruce F. "Agricultural Productivity and Economic Development in Japan." *Journal of Political Economy*, 1951; 59:6, pp. 498–513.

Kaplan, Robert D. "The Coming Anarchy." *The Atlantic Monthly*, February 1994.

Koehring, John W., team leader. *AID's In-Country Presence—An Assessment*. AID, Center for Development Information and Evaluation, October 1992.

Knight, John B. and Richard H. Sabot. *Education, Productivity, and Inequality—The East African Natural Experiment*. New York: Oxford University Press, 1990.

Kull, Steven, principal investigator. *Americans and Foreign Aid—A Study of American Public Attitudes—Summary of Findings*. University of Maryland, January 23, 1995.

Kull, Steven and I. M. Destler, principal investigators. *An Emerging Consensus—A Study of American Public Attitudes on America's Role in the World—Summary of Findings*. University of Maryland, July 10, 1996.

Lindauer, David L. and Michael Roemer, editors. *Asia and Africa: Legacies and Opportunities in Development*. Cambridge, MA: Harvard Institute for International Development, January 1994.

McClelland, David C. *The Achieving Society*. New York: van Nostrand, 1961.

McClelland, Donald G. *Investment in Agriculture: A Synthesis of the Evaluation Literature*. AID, July 1996.

McClelland, Donald G., Robert Muscat, Lisa Smith, and Bruce Spake. *Food Aid in Bangladesh—A Gradual Shift From Relief to Reform*. USAID Center for Development Information and Evaluation, Impact Evaluation 5, 1997.

Meier, Gerald M. *Leading Issues in Economic Development*. 5th edition. New York: Oxford University Press, 1989.

Mellor, John W. *The New Economics of Growth: A Strategy for India and the Developing World*. Ithaca, NY: Cornell University Press, 1976.

Mellor, John W. and Uma J. Lele. *Growth Linkages of the New Foodgrain Technologies*. Occasional Paper No. 50, Ithaca, NY: Cornell University Department of Agricultural Economics, May 1972.

Mohan, Charles, and Joe Stepanek. *Zambia: Crisis to Crisis Grows More Costly—The Year 1995 in Review*, Lusaka: AID, November 25, 1995.

Mule, Harris, chairman. "Partnership for Capacity Building in Africa: A Report of the Working Party on The Impact of Bank Policies, Instruments and Operational Practices on Capacity Building in Africa." Washington, D.C.: World Bank, October 1996.

Mwanawina, Inyambo and Howard White. "Swedish Balance of Payments Support to Zambia: Draft Final Report." Lusaka: Swedish International Development Authority, draft, February 1995.

Ndulu, Benno, and Nicolas van de Walle. *Agenda for Africa's Economic Renewal.* New Brunswick, NJ: Transaction Publishers, 1996.

Olson, Jr., Mancur. "Big Bills Left on the Sidewalk—Why Some Nations Are Rich, and Others Poor." *Journal of Economic Perspective,* 10:2, Spring 1996.

Organization for Economic Cooperation and Development, Development Assistance Committee. *Development Cooperation—Efforts and Policies of the Members of the Development Assistance Committee,* Paris: OECD, DAC Annual Reports, 1995, 1996, and 1997.

Pinstrup-Andersen, Per, Rajul Pandya-Lorch, and Mark W. Rosegrant, *The World Food Situation—Recent Developments, Emerging Issues, and Long-Term Prospects.* Washington, D.C.: International Food Policy Research Institute, 2020 Vision Food Policy Report, December 1997.

Polhemus, James. "Democracy Betrayed: Zambia's Third Republic." Prepared for the Annual Meeting of the African Studies Association of Australia and the Pacific, Australia, Canberra, September 25–27, 1997.

Rakner, Lise. "Reform as a matter of political survival: Political and economic liberalization in Zambia 1991–1996." Bergen, Norway: Chr. Michelsens Institute, 1996.

Ranis, Gustav. "On Fast-Disbursing Policy-Based Loans." Washington, D.C.: Center for Strategic and International Studies, Task Force on Multilateral Development Banks, draft, 1996.

Ranis, Gustav and John C.H. Fei. "A Theory of Economic Development," *American Economic Review,* 51:4, September 1961, pp. 533–65.

Rich, William. *Smaller Families Through Social and Economic Progress.* Washington, D.C.: Overseas Development Council, January 1973.

Richburg, Keith. *Out of America.* New York: Basic Books, 1996.

Rodrik, Dani. "King Kong Meets Godzilla: The World Bank and The East Asian Miracle." London: Center for Economic Policy Research, Discussion Paper No. 944, April 1994.

Roemer, Michael and Mary Kay Gugerty. *Does Economic Growth Reduce Poverty?* Cambridge, MA: Harvard Institute for International Development, Consulting Assistance on Economic Reform II, Discussion Paper 5, April 1997.

Ruttan, Vernon W. *Why Food Aid?* Baltimore, MD: Johns Hopkins University Press, 1993.

————. *United States Development Assistance Policy—The Domestic Politics of*

Foreign Economic Aid. Baltimore, MD: Johns Hopkins University Press, 1996.

Sahn, David E. *Economic Reform and the Poor In Africa*. Oxford, U.K.: Clarendon Press, 1996.

Schultz, T. Paul. *Human Capital in Women and Men: Macro and Micro Evidence of Economic Return*. San Francisco, CA: International Center For Economic Growth, 1994.

Schultz, Theodore W. "Investment in Human Capital," *American Economic Review*, 51:1, March 1961.

———. *Transforming Traditional Agriculture*, New Haven, CT: Yale University Press, 1964.

Schumpeter, Joseph A. *Capitalism, Socialism and Democracy*. New York: Harper, 1942.

———. *The Theory of Economic Development—An Inquiry into Profits, Capital, Credit, Interest, and the Business Cycle*. New York: Oxford University Press, 1961.

Seckler, David, Doug Gollin, and Pierre Antoine. *Agriculture Potential of Mid-Africa—A Technological Assessment*, Washington, D.C.: Winrock International, July 1992.

Seckler, David and Michael Rock. *World Population Growth and Food Demand to 2035*. Washington, D.C.: Winrock International, September 1996.

Shaw, Robert d'A. *Rethinking Economic Development*. Washington, D.C.: Overseas Development Council, March 1972.

Stepanek, Joseph F. *Bangladesh: Equitable Growth?* New York: Pergamon Press, 1979.

———. *Monograph on Tanzania's Development—Discussion of Issues*. Dar es Salaam: AID, July 24, 1991.

Svasand, Lars, Jorgen Elklit, Knut Frigaard, Carl-Goran Gustafsson, and Aanund Hyllan. *Report on Improvement of the Electoral Process in Zambia*. Bergen, Norway: University of Bergen, January 23, 1995.

Timmer, C. Peter. "The Macro Dimensions of Food Security: Economic Growth, Equitable Distribution, and Food Price Stability." Cambridge, MA: Harvard University, draft, June 1998.

United Nations Development Programme. *Human Development Report 1996*. New York: Oxford University Press, 1996.

USAID. *U.S. Overseas Loans and Grants and Assistance from International Organizations*. July 1, 1945–September 30, 1996.

von Hayek, Friedrick August. *The Road to Serfdom*. University of Chicago Press, 1944.

Weisblat, Abe and Bryant Kearl. *Building National Capacity in the Social Sciences: Insights from Experience in Asia*. Washington, D.C.: Winrock International, April 1989.

Wolgin, Jerome M. "Evolution of Economic Policymaking in Africa," *American Economics Association Papers and Proceedings*. May 1997, pp. 54–57.

The World Bank. *Annual Report,* 1997.
———. *Global Development Finances 1998.* Analysis and Summary Tables.
———. *World Bank Atlas,* 1996, 1997, and 1998.
———. *World Debt Tables: External Finance for Developing Countries, 1994–95,* Volumes I and II.
———. *World Development Indicators,* 1996, 1997, and 1998.
———. *World Development Report,* 1996 and 1997.

Index

About the Author

JOSEPH F. STEPANEK currently is a Visiting Research Fellow at The International Food Policy Research Institute. Dr. Stepanek's career with the United States Agency for International Development took him to Indonesia and Kenya, and then to Tanzania, and Zambia, where he served as AID Director. His earlier food and agricultural policy study was *Bangladesh*: *Equitable Growth?* (1979).

ISBN 0-275-96505-8

EAN

HARDCOVER BAR CODE